The Memoirs of General Grivas

THE MEMOIRS OF

General Grivas

Edited by
CHARLES
FOLEY

LONGMANS

LONGMANS, GREEN AND CO LTD
48 Grosvenor Street, London W1
Associated companies, branches and representatives
throughout the world

Printed in Great Britain by
Richard Clay and Company, Ltd,
Bungay, Suffolk

Contents

Illustrations

Acknowledgement

THE publishers are indebted to Sir Hugh Foot, GCMG, KCVO, OBE, and to Mr Francis Noel-Baker, MP, for permission to quote letters from them to General Grivas.

Editor's Note

THIS book is based primarily on an account of his Cyprus campaign written by General Grivas in Greek. While preparing the text I have worked in co-ordination with him and a quantity of fresh material from his private papers, letters and diaries has been introduced. During a series of meetings in Zurich and Athens he answered questions about his early career and other matters of special interest. He also supplied official reports on his work in the resistance during the occupation of Greece and against Communism in the Greek civil war, along with a number of photographs, photostated letters and other documents. He arranged for me to interview some of his prominent followers and provided written documents from others. He has corrected and supplemented the work in progress and approved the final text.

CHARLES FOLEY

CHAPTER ONE

By Way of Introduction

A broken promise – Childhood and schooldays – Athens Military Academy – The Asia Minor campaign – My part in the First World War – The German occupation – The truth about 'Xhi', my wartime resistance movement

DURING a lifetime devoted to the arts of war I have fought three times with the British: twice, in world conflicts, alongside them, and once, in a struggle of my own making, against them. History will vindicate my claim that on each occasion I was fighting for the same ideal: freedom.

It was with deep regret, but a high sense of duty, that I took up arms against an old friend and ally in 1955. I held Britain in admiration and respect and my quarrel was not with a great nation and people, but with a band of politicians who denied even the hope of freedom to my fellow-countrymen in Cyprus. It is on their heads that the guilt rests for the deaths of so many men, women and children in the tragic years that followed.

Like all successful soldiers I am a rigid disciplinarian, but I am also a man of strong liberal principles, and when these are assailed I cannot compromise: I shall always be found on the side of those who oppose the domination of the small and weak. Cyprus was my motherland. Cyprus was small and weak. Over the centuries she had suffered a long succession of alien occupations until the day in 1878 when Turkey sold her, for a few thousand pounds, to Britain. The Cypriots welcomed the British, for they remembered that only a dozen years before Britain had freely restored the Ionian islands to Greece, and everyone believed that the island's plea for *Enosis*, made to the first British Governor as he landed at Famagusta, would soon be granted.

These hopes were never realised; yet the British had always recognised the inalienably Greek character of Cyprus. Sir Winston Churchill stood at the head of a long line of British personalities who had publicly acknowledged that the Cypriots were Greek-speaking, Greek-thinking, Greek-feeling and in every other way Greek. During the First World War the island was, in fact, offered to Greece in return for her participation on the

I

allied side; but owing to the chaotic politics of Athens at the time, the offer was not taken up.

When, in the Second World War, the Swastika flew over the Acropolis in Athens, our hopes were kept alight by the promises of Britain and America: 30,000 Cypriots were induced to join the British army by assurances that they were fighting 'for Greece and freedom'. Like every other Cypriot, I believed that we were also fighting for the freedom of Cyprus. But when the war was over and democracy was safe once more, these promises were broken and the principles for which we had struggled were trampled into the dust. As the empty post-war years went by I was forced to realise that only in one way would the island win the freedom which it had sought so long: by fighting for it.

*

Before embarking on the story of my personal intervention in Cyprus it may be as well to disperse the mystery with which certain writers have surrounded me by briefly describing my early life, my service in two world wars and my work with the resistance during the occupation of Greece: the events, in fact, which made me the man I was when, at the age of fifty-eight, I plunged into my most difficult task, the liberation of my motherland.

I was born on 23 May 1898 in the village of Trikomo, which lies in good farming land a mile from the sea in the district of Famagusta. My father was a prosperous cereal merchant and we had the handsomest house in the village, a two-storeyed building of a dozen rooms, in traditional Cypriot style, with a spacious hall, overhanging balconies and a garden filled with fruit trees. My earliest memories are of the Greek pictures and ornaments collected by my parents, and of the twelfth-century village church, dedicated to the Blessed Virgin Mary, where the wonderful Byzantine paintings of saints and sinners on the walls mirrored the faces and attitudes of the peasants at prayer; they told the story of the Cypriots' patient suffering better than any words.

I was the fourth child in a family of six, of whom four were girls. My elder brother Michael had a quiet and ruminative nature, in sharp contrast to mine, which served him well when he later studied medicine and became a general practitioner in Nicosia. Michael liked to work about the house and tend the animals, while my idea of heaven was to gallop a horse across the fields, down to the sea and along the sands. Nonetheless, we were good friends and shared a passion for collecting stamps.

The village school was firmly disciplined and transgressors could count on a beating with a raspberry cane, but I enjoyed my studies, in which the glories of Greek history always took first place. I was particularly fascinated by the legends of Dighenis Akritas, the half-mythical guardian of the frontiers of Alexander's empire. Not far from Trikomo was a huge rock, which the village elders assured me had been hurled there by Dighenis, and my mother often sang folk-songs recounting his acts of heroism.

Mine was a happy childhood, and happiest of all when I marched behind the blue and white banners on some national day and felt the Hellenic passion for liberty burning in us all.

At the age of eleven I went to live with relatives in Nicosia, where I attended the Pancyprian Gymnasium. Like all the other secondary schools of Cyprus it was staffed by teachers from Greece who brought fresh fervour to our nationalism. At that time Greece was winning one victory after another in the Balkan wars and popular feeling towards the crusade for a greater Greece ran high. I decided to become a soldier and play my part in this struggle, in the hope that it would lead, one day, to the liberation of the country of my birth. To harden my body I put myself through a rigorous course of athletic training, and in my last year at the Gymnasium I won first prize for the 100, 200 and 400 metre races as well as for the high jump.

In 1916, when the deep thunder of the First World War was heard, I went to Athens determined to gain entrance to the Military Academy. I was seventeen, alone, friendless and very poor, for my father's fortunes had declined in recent years. The Academy was known as the 'School of the Promising Ones', for only one candidate in ten could be accepted. After the stiff entrance examinations we gathered each day to see the lists of those who had succeeded, subject by subject; each day our numbers dwindled, until only the handful who had passed with the highest marks remained. I rejoiced to find myself among them. To celebrate my success I bought one of Moltke's works on strategy; I thought him second only to Napoleon in military genius.

Life at the Academy was spartan, and there was little respite from reveille at 6 am to lights out at 9 pm. We had three minutes in the morning to dress and reach the stadium for exercise; a quick breakfast was followed by study until 8 am, then kit inspection, prayers and bed. This routine was slightly relaxed during the holidays, when those who had no homes in Greece had to stay on in school. We rarely left the grounds and always wore uniform – we had two sets of khaki battledress, run up from coarse local cloth because of the blockade.

When the allied victory came in 1918 Greece had to fight on to secure the territory she had been given in Asia Minor. My requests to break off my training and go to the front were rejected, but I passed out among the first in the following year and was immediately placed on active service. The Greek army was advancing steadily through Turkey and my division was ordered to mop up guerrillas under the leadership of Mustafa Kemal in the mountains behind Smyrna. It was in this rugged region that I had my first taste of guerrilla warfare and began to realise its possibilities. I was fascinated by the ease with which a band of irregulars armed only with rifles successfully delayed our division near Nikomidia for a full day, even when artillery was brought up to shell their positions.

I served in Asia Minor until the end of the campaign and my division advanced to within sixty miles of Ankara before we were forced to retreat after heavy fighting. We withdrew in good order by way of Broussa; thus I was spared the sight of the sack of Smyrna and the appalling massacre which followed the evacuation of the Greek army. Later, with a wound and a war medal, I was sent to Eastern Thrace, where I commanded a company in the army which was formed to attack Constantinople.

With the unhappy end of the war, brought about by the brilliance and tenacity of Turkey's new leader, Mustafa Kemal, who had renamed himself Ataturk, I was gazetted captain in the peace-time army at the early age of twenty-six and won a scholarship which took me to France for studies at the École de Tir and the École d'Infanterie at Versailles. I also had the privilege of joining the staff of the 8th French Army Division for an advanced course. During the years between the two world wars I served with various units of the Greek army, won awards which took me to the École de Guerre in Paris and lectured on tactics at the War School in Athens.

*

Italy's invasion of Greece in October 1940 found me serving as a lieutenant-colonel in the operations room of the General Staff, but in a few weeks I was sent, at my request, to the mountain front as Chief of Staff to the 2nd Army Division. The journey was made through deep snow by mule and on foot. I found my new unit, which formed part of the 1st Army Corps, was living up to its name – the Iron Division – on the Epirus front. Not only did we hold the Italian army, but we succeeded in throwing enormously superior forces back across the border as we fought our way slowly forwards through the wild, mountainous frontier region into Albania. That winter the world watched Greece in admiration and wonder.

When Hitler came to Mussolini's rescue in April 1941 we had little hope of withstanding their combined forces: the German armies, striking from the flank, cut us off and there was no alternative but a fighting retreat. I conferred with my divisional commander and we decided in no circumstances to surrender; my plan was to move into the high Pindus mountains and organise guerrilla warfare against the occupying forces. Unfortunately certain superior officers in Athens, who had decided to capitulate, guessed from our movements what we meant to do, with the result that we were intercepted by the Germans outside Janina and forced to split up. Escaping with other staff officers, I hid in the hills for some weeks and there we buried our arms. However, I retained my revolver and it was with me when I made my way back to Athens.

The occupation was a terrible time for Greece, but the brutality of the Nazis spurred the people to revolt. Resistance movements sprang up everywhere. I was among the first to try and build up a fighting organisation in Athens. In 1943 I was in contact with General Papagos, Commander-in-Chief of the disbanded Greek army and with Achilles Kyrou, an influential newspaper editor who was working to bring the nationalist forces together. My activities were soon noticed by the Germans, who ordered my arrest on 24 March 1943. Luckily I was visiting the law courts when the Germans came to my office at the War Ministry so that my aide, Lt. Homer Papadopolous, was able to warn me in time. From that moment I went underground and began my work in secret. Within a few months I had formed my first groups, which consisted entirely of trustworthy Greek officers, in Athens, Piraeus and their suburbs. This was the start of my 'private army', which I called Xhi, after the Greek letter X which symbolises the unknown.

During the Cyprus struggle British propagandists frequently attacked Xhi and used it as a stick to beat EOKA, giving a completely false picture of its activities and methods. It was an easy matter to draw fanciful parallels between the two organisations, since the work of Xhi was largely unknown outside Greece, and the British did their best to present it in the most sinister light. The true facts about the movement are here described fully for the first time, so that the reader may judge it for himself.

From the outset, the Greek resistance forces fell into two factions, the nationalist and the Communist. It is true that the Communists, who had long thrived on secret conspiracy, were better organised at the start and could act more decisively. Papagos, who might have done much for us, was arrested and the Communists set up a pseudo-patriotic front called EAM to persuade the British that they intended to offer serious resistance to the Germans; in fact, their only purpose was to seize power as soon as the Germans left. Meanwhile they collaborated with the occupiers and worked against the nationalist forces. The British were completely deceived and poured weapons into the Communist arsenals: they neither foresaw nor cared what would happen at the end of the war.

Again and again my efforts to arm guerrillas and send them out against the Germans were frustrated by this pro-Communist policy and by the attitude of the Greek Government in exile at Cairo. One of my first attempts to get support was through a Government agent who had landed secretly in Greece. We met at the home of Archbishop Chrysanthos and I explained my plans and requirements and the capabilities of the organisation. All he could find to say was that we should carry on with the good work.

When it became obvious that the Germans would be forced to withdraw from Athens I drew up a plan to seize the Ellikon–Kitheron area, which would make an excellent base for operations against their retreating columns. Eventually I succeeded in contacting a leading figure in the British secret service in Greece, Captain P. Lycourezos (known to me as 'Kodros'), and explained the plan. He promptly radioed GHQ Middle East in Cairo explaining what I wanted to do and asking for an airdrop of arms and equipment 'to help this officer to form his guerrilla organisation as his sentiments are undoubtedly patriotic and pro-British'. The offer was accepted, with the stipulation that I must find a British liaison officer operating in Greece who would witness my signature to a 'national agreement' uniting the right-wing groups and putting them under British command. I agreed to do this at once, only to discover that the liaison officers were so deeply involved with the Communists that they wanted nothing to do with us. Again I sent a radio message to Cairo, asking GHQ to find another means of implementing the arrangement, but though they promised to do so, nothing happened.

A month later the British sent Captain Donald Stott, a New Zealander (known to us at the time only by his *nom de guerre* 'Captain Don'), with the task of co-ordinating the nationalist groups. These, including Xhi, willingly signed a promise to give all the help they could to any allied invasion force. We agreed to prevent enemy sabotage of roads and installations, harass retreating forces, guard the capital until the allies arrived and then place our entire forces at their disposal, accepting GHQ Middle East as supreme authority. Captain Don returned to Cairo, but we heard no more of him, or his agreement, until long after the war was over.[1]

[1] In a book called *Apple of Discord*, Colonel C. M. Woodhouse, head of the British military mission in Greece during the occupation, revealed that Stott was abruptly removed by higher British authorities because his 'courage and originality' involved him in 'perilous activities': these included the risk of entering into

The situation was further aggravated by the fact that a group of anti-monarchist officers had worked their way into power in the Greek intelligence wing of GHQ Middle East: these intriguers persuaded the British to abandon King George of the Hellenes, who had proved his loyalty to Britain under fire, in favour of a band of unknown men whose only allegiance was to Moscow. So, while the real patriots were starved of all supplies, the flow of arms into the hands of EAM, and its army in the field, known as ELAS, continued.

Not until the capitulation of Italy, following Mussolini's downfall in the summer of 1943, was I finally able to secure a few arms, buying them from the decamping Italians with money supplied by a committee under Archbishop Chrysanthos. Again, in December, I was assured of plentiful supplies by a British secret agent, but none ever came. Meanwhile we were harried by the Germans and their puppet government in Athens. I kept in touch with Captain Lycourezos and provided recruits for other nationalist organisations which were in a better position to use them: a team of officers headed by my chief of staff, Vassilios Papayannis, was sent to join General Zervas, the right-wing guerrilla leader in the mountains.

In May 1944 the Greek administration again ordered my arrest, after I had failed to comply with their order to report for duty with the so-called 'security battalions' which were policing the countryside for the Germans.

'negotiations of a complicated nature with the German occupation forces'. I do not know why Stott's removal for completely unrelated causes should affect the agreement which we all signed; it can only be supposed that the British General Staff were too firmly wedded to the policy of arming the Communists to honour their pledges to us. Colonel Woodhouse's assertion that Xhi took no action against the Germans was often quoted by anti-EOKA propagandists; indeed, he went so far as to say that no resistance organisation of the Right was active during the occupation. I hope I have made it clear that if the nationalists were not able to do all they wished against the Germans, it was mainly the fault of Colonel Woodhouse and his masters in Cairo. This view is generally accepted, even by British authorities: Air Vice-Marshal A. Gould-Lee writes in his book, *The Royal House of Greece*, that British agents used the Communists from the first as a ready-made machine. 'The Government thus found itself committed to a dubious and dangerous line of co-operation . . . this course was followed with great deliberation and it is no exaggeration to say that British intelligence built up the Communist army there.'

Conclusive evidence is supplied by Sir Winston Churchill, who told the House of Commons after the Greek civil war: 'It was not against the Germans that they were trying to fight, but to a great extent they were simply taking our arms, lying low, and awaiting the moment when they could seize power and make Greece a Communist state, with totalitarian liquidation of all opponents.'

Failing to find me, they tried to arrest my wife, and she too was forced to go into hiding.

Throughout the occupation I ran Xhi from my headquarters in Thyssion, a district which lies on the hill below the Acropolis, moving from house to house among friends who gave me shelter. I had 300 men, mostly officers, who were scattered in teams of fifteen to twenty all over Athens, and numerous civilian helpers. These were mainly engaged in collecting information for allied intelligence. My official report to the Greek High Command on the work of Xhi during the occupation shows that we furnished GHQ Middle East with ninety-five separate and detailed accounts of enemy dispositions all over Greece. These included reports on German army strengths, troop movements, the location of camps and petrol dumps, plans of minefields in the harbours of Piraeus, Salonika, Patras, etc., etc. We also raised morale in Greece by distributing leaflets attacking the Germans, and gave help to various allied intelligence officers, such as Captain Fraser of Force 133 (an intelligence organisation), whom we supplied with a team of officers and civilians who procured a mass of information about German fortified positions.

The British were finally woken from their complacency when Communist-engineered mutinies broke out in the free Greek Army in Egypt and Rhodesia, while a naval mutiny kept forty-three Greek warships and merchantmen idle at Alexandria at a time when they were urgently needed for the invasion of Italy. These events showed the British where their policy was leading and, almost too late, they withdrew their support from the Communists in Greece and gave it instead to the nationalists. General Spiliotopoulos, a monarchist, was put in command of the underground forces in Attica and I at once placed myself under his orders. I formed an infantry regiment which absorbed two smaller resistance units and we undertook to take charge of a large shipment of arms which was to be landed in Greece. On 11 September 1944 I sent a hundred men to Porto Rafti to receive the arms, but the ship was delayed and we had to fight off strong attacks from Communists who were determined to seize the cargo for themselves. We brought the guns safely to General Spiliotopoulos in Athens, and also guided three British intelligence officers with radio equipment; we gave these men shelter in Athens before they moved on to a secret destination.

When the Germans began to withdraw later in September 1944 they passed through country controlled by the ELAS army of 40,000, yet their convoys were not hindered in any way. The only action taken by ELAS during the German retreat was to close in on Athens. They ignored orders from the Greek military commander in the capital and from GHQ Middle East.[1] OPLA, the Communists' professional assassination squad, set about eliminating their enemies.

The German evacuation of Athens began at 2.30 pm on 8 October 1944: this was the signal for ELAS to clear my forces out of Thyssion, where we were strongest, and gain control of the city centre. Although ELAS attacked in strength with nearly 1,500 men, we held them off for thirty hours until, on the evening of 9 October, fighting was suspended by the intervention of the Athens Military Commander. The first British troops arrived a few days later, closely followed by the Greek Government, accompanied by Mr Harold Macmillan, British Minister Resident in the Middle East. Meanwhile the ELAS army waited on the hills around Athens: by the end of November, Lt-General Scobie, the British Commander, decided that the Communists had no intention of keeping their promise to put themselves under his command.

On 3 December 1944 the wheel of British policy turned full circle: I was asked by Athens military HQ to place my forces at the disposal of a national guard being formed to meet the Communist threat. With twenty of my officers I went at once to the Ministry of Defence. The Minister warned me that the Communists were expected to strike at any moment and said I should return to defend Thyssion, since ELAS forces were already moving in that direction. At the same moment the Communists were stage-managing a demonstration in Constitution Square, the heart of the capital, which was certain to cause trouble: inevitably the police lost control and opened fire. These were the first shots in a civil war which lasted for the next four years.

My main force at the time amounted to only eighty or ninety men in the centre of Thyssion, with another forty based in houses not far off. Against this, the Communists threw 3,000 of their best troops, armed with modern British weapons. We repulsed one attack after another throughout the first day, heavily punishing our assailants. On the second day we asked help from the Athens military HQ, and at about 3 pm, when he had suffered about forty casualties, but inflicted several hundred, two British tanks arrived at the scene. I was assured by the officer in charge that the lives of nationalists in the area would be safeguarded, so I called a cease-fire and accompanied him in a tank to the ELAS headquarters. Here he had a talk,

[1] Documentary proof is available of a typical agreement signed by the Germans and a representative of the 11th ELAS Division in Macedonia, which undertook not to impede the German retreat on condition that they left intact for the Communists the war material they had to abandon.

9

out of earshot, with their leaders, and on receiving the necessary assurances I ordered my men to withdraw to a nearby police station which was regarded as neutral ground. But the Communists could be relied on for nothing but bad faith. They swarmed into Thyssion, attacked our helpless nationalist friends and finally surrounded the police station where we were sheltering; the British were obliged to evacuate us in lorries.

During the next week our men were enrolled in the national guard and served faithfully until, in February 1945, the Communists were forced to leave Athens. I then dissolved the Xhi organisation, believing that it had served its purpose. The Communists, however, had withdrawn from the capital only to continue their excesses elsewhere. For the next four years a full-scale civil war was fought out between the new Greek army, aided by the British, and ELAS, supported by Russia and the Balkan countries which she had occupied. Both Britain and Greece paid heavily for their mistakes: in the first few days alone 120 young British soldiers, who thought that they would soon be going home, were killed in Athens; and before the struggle ended 20,000 men, women and children had been massacred by the Reds in their ruthless bid for power. Greece was devastated, her economy ruined, her people starving and her honour stained by the atrocities which the Communists committed against their innocent countrymen.

I had, up to that moment, always been whole-heartedly pro-British; but in the years that followed I found it hard to forget the frivolous role played by the rulers of Britain in the tragedy of Greece.

Today I am often asked to what extent my experiences in the resistance and the Communist revolt guided me in my fight against the British. My answer is that our success was due, not to experience, but to my deep understanding of Cypriot psychology and my 'sense of war' – the quality of judgement that brings correct decisions in moments of crisis. I based my actions on a thorough study of every situation (my opponent, the terrain, resources, etc.), and applied my general knowledge of guerrilla warfare to the special circumstances before me.

Naturally my experience in action was valuable. But I should point out that during my military education in Greece, my studies at the highest military academies in France, and my years as a staff college lecturer in Athens, guerrilla warfare had no place on the formal agenda and was rarely mentioned outside it. One result of this indifference was that the resistance movements of the Second World War failed to realise their full potentialities. The much-publicised guerrillas of Greece and Yugoslavia, to take an example from my own sphere of activity, sat in the mountains and said they were making war while the trains continued to run on time, the roads were clear and the Germans were freely supplied from Europe: this, though all main Balkan routes run through defiles which invite attack. I do not say that these guerrillas lacked courage; but I fear their chief achievement was to use up German manpower in chasing them and guarding installations. The reasons for this were the lack of a unified command and the total absence of planning and preparation. It is not too much to say that the German forces in the Balkans could have been devastated by a combined force of Greek and Yugoslav fighters under one leader, with a realistic plan of action. As it was, the Greek groups spent much time quarrelling among themselves. Lack of foresight was to blame.[1]

Any country may be occupied in war: once the psychological barrier which seems to prevent governments from realising this is overcome, it is a simple matter to cache arms and explosives in advance and to appoint men who can lead and hold a population's loyalty. You may be certain that Russia and China, who set the highest value on large-scale guerrilla action, have already trained powerful forces to fight behind the lines of any future invader. But if NATO's supreme commander were asked tomorrow what has been done to prepare for guerrilla warfare if Western Europe is overrun, I am equally sure that the honest answer would be: nothing. It has been left, as usual, to improvisation. Great things can be done with poor material, as we proved in Cyprus. But when proper resources are available, the horizon is boundless.

[1] Total Greek guerrilla forces during the occupation were about 100,000 well-equipped men. German forces at the end of 1944 numbered 250,000–300,000.

CHAPTER TWO

Birth of a Revolution

*Government House is burned down – The British reject all appeals – I decide
we must fight – Contacts with Marshal Papagos – Reconaissance in Cyprus –
Makarios is dubious – A revolutionary committee is formed – A shipload of
guns – I sail for Cyprus in secret – Organising EOKA – The loss of the
St George and our explosives – My first underground headquarters*

Throughout the first half of this century the British were never allowed to
forget the Cypriot desire for freedom: many written appeals were made to
successive governments, and delegations were sent to London to put our
case personally; but these, if they were received at all by British Ministers,
met with patronising indifference or outright rejection. Events reached a
climax in 1931 when, during a short-lived revolt, Government House was
burned down by demonstrators and fierce reprisals were taken against the
Cypriots: troops were rushed to the island, the leaders of the Enosis movement (including two bishops) were arrested and deported, hundreds
of people were jailed and the constitution was abolished. Church bells
were silenced, Greek flags torn down and it became illegal even to
speak of union with Greece. All this was done under the Governorship of Sir Ronald Storrs, a self-proclaimed Philhellene, who later wrote,
in his autobiography: 'I would not have had the results otherwise . . .
for though the scale of the disturbances was relatively small, the issues
were as great and as universal as any which can arise in far larger
territories.' This was the attitude of a prominent liberal, and the attitude
of his masters in the Conservative Party was, of course, a great deal
more rigid when the subject of any change in the status of Cyprus was
brought up.

After the Second World War, in which the Cypriots fought gallantly,
side by side with British troops in many parts of the world, the United
Nations Charter proclaimed for all peoples the right of self-determination.
In Britain, the Labour Party came to power and gave independence to
many countries under British domination; but when a Cypriot delegation
went to London in 1947 to plead the island's right to choose its own future
they were told by the Colonial Secretary of the day that there could be no
change of sovereignty for Cyprus, and that the matter could not even be

discussed. More and more it seemed to me that only a revolution would liberate my homeland.

I always take my decisions after careful thought, but once taken they are, for me, irrevocable; thus I set out on a path from which there was no turning back when, in May 1948, I first put my thoughts into words to my old friend Christodolous Papadopoulos, a brother of my former aide in Xhi, Homer Papadopoulos. Christos was a lawyer from Cyprus and a member of the Cyprus Ethnarchy, the church council which led the crusade for union with Greece; he had lived in Athens for many years. At my request he visited Cyprus in August 1950 to study the situation, returning to tell me that the passion for Enosis was, if anything, higher than ever before.

I turned next to General G. Kosmas, Chief of the General Staff, formerly my colonel in the 30th Infantry Regiment: he was in the confidence of Marshal Papagos, who was soon to become Premier of Greece. I hoped in this way, although I was at the time retired on pension from the army, to win some kind of official backing for my plans, but it was slow in coming. Kosmas eventually promised his full support and at a meeting in his office on 27 January 1951 he said he agreed with me that only force could liberate Cyprus. I asked him to try and bring Papagos around to the same point of view.

At the same time I contacted a man of great influence and prestige in Greece, Mr George Stratos, a former War Minister, and explained my aims. So it came about that on 1 May 1951 at the Tsitsas Café in Athens, a meeting was held between Stratos, myself and the brothers Savvas and Socrates Loizides, two exiled political leaders who were members of the Ethnarchy Council. The outcome of this discussion was a proposal that I should undertake the leadership of an armed struggle to throw the British out of Cyprus. I accepted immediately, making only one condition: that I should be allowed to visit the island, study the situation and prepare the revolution in my own time. My colleagues readily agreed and from that moment the liberation movement passed from the sphere of abstract idealism into the field of action.

*

There was no secrecy about this visit to my homeland, my first for twenty years. I travelled under my own name, with my own passport, and took my wife, Kiki, with me.[1] We arrived on 5 July 1951 and stayed first in Nicosia with my brother Michael, who was now a doctor with a large practice. I

[1] General Grivas married Miss Vassiliki Dekas, niece of a brother officer, in 1938.

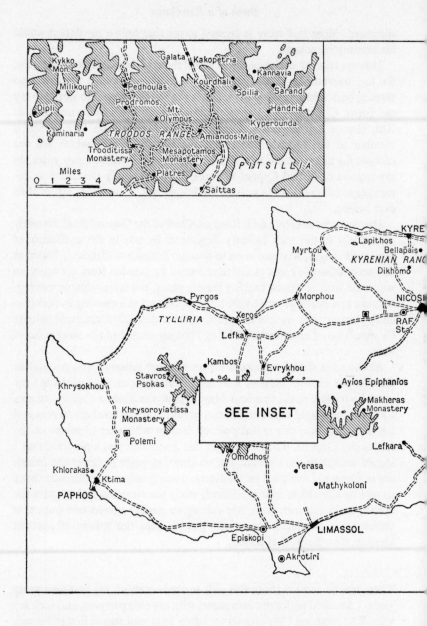

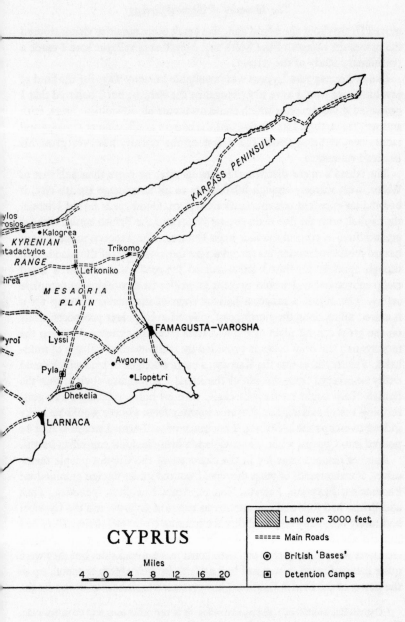

KARPASS PENINSULA

ylos
rosios
● Kalogrea
KYRENIAN
ntadactylos
RANGE
Trikomo
Lefkoniko
hrea
MESAORIA
PLAIN

yroï
● Lyssi

FAMAGUSTA–VAROSHA

Pyla
● Avgorou
● Liopetri
Dhekelia

LARNACA

CYPRUS

Miles
4 0   4   8   12   16   20

Land over 3000 feet
Main Roads
⊙ British 'Bases'
▣ Detention Camps

moved freely about the island and, like every other summer visitor, toured the mountain villages of the Solea and Marathassa valleys: here I made a preliminary study of the terrain.

I knew already that Cyprus was unsuitable in many ways for the kind of revolution we would have to fight against the British; but I believed that I possessed three weapons which could overcome all difficulties: heart, faith and will for victory. I knew also that the correct application of strategy and tactics would bring about the defeat of the enemy, however great his material resources.

The island's major disadvantage was its size: no more than half that of Wales, with scarcely enough inhabitants to fill an average British city, it boasted an excellent communications system. Good roads linked Nicosia, the capital, with the five main coastal towns and the British could, without great difficulty, control the four main features. The Troodos range, a haphazard jumble of mountains spread across the south-west of the island, was, though sparsely inhabited, criss-crossed by roads which allowed rapid troop movement and would prevent guerrillas from working in complete safety. The Kyrenia range, a narrow strip of mountains running for a hundred miles along the north coast, offered even poorer prospects, while on the great central plain of the Mesaoria (the name means 'between the mountains') the only cover is provided by white-washed villages of mud-brick. Finally, there was the Karpass, a narrow tongue of land which could easily be severed from the rest of the island.[1] It was also obvious that the British Navy could create a blockade without much difficulty: any gun-running vessel making the 500-mile journey from Greece would be lucky indeed to escape the radar net. Thousands of well-armed troops would be poured into Cyprus, while we struggled to bring in a few contraband arms.

Another disadvantage lay in the character of the Cypriot people themselves. For thousands of years they had laboured under foreign domination: Phoenician, Egyptian, Persian, Roman, Arab, Lusignan, Venetian, Turk and Briton had followed one another as rulers of Cyprus, and the Cypriots had rarely taken any responsibility for running their own affairs. They had resisted the occupiers and their alien cultures passively; their national character was wholly Greek and their spirit was unbreakable; but they were quite inexperienced in war and had no faith in their ability to match up to the power of the British Empire. They preferred to sit back and wait for the

---

[1] Cyprus has an area of 3,584 square miles: it is 140 miles long and 60 miles wide. The estimated population on 1 January 1956 was 523,800, of which 421,000 were Greeks and 92,000 Turks. It is the third largest island in the Mediterranean, smaller than Sardinia and Sicily, larger than Corsica and Crete.

tyrant to fall. My task, as Leader, would be to give them that faith. The tremendous odds did not dismay me. Many military writers maintain that a leader's capabilities can only overcome a superior force of limited size, but I do not accept this doctrine. In fact, I never seriously took into account the numerical superiority of the British. Brains, subtlety and good planning in an underground movement can defeat any odds. The struggle for Cyprus proves, I believe, the accuracy of this claim.

On this first visit to the island I found little but scepticism towards the idea of a rising against the British; but I knew that the Cypriot temperament could be fanned into flame by one strong breath.

Soon after my arrival I met Archbishop Makarios[1] and told him I thought we had a good chance of success. We discussed the whole question and I explained that I had made a study of the prospects of guerrilla warfare in the island. He seemed reserved and sceptical and when, a month later, I saw him again, on 3 August 1951, and told him the results of my reconnaissance, it was plain that he had grave doubts; on the surface he appeared to agree with everything I said, but I had the impression that he was not really convinced. Apart from Makarios's attitude I left Cyprus satisfied with what I had found. I had decided that the fight could be carried out on two levels: by small, compact guerrilla groups working on a limited scale in the mountains and by saboteurs in the towns, where there were plenty of military targets.

*

As soon as I returned to Athens I set to work to build up a revolutionary committee which would provide the movement with moral and material support. But wherever I turned for aid I was faced by arguments of political expediency or the Greek feeling of sentiment towards an old ally. Marshal Papagos would do nothing. I was informed through General Kosmas that he thought a liberation campaign would be 'premature': it was not that he did not wish to support us, but as leader of the Opposition he was deeply involved in a bid for power and could not risk exposure as a revolutionary plotting against Britain. In these circumstances it was not until 2 July 1952 that we were able to organise the first meeting of a secret liberation committee in Athens, under the chairmanship of Archbishop Makarios. Around the table were George Stratos, the Loizides brothers, General

---

[1] I first met Archbishop Makarios in 1946 when, as a Deacon in Athens, he contributed some articles attacking Communism from a Christian viewpoint to the newspaper published by 'X', my resistance movement, which I had turned into a political party to fight the elections.

Papadopoulos, who was also a Cypriot, Colonel Alexopoulos, a former member of Xhi, two Athens University professors and a lawyer.

When I began by declaring that we should prepare a two-pronged attack, based on guerrillas in the mountains and saboteurs in the towns, Makarios interjected: 'Not fifty men will be found to follow you.' I replied: 'I know the Cypriots well. I am sure they will respond to our call.' Stratos agreed with me, saying: 'Nobody is born brave, but they can find bravery under the right leadership.' The meeting ended inconclusively, but after a second discussion on 21 July we agreed to set up two committees, political and military, which would both come under the chairmanship of Stratos while the Archbishop was absent in Cyprus. Before leaving, Makarios asked me not to visit the island again until he sent for me, but the committee later decided that it was essential that I make a further, more detailed, reconnaissance on the spot. Stratos then called on Archbishop Spiridon of Athens, Primate of all Greece, who promised us his full support and agreed that I should go again to Cyprus. He told us that he doubted whether Makarios really wanted a forceful solution; but, he added, 'Freedom is never won without bloodshed'.

I arrived in the island at the start of October 1952 and this time I devoted five full months to a thorough study of the problems I would have to face. My difficulties were increased by the need to work in the utmost secrecy, for surprise would be the key to the success of our first attacks. On the basis of a close personal survey I decided that there was definitely scope for guerrilla forces in both mountain ranges, although this would be on a small scale, to allow greater freedom of movement and simplify problems of concealment and supply.

I also sketched out a plan for smuggling arms to Cyprus before the fighting began. It was at this time, in November 1952, that I first met Andreas Azinas, a young protégé of the Archbishop who came to the door of my brother's house in Nicosia to offer his assistance. With him I chose the landfall for our first gun-running caique: this was a small sandy bay on the west coast a few miles from Paphos, where a path would take us up from the beach to Khlorakas village, the home of Azinas's family. It was arranged that his relatives and friends would receive the arms and hide them in their fields. Azinas was to supervise the whole operation, under my orders. His position as Secretary-General of PEK, the Farmers' Union, gave him an excuse for constant travels round the island and for trips to Athens on agricultural business. He became liaison between Makarios and myself.

We nearly ran into trouble before we had begun. A caique loaded with

General Grivas at the Rhodes bay from which he embarked for Cyprus

The guerrilla Harilaos Xenofontos, repairing the Spilia hideout.
It was he who placed the time bomb, designed for Governor
Armitage, in the Pallas Cinema, Nicosia

Students demonstrating with the Greek flag at their head

pottery was sent from Greece to Paphos for a trial run to allow the captain to inspect the landing points. It was spotted by the police, who thought it was acting suspiciously and arrested the captain; however, nothing could be found against him, and he was released after questioning. This unfortunate incident had at least the advantage of impressing the need for secrecy on everyone.

Meanwhile the leaders of the two Christian Youth movements, Father Stavros of OXEN and Stavros Poskottis of PEON, were selecting a handful of reliable young men to receive and store guns in other parts of the island. The actual fighters would be picked from these organisations when I returned to prepare our first attacks. I had decided to use only Cypriots in the fight, to show the world that our campaign was purely Cypriot in origin and conduct; I knew, besides, that if I began recruiting men on the Greek mainland, the secret would be all over Athens in a few days.

On my return to Greece in February 1953 I drew up an overall plan which, with only minor modifications, acted as a guide to my operations from start to finish of the struggle.[1] It may surprise the reader to learn that a document forecasting the pattern of events so accurately could be drawn up more than two years before the campaign began, but this is the case. Copies of the plan were given to Makarios and George Stratos at the time of its conception. I should add that I was expected to work on the basis of the Archbishop's estimate that the fight would be brought to an end within three to six months by a political settlement; I never believed this, and for that reason I insisted on the dispatch of more arms and made provision for a prolonged struggle.

The sum needed to buy arms and ship them to Cyprus was not large, but procrastination and sometimes blunt refusal to give me financial aid made it a difficult task. I brought out of store guns which had been hidden since my days as leader of Xhi and bought others from the stocks hoarded by various people after the end of the civil war of 1945. All my energies were concentrated on advancing the start of the revolution, for every day increased the chances of discovery; it was obvious, too, that the passage of time was making Britain more obstinate in her refusal to leave Cyprus, which was on the way to becoming her last foothold in the Middle East.

A new meeting of the liberation committee was called on 7 March 1953, when Archbishop Makarios returned from a visit to the United States, and the twelve members present took this solemn oath of secrecy and obedience:

[1] This plan is given in Appendix 1.

I swear in the name of the Holy Trinity to keep secret all I know or come to know about the cause of Enosis, even under torture or at the cost of my life. I shall obey without question the instructions given to me at all times.[1]

Three days later Makarios and Savvas Loizides came to my flat in Athens to discuss the results of my visit to Cyprus. My recommendations were not well received. Makarios, while accepting the need to use force, wanted to restrict my operations to sabotage. I insisted on my original plan, which included the use of guerrilla groups, and we parted on a note of disagreement.

Marshal Papagos had now been elected Prime Minister of Greece with a sweeping majority and I had again appealed to him for support. Four days after my talk with Makarios I received Papagos's answer: he did not wish to become involved with the movement, nor did he wish it to be known that he had been informed of my plans. This was the start of a series of threats and warnings designed to make me abandon the whole affair. On 30 March a high-ranking staff officer told me that a liberation struggle was unlikely to succeed and suggested that I would do best to leave the problem in the hands of diplomacy; two months later he called me to General Headquarters and accused me of trying to obtain arms from military stores. I denied this and told him that no-one could stop me from building up a revolutionary movement in Cyprus: it was my right and my duty as a Greek Cypriot.

While blocking this sort of interference from the Greek Government I had to deal simultaneously with the Archbishop's timidities. Once more, on 7 June 1953, Makarios sent word, through Andreas Azinas, that he wanted only sabotage: mines and grenades could be sent to Cyprus, but not guns; nor did he want anyone to come from Greece. This, of course, meant me. I was amazed at his attitude. How could he expect to impose our will on the British without plan, programme or a capable leader? Did he really suppose that they would give way to a few sabotage attempts after three or four months? I began to believe that Makarios did not want to use force at all, and that he had merely yielded to pressure in going this far. I could only assume that his hesitations were due to a fear that he would be exiled if a revolution began. I told Azinas that I could not associate myself with these tactics which, while they would mean hardship and reprisals for

[1] The signatories to this oath were: Makarios, Archbishop of Cyprus, Nicolas Papadopoulos (General), George Stratos, Yerasimos Konidaris (Professor), Antonios Avgikos (lawyer), Savvas and Socrates Loizides, George Grivas, El. Tsatsomiros (craftsman), D. Stavropolos (railway official), Demetrios Vezanis (Professor), Elias Alexopoulos (Colonel).

the Cypriots, would certainly not compel the British to negotiate. Other members of the committee agreed with me and said that we should go ahead regardless of the Archbishop's views. This had its effect, for on 23 June 1953 I received a letter from my brother Michael, who wrote: 'Archbishop Makarios agrees with what you told him through Azinas and you are to prepare the material for transport.' At the same time Savvas Loizides received money from Makarios to buy arms.

Over the years Greece had hoped to settle the Cyprus problem in friendly discussion with Britain, but in the autumn of 1953 Marshal Papagos, in his new role as Premier, announced that the question would be brought before the United Nations for the first time in the following year. Even then the attempts to hinder my work continued. On 28 September 1953 I was called to the office of a Government Minister, who warned me that unless I dropped my plans he would 'unhappily' have to arrest me! I carried on with my work exactly as before and heard nothing more from this gentleman.

We were still far from fixing a starting date for the revolution. Savvas Loizides told me that the Greek Foreign Minister, Stefanos Stefanopoulos, feared that any action taken before the United Nations debated Cyprus would be regarded as blackmail. I protested that the tides of international politics were moving against us at an increasing rate, and that every day we wasted more British troops arrived in the island from the Suez Canal bases: the British had already decided to withdraw from Egypt and make Cyprus their Middle East Headquarters. I put these arguments with some force, and at a meeting of the liberation committee on 29 January 1954, it was at last agreed that action should begin as soon as possible: agreed, that is, by everyone except Makarios, who arrived in Athens a month later, when the first shipload of arms was ready to leave. When we met I realised at once that he had still not made up his mind to use force. To pin him down once and for all I asked Admiral Sakelariou, the former Commander-in-Chief of the Greek Navy who was helping me with the arrangements over the arms caique, to see Makarios with me and urge him to go forward more boldly. The Admiral is a man of great personality and persuasiveness and between us, we were able to dispel some, at least, of the doubts in Makarios's mind. One week later Andreas Azinas flew from Cyprus to receive my orders about the reception of the shipment at Khlorakas. On 2 March 1954, on a lonely stretch of coast in Attica, the following arms were loaded aboard a small caique, under cover of darkness:

3 Brens (British)
3 Beretta machine-guns (Italian; one in poor condition)

4 Thompson sub-machine-guns (American)
17 automatics; stens (British) and marcips (German)
47 rifles (of various origins and ages)
7 revolvers (ditto)
32,150 rounds (various calibres)
290 hand grenades
20 kilos explosive, with fuse.

The cost of the heavy material in this list, plus packing and transport to the loading point, was no more than 50,000 drachmae (approximately £600). The cargo was safely unloaded at Khlorakas under Azinas's personal supervision and concealed in the fields around the village. It was with these arms, and these alone, that I kept the fight going for almost a year without any appreciable reinforcements.

I began at once to prepare a second boatload, which was to consist chiefly of explosives; but despite the backing of the committee I could not get Makarios to see the importance of sending a good supply before operations began. He offered the scantiest means and was slow in doing so, while the Greek Government, far from offering to help, continued to interfere, in a feeble way. The Foreign Ministry advised me in April 1954 that recourse to violence would cause 'incalculable damage' to the Cyprus question which was making good diplomatic progress. A month later General K. Venderis, Head of the Royal Household, who had collaborated with me as chief of the resistance organisation 'RAN' against the Germans and the Communists during the occupation, passed on another message from Papagos insisting that we should do nothing to upset Britain; he also hinted that the Marshal had taken steps in Cyprus to spoil my chances. I had to make up my mind: faced with such a miserable lack of support, should I abandon the struggle, or should I carry on in spite of everything? Anyone else, meeting with such discouragement, over so many years, might well have given up: but I had taken my decision to get to Cyprus as soon as possible, and no human power could prevent me from carrying it out. Luck is always on the side of the daring. Herodotus says somewhere that great things are never achieved without great dangers.

The Greek appeal had not yet been lodged with the United Nations and I heard that the Foreign Ministry were divided as to whether to persist with it. I was quite sure that we would achieve nothing in this sphere unless a strong fighting force was present in Cyprus to support Greek diplomacy, and when Azinas next visited me, on 16 July 1954, I told him to prepare for my arrival at once. He must find houses where we could hide, mark down sabotage targets for my approval, locate army and police units, note British agents, find new landing points for arms caiques and, finally, arrange for my reception at Khlorakas. There was no question of my entering Cyprus openly this time; because of the heightened feelings against Britain in the island, the Cyprus Government had begun to refuse visas to visitors from Greece, and my application was among them. I would have to land in secret from a fishing boat.

My brother wrote in August to say that Makarios was sending money for that essential second load of arms and explosives. A fortnight later Greece's appeal was submitted to the United Nations: Savvas Loizides told me that diplomacy could do no more, for the time being. I assured him that I would push ahead even if I did so alone, and I began to prepare for my departure. By the first week in October the new shipment of arms was ready. Some had been contributed by well-wishers and it had cost 80,000 drachmae (£950) to buy the rest, and to pack and load the consignment. It included:

34 pistols with 656 rounds
4 Steiger automatics with 4,000 rounds
4,000 rounds 9 mm ammunition
350 kilos dynamite
300 lb Nobel 808 explosive
100 mines
300 hand grenades
700 canisters fulminate of mercury
100 smoke bombs
1,100 metres slow-burning fuse
120 coloured flares
Cameras, binoculars, etc.

This material was to be loaded on to a caique as before and sent to Khlorakas under the same captain.

A new Makarios passed through Athens in October 1954, on his way to the United Nations in New York. Now he wanted to speed the dispatch of arms to Cyprus: he told me he had given Savvas Loizides money to pay for the caique and that both he and the Foreign Minister, Stefanopoulos, were eager for me to leave at once. It was now considered that action was required *before* the debate at the United Nations, so as to persuade the Americans that an adverse attitude would start trouble in Cyprus, and thus in the Middle East. But even at this stage Makarios dithered: when we met for a third time he said he would signal from America when he wanted us to strike; and at a fourth meeting he told me to attack as soon as I arrived. Obviously this was impossible in an island where no one but myself was capable of performing the simplest sabotage operation, but I listened calmly and did not try to discourage him. The important thing was that I should land in Cyprus as quickly as possible. I would strike when we were ready. My progress in setting up the organisation, not the hasty and unrealistic decisions of Makarios, would determine the start of action.

*

When, on 26 October 1954, I took leave of my wife and, armed only with faith, set out for Cyprus, I knew that I had begun the hardest task of my life. But I knew also that all roads are open to the brave, and I closed my diary on a note of hope with the words: 'God guide me. . . . I leave with faith and courage. . . . I shall succeed.'

I sailed from Piraeus on the ss *Aegean* for the island of Rhodes, where a caique was waiting to take me the last 200 miles to Cyprus. Socrates Loizides, the younger of the two exiled Cypriot brothers, travelled with me. A fierce storm was blowing when we entered Rhodes harbour and it continued unabated for the next twelve days. We stayed the night at a guest house run by Mrs Syzmani, of the local tourist office, but next day we moved to a room in the old part of the town which had once served as a masonic lodge. We had to keep out of sight in case government agents tried to stop us from reaching Cyprus. Here, for ten more days and nights, we waited while the rain poured down and the wind howled, whipping up huge seas: at one stage we thought our caique, the *Siren*, had foundered in the storm, when a messenger told us she was missing from her anchorage; but she had only taken refuge further down the coast, since the captain could not give himself away by entering the harbour.

At last, on the afternoon of 8 November, the weather cleared and we were able to sail at midnight from the little bay of Kallithea. Before dawn a new gale arose, more violent than the one that had gone before. Mountainous seas were breaking over our 30-foot boat as we passed Castelorizon island, off the Turkish coast, and the captain wanted to run for the safety of the mainland. I told him I would rather we all went to the bottom than fall into the hands of the Turks, destroying everything that had been achieved so far. All through the next day and night we fought our way slowly south, until towards noon on 10 November we sighted the thin line of the Cyprus coast. We approached Khlorakas at dusk and rowed ashore in the dinghy at 8 pm. When we were a few yards from land a voice called, 'Who is there?'

I replied, 'Dighenis is here!'

And the correct response came back: 'Akritas is here.'

We stepped ashore and shook hands with the men who had come to meet us and guide us to the village. The storm had ceased and everything was calm.

Next morning the arms which had already arrived in Cyprus were brought from their hiding places to be cleaned and distributed. This was the first task, and for the next fortnight I was kept busy organising groups and training men from OXEN and PEON, the youth movements. Soon the nucleus of the organisation was formed in the five main towns and in seven key villages. To every member was administered this solemn oath:

I swear in the name of the Holy Trinity that:

I shall work with all my power for the liberation of Cyprus from the British yoke, sacrificing for this even my life.

I shall perform without question all the instructions of the Organisation which may be given to me and I shall not bring any objection, however difficult or dangerous these may be.

I shall not abandon the struggle unless I receive instructions from the Leader of the Organisation, and after our aim has been accomplished.

I shall never reveal to anyone any secret of the Organisation, neither the names of my chiefs nor those of any other members, even if I am captured and tortured.

I shall not reveal any of the instructions which may be given me, even to my fellow fighters.

If I disobey this oath I shall be worthy of every punishment as a traitor, and may eternal contempt cover me.

The only way to train guerrillas in Cyprus was by putting them through actual combat: this must wait until the fight began and I could lead the groups myself. Meanwhile, to start the simpler task of training saboteurs, I moved at the end of November to Nicosia. Lefkios Rhodosthenous, who was later to lead the Limassol groups, drove me through the huge British bases then under construction on the south coast, which would soon house the new Middle East Headquarters. As we passed through one half-finished camp a few miles from Limassol our car sank into the mud. I called out to an army truck nearby and the soldiers obligingly pulled us out with rope and tackle. We continued our tour of inspection, with the boot full of weapons, through Larnaca and Famagusta, arriving in the capital after dark.

I immediately began interviewing young men selected from the ranks of OXEN and PEON as possible group leaders. Among them were men like Markos Drakos, the twenty-two-year-old clerk of a mining company who became one of EOKA's greatest heroes; Haralambos Mouskos, who died in a gun-battle with the British army; and many who are still alive today – Yannakis Droushiotis, who left his job in a weaving factory to become leader of the Paphos area; Lambros Kafkallides, a grocer who became my tireless personal servant and aide when I formed the first guerrilla bands. But even men of this calibre needed training and guidance at every step; and there were many who fell below their standard of intelligence, loyalty and enthusiasm. However, we soon had three rudimentary teams of PEON boys in Nicosia, eighteen men in all, and I could see that there was plenty of good material among them.

We needed several houses around Nicosia in which we could hold meetings, store arms and build underground hideouts. Father Stavros, head of OXEN, was detailed to find them. Owing to our elaborate security precautions it took me until mid-December to get the guns safely into the hands of those who were to use them and into caches all over Cyprus. Socrates Loizides, my companion in the *Siren*, went to Limassol district to organise groups there, while another assistant whom I had brought from Greece came to join me in Nicosia; both these men had served in the Greek army and were able to give some rough and ready weapon-training to others. More than this they could not do and I had personally to supervise every detail of the Organisation's construction, training, administration and strategy; where this was impossible, since I could not be everywhere at once, I issued long instructions and orders. A good example is an order made in February 1955:

ORGANISATION OF THE OUT-OF-TOWN POPULATION

1. AIMS

The initiation of persons in order that they should be able to offer the following assistance:

(*a*) by taking part in mass demonstrations in villages, mass protests, etc.;

(*b*) concealing and giving asylum to members of the Organisation;

(*c*) participation in acts of violence, if necessary with arms;

(*d*) obtaining and passing information as regards the object and nature of any movement of troops and police;

(*e*) observing government agents.

They are not to be used for any political or party purposes.

2. ORGANISATION

The Organisation will be temporary and is to be modified in due course. In every province there is to be a section of the Organisation with district HQ in the capital of the province. At the head of this section will be a District Leader, who is to be assisted by a staff which, for the present, he will be able to pick at his discretion.

District Leaders will have the power to appoint local leaders who will be responsible to the District Leader for the Organisation, etc., in each town, locality or village.

District Leaders will be responsible exclusively to the Leader of EOKA, from whom alone they will receive their orders.

3. SELECTION AND INITIATION OF MEMBERS

The initiation of persons must be done in absolute secrecy in order that the existence of the Organisation should not be revealed to the authorities or un-authorised persons.

Personnel will be bound by oath to obey all orders issued by the Organisation and to keep absolute secrecy.

Members must be made to realise that any disobedience will be severely punished.

At every locality (town, village) a nucleus of one or two persons will be formed to start with, according to local requirements. This is to be done in absolute secrecy and these nuclei are then to expand by initiating further members of their communities in accordance with local requirements and conditions. The object, however, is not NUMBERS but QUALITY.

The initiation of new members will be limited to nationalists who have proved themselves reliable or whose trustworthiness or courage can be relied on.

Persons who are taken into the Organisation in each locality must be divided into categories (*a*), (*b*), (*c*), (*d*), (*e*), according to the work they will be used for (see under subheading 'AIMS').

Steps must be taken to prevent indiscretions even between members so as to preclude the possibility of leakages which can give our members away and information about our intentions. For this reason, and in so far as it may be practicable, one member should not know any other member in the same locality or elsewhere particularly as regards members who have been given responsible tasks such as the concealment of wanted men. In this case it is particularly important that both the members themselves and their work should be unknown to other members.

As for members directly concerned, they are to be very careful in their con-versations with other people and in their activities, so as to give no grounds for the slightest suspicion which could result in attracting the attention of the authorities.

4. In order to make good and rapid communications possible and in order to ensure that members can be contacted at short notice it is essential that quick

and safe couriers should be established. This will be the responsibility of the District Leaders.

The setting up of the Organisation will begin at once.

The Leader of EOKA is to receive every Sunday evening from his District Leaders their reports on what was accomplished in their respective districts in the course of the preceding week, and also any recommendations that they may have to put forward.

The Leader,
Dighenis.

Good intelligence and courier services were a first essential. Our early system was rudimentary and the couriers broke every rule of security. I had to make superhuman efforts to train them up to my standards but finally I succeeded, and our ultimate victory was due in no small measure to their efficiency. I never tried to use radio, telephone or any scientific means of communication which might give our positions away. I relied entirely on delivery by hand, and my messengers, after instruction from me, developed great ingenuity in inventing hiding places and concealing EOKA correspondence. Daily they passed unharmed through road block, curfew and search. The cream of British intelligence was sent to Cyprus to smash this system, yet during four years of fighting they captured only a few letters; and the information they did obtain was followed up with deplorable slowness. Several times the police had information in their hands which could have led them to my hideout, but I was always able to snap the thread before they acted. This high standard was achieved through the rigid application of discipline. I issued frequent warnings that I alone would give orders and that everyone would obey: disobedience would be punished by death.

There were two other factors to which I attached prime importance: public support and the organisation of a youth movement. I knew that with these on our side, applied with the proper strategy, the size of the material forces against us would be irrelevant. The use of young people in a battle of this kind was entirely my own idea. I know of no other movement, organisation or army which has so actively employed boys and girls of school age in the front line. And yet there is every reason to do so: young people love danger; they must take risks to prove their worth. I had some experience of working with the young during the occupation, and later during the civil war in Greece, when time and time again, boys of sixteen and seventeen proved themselves equal or superior to mature men. I began the youth organisation by appointing an agent in each town: his task was to choose a leader at every school, who would, in turn, set up class leaders. There was a separate organisation for youths of school age who were working. Cypriot youth first showed its strength in December 1954, when the United Nations rejected the Cyprus appeal with the remark that it was 'not the appropriate time' to discuss the matter. The students received the news with spontaneous strikes and demonstrations, during which the army opened fire on a crowd and wounded three young boys. There were bitter feelings in Cyprus and Greece over this incident.

Archbishop Makarios, who had been in New York for the debate, returned on 10 January 1955, and next day we met in the Larnaca Bishopric. He told me of events at the United Nations, where America had opposed us and said that Marshal Papagos was now in full agreement with our activities. I was glad to hear it, for the Greek Premier, up to that date, had offered no support at all, and everything we had done, we had done despite him. I told him we must give the organisation a name, and suggested EOKA.[1] We also discussed a date for the start of the revolution. Makarios wanted to begin on 25 March, Greece's independence day; but I suggested that if we left it so long, we might lose the element of surprise: so far the British had taken no precautions whatsoever and army camps and government offices were almost unguarded. We should also make use of the long winter nights to operate. The question was left undecided, and before we could strike, disaster intervened.

*

The boatload of arms and explosives which was supposed to follow me out to Cyprus had not arrived. This was bad: we must have explosives before we could start. I sent an urgent note to Athens to speed a new caique on its way. Andreas Azinas informed me that the Archbishop, on his way back from America, had paid out 65,000 drachmae (£795) in Athens for a new shipment, and another instalment of 48,000 drachmae (£480) would be paid when the material arrived.

The caique *St George* left Greece on 13 January 1955, and I ordered the Khlorakas group to prepare for her reception. Two days later Archbishop Makarios warned me that someone had betrayed us: the British had wind of an arms cargo and had put a special watch on the western half of the island. We had no way of contacting the *St George* at sea and we waited, hoping against hope that all might be well, for two agonising weeks. I felt sure that she was only delayed by bad weather, as the *Siren* had been, in Rhodes. But luck was against us: on 26 January 1954 the caique was intercepted by a British destroyer off the Khlorakas coast and both the

[1] Ethniki Organosis Kyprion Agoniston: National Organisation of Cypriot Fighters.

crew and the shore party were arrested, including Socrates Loizides, who had planned to return to Greece aboard her.

This was a staggering blow. We had lost the vital explosives, almost the entire stock for the sabotage campaign with which we were to begin action and the whole movement was in danger of discovery. I left Nicosia at once and took refuge in the mountain village of Kakopetria after ordering all training to cease. But the authorities seemed satisfied with their prize and took the matter no further, so after a few days I returned to the capital and began work once more. I intended to keep to the original plan for sabotage if we could obtain enough explosives from the mines and from army stores; if not, I should have to train my best men in small arms and start the fight with guerrillas.

To help me with this problem I turned to a young man from Lyssi, called Gregoris Afxentiou, who had served as an officer in the Greek army, and whom I had placed in charge of Famagusta district, which he knew well. Afxentiou first had the idea of getting explosives from the sea bed: it was well known that fishermen in the area were dynamiting fish and that they got their material by diving in shallow water off the Famagusta coast to recover some of the hundreds of surplus shells dumped there by the British at the end of the war. Extracting the contents was dangerous work, but Afxentiou and his group were able to collect large quantities of TNT; and so I was able to open our attack with sabotage, according to plan. Afxentiou later became the finest of my lieutenants, brave, humble, disciplined and frugal, inspiring respect and affection in all who knew him.

We also arranged a network of men to smuggle dynamite in sticks from the local mines at Amiandos and elsewhere. From these two sources we created our own crude bombs, making them from whisky bottles filled with petrol, to which sticks of dynamite were attached with adhesive tape; and from metal pipe-joints with screw caps, through which protruded a length of fuse-wire, to be lit with a cigarette.

Before the fight began I had to find a secure and permanent headquarters. It was necessary, for the present, that I should stay in Nicosia and personally supervise operations; in the capital, too, I could best maintain contact with the five towns – the ports of Famagusta, Larnaca and Limassol and the smaller towns of Ktima and Kyrenia. All roads in Cyprus lead to Nicosia, which lies in the centre of the Mesaoria plain, broiling in summer temperatures of 110°F, and over.

Nicosia is divided into two parts, the old town and the new. The old quarter, a maze of winding streets and tumbledown buildings, is contained in an exact circle by the city wall, built 500 years ago by the Venetians as a defence against the Turks. There are good hiding places here, but this densely packed, noisy heart of the island is easily isolated: the British need only place road blocks at the main gates in the 40-foot high walls to cut it off from the outside world. So it was in the suburbs which spread for miles around that I looked for a suitable house. We rented a small, red-roofed bungalow on the outskirts of the town, new and clean and set in an area occupied largely by British families. Beneath the tiled floor of the bedroom we excavated a secret cellar in which we could take refuge with our arms in case of danger. This hideout, when completed, was a tiny, cement-lined box, just large enough for a man to crouch in. It was a most uncomfortable spot, but the entrance was impossible to find unless one knew exactly what to look for: a section of the tiled floor which could be raised like a man-hole cover, revealing a narrow tunnel with a ladder going down. For the next few months this little villa was EOKA's headquarters in Cyprus.

Our recruiting and training was making good progress, but it would not be easy to impress on the island that a serious revolutionary movement had arisen. We could make up for this, in part, by careful selection of targets and assault techniques. I personally inspected all government offices and military installations before making out this final list:

NICOSIA: Cyprus Broadcasting Station (government radio); Forces Broadcasting Station; Wolseley Barracks (Cyprus Military HQ); the Secretariat; the Education Office.

FAMAGUSTA: Dhekelia Cantonment; Pergamos Water Supply Point; 625 Ordnance Depot.

LARNACA: Police HQ; the Courts; Administration Offices; homes of the District Commissioner and Police Chief.

LIMASSOL: Police HQ; Episkopi Power Station.

Sabotage groups, each of five or six men, were ready in all these towns: the Organisation's total fighting strength was not more than eighty men. The British, despite the capture of the *St George*, had not the slightest idea of what was coming and their forces at this time appeared to be ill-equipped and ill-organised. The police, in particular, were of low standard, thanks to poor pay and conditions: they were unarmed, short of transport, without radio, while many village police stations did not even have a telephone. Nor was the army in any state to deal with a revolution. The British withdrawal from the Canal Zone was in full spate and Middle East Land Forces HQ had recently moved into Wolseley Barracks, Nicosia. Later, this Headquarters would move to the new bases at Episkopi and Dhekelia, but they were far from completion; large numbers of troops were engaged on construction and administrative work and there were virtually no security precautions. Even so, my small force was outnumbered by more than a hundred to one. But, as I have said, this made no difference to the type of subversive warfare I was planning.

By the middle of March 1955 my preparations were complete and after consultation with Makarios I decided on the night of 31 March for the start of the struggle. I summoned the area commanders from the towns and gave them my last orders, urging them to inspire their men with daring, for there must be no failures in this first assault. I had already taken as my *nom-de-guerre* 'DIGHENIS', the great hero of Byzantine legend. Now I drew up my first revolutionary proclamation, calling on the people to throw off the English yoke and be worthy of the Greek heroes, the 300 of Leonidas and the fighters of 1821. I warned that the struggle would be hard, but we would win, for right was on our side. I ended with these words:

Diplomats of the world – Look to your duty. It is shameful that, in the twentieth century people should have to shed blood for freedom, that divine gift for which we too fought at your side and for which you, at least, claim that you fought against Nazism. Greeks – . . . Forward all together for the freedom of our Cyprus.[1]

[1] For complete text of this proclamation, see Appendix 2.

CHAPTER THREE

The Struggle Begins

As midnight approached on 31 March 1955, I waited in our Nicosia house for the attack to begin; with me were my bodyguard Gregoris Louka and the houseowner. At the appointed time, 0030 hours, the electric light flickered briefly, and I realised that the attempt to cut the current had failed. But within seconds we heard the first explosions: they echoed over the sleeping town and a brief silence followed; then came a second series of muffled thuds which shook the foundations of the house and finally a single bang, the loudest of all. We sat up listening until 3 am, but there was no other sound, and we turned in for the night.

I was up at 6 am as usual and sent Gregoris Louka out to buy the morning papers; their reports showed that the attack had gone well. In the evening Yannakis Droushiotis, my chief aide in Nicosia, brought further details. A four-man group under Markos Drakos had scored the greatest success, with a raid on the Government radio station: they had broken into the building, gagged and bound the watchmen, then planted bombs in the machinery. The roof had been blown off and transmitters and other vital equipment destroyed; total damage was estimated at nearly £60,000. Haralambos Mouskos's group of seven had walked into the unguarded Secretariat, flung their bombs through the government office windows and walked out again. A team under Christakis Eleftheriou had thrown bombs over a fence around Wolseley Barracks into some wireless installations.

Results elsewhere were less satisfactory. At Limassol the two main police stations had been bombed and the Episkopi power plant dynamited, but several members had been arrested. At Larnaca, the Courts, the Commissioner's Office and Police HQ had all been shattered by bombs, but the town leader, Poskottis, had been caught with two of his groups. At Famagusta the attacks had failed – the bombs had been thrown but they had failed to explode, and Gregoris Afxentiou was wanted by the police. A poster was issued offering £250 reward for his arrest, which was soon raised to £1,000. Our only casualty was a young member of the Famagusta group, Modestos Pantelis, who was electrocuted in the attempt to cut the electricity supply: he had thrown a rope, damp with dew, over the high tension wires and it had exploded in a blinding flash, leaving him dead at the foot of a pylon.

These losses did not weaken the Organisation, for the gaps were quickly filled by young fighters from the ranks. Michael Rossides, a mines clerk, aged twenty-one, took over in Larnaca; Pavlos Pavlakis, who worked for a British shipping firm in Famagusta, replaced Afxentiou, whom I made commander of Kyrenia district.

The attack took the world by surprise; but none were more shocked than the British officials who ran Cyprus. Both they and their military advisers appeared stunned and panic-stricken: absurd efforts were made to recruit Cypriot civil servants into a special constabulary to guard government buildings and pathetic bleats of protest and condemnation were broadcast. These were supported by the Cypriot Communists, who disowned the attack as the work of 'hooligans', 'pop-gun wielders' and the like. Nor did we receive the proper encouragement from Athens: the 'Voice of the Fatherland' programme, beamed to Cyprus, was so feeble that I was obliged to complain to Makarios.

I continued action over the next few days to make it plain that we were fighting a deliberate and systematic war, then ordered a halt while I regrouped my forces for a heavier attack. Our success had electrified the island and young men pressed forward to join EOKA's ranks: there was no shortage of good men, but I had to ensure that we had sufficient arms and explosives for a long fight. Unlike Makarios, I did not expect an early solution from Britain or the United Nations and my plan was that the first stage of the offensive should last until October, when the Security Council would again debate the Cyprus problem. The outcome would determine the next stage and final form of the campaign.

Meanwhile I began the battle for the minds of the population in earnest; above all, I concentrated on the young. I intended to turn the youth of Cyprus into the seedbed of EOKA, and early in May 1955 I issued orders that students of both sexes should be enrolled in the Organisation to distribute leaflets, watch British agents and police, and take part in mass demonstrations. The liveliest and bravest boys would graduate later to the fighting groups.

Our first major demonstration was on 24 May 1955, when some 700 pupils threw themselves into the struggle with such determination that the police bolted before them, pursued by a hail of stones, and the army had to be called out. After that, nothing could hold the schools back. They learned to act as one in blind obedience to my orders and developed into one of the chief factors in our victory. The British were baffled to find that

A captured priest being led to prison

The Rhegaina peak in the 'Alonoudi' region where Grivas camped for a fortnight with a wounded guerrilla, Styllis Xapolytos of Galata

Markos Drakos's group
of guerrillas

The spot in Nicosia where General Kendrew's car and that of his escorts struck
an electrically detonated mine

the enemy throwing bombs was a sixteen-year-old schoolboy, or that those distributing revolutionary leaflets were ten-year-olds from the primary schools. They tried to frighten children away from the movement and persuade parents to keep them indoors. There were also certain Cypriots in authority who tried to put obstacles in my path. I was forced to announce that I would take severe action against anyone who interfered; and my threat was carried out in the case of some incorrigible teachers. Today, however, I often receive letters from Cypriot educational institutions, thanking me for saving the youth of the island, and placing them on the path of honour, duty, prosperity and progress.

The Cypriot Press also required much encouragement in these early days. It would allow repressive laws to be passed without a murmur, because editors lacked faith in our ability to stand up to the Government. I was forced to order a boycott against weak-spirited newspapers: these, when they saw sales fall and realised our strength, quickly complied with my directions. Later they played an important role in the struggle. So, indeed, did every Greek organisation and institution, with the solitary exception of the Communist Party, AKEL. In opposing us, the Cypriot Communists were simply taking orders from behind the Iron Curtain; this was clearly shown in the first month of our campaign, when, in a broadcast from Moscow, the leader of Greece's Communist Party, Zachariades, denounced EOKA and treacherously revealed the identity of 'Dighenis', which he had learned from one of his Athenian spies. Comically, the British did not take this piece of information seriously: the idea of an elderly retired officer as the Leader of EOKA was too strange for them to accept.

★

At this time I was moving frequently about Nicosia, both by car and on foot, to meet the group leaders, who needed constant encouragement and clear orders. I often wondered, as I drove through the streets, what would have happened if someone had told the soldiers and police we passed that the man in dark glasses, sitting beside the driver of our old black Austin saloon, was their arch-enemy, Dighenis. Probably, like the authorities, they would have disbelieved it. Far more real was the danger of being recognised by friends or relatives who would want to know what I was doing in Cyprus. I adopted some simple disguises – dark glasses, a clipped moustache, a battered old hat – but I was twice spotted by friends of my sister-in-law, who hurried off to complain to her that I had ignored their greetings. She said they must be mistaken and my brother Michael assured them that I was still in Athens. On another occasion I was returning from a visit to the mountains when we were passed by a car containing a British police officer. I told our driver to tag on behind him, and we were waved on at road blocks as if we were his escort.

One trip took me to a small house in Strovolos, which we kept for meetings: here I met eight Cypriot students, all in their teens or early twenties, who had hurried to Cyprus from Greece on learning of our first attacks. They had all received some elementary arms training in Athens and I saw that I had here the nucleus of my first mountain guerrilla groups. They were keen and energetic boys, and among them were three who later played an important part in the fighting – Renos Kyriakides, younger brother of the Bishop of Kyrenia, who led the Pitsillia guerrillas; Tassos Sofocleus, who became Kyrenia leader and was savagely treated on his arrest; Photis Papaphotis, Karpass leader, who lost a hand in a bomb explosion. For the time being I sent them to various groups to complete their training for the next big attack, which I planned to begin in June.

Since the opening offensive there had been only isolated assaults on 'opportunity targets', chief among them being the Governor of Cyprus, Sir Robert Armitage. As part of the Empire Day celebrations at the end of May, he had agreed to attend the première of a new British film at the Pallas Cinema in Nicosia. Markos Drakos worked out a plan to kill him: he chose from his group Haralambos Xenofontos, a municipal worker, and gave him a bomb made out of a Coca-Cola bottle packed with explosive. Xenofontos went to an early showing of the film and planted it, only seconds before the Governor's party arrived, under a seat on the balcony. The time-pencil burned slowly away for the next two hours, a few feet from Armitage's chair. But the film ended five minutes before the scheduled time and the Governor and audience had just left the building when the bomb exploded, wrecking the gallery: seven rows of seats were shattered and the ceiling was peppered with holes caused by flying fragments of wood and metal.

On the eve of the second full-scale attack in June 1955 I drove into the mountains for a meeting with my group leaders. Renos Kyriakides, whom I had charged with the creation of the first guerrilla group, was there; I gave him the code name 'Romanos'. We talked and lunched among the pines at the deserted monastery of Mesapotamos and I issued my final orders. Some time was spent discussing the first raids to be made on police stations. As we drove back to Nicosia, we were startled to see a police patrol standing in the road waving us down. Both my escort and myself were heavily armed and we were just about to pull out revolvers when the sergeant in charge called out to ask if we would take a man wounded in a village quarrel to hospital; we refused, politely, pointing out that the car was full.

The offensive went off according to plan on the night of 19 June 1955: this time we used powerful and deadly bombs filled with shrapnel placed so as to cause maximum damage. The first death from EOKA action occurred when one bomb, which blew a gaping hole in the wall of Nicosia Divisional Police HQ, killed a man and wounded sixteen others. Renos Kyriakides's group attacked Amiandos Police Station, killing the sergeant in charge, and several other stations were attacked. A target that I had personally selected was the Commander-in-Chief, Middle East Land Forces, General Keightley, who drove daily to Nicosia from his home on the Kyrenia coast. I found a good place for an ambush on the pass over the Kyrenia mountains, but Makarios vetoed the plan and the idea was abandoned. That did not deter us from throwing a grenade at his house: night after night the homes, the bars, the hotels frequented by the British were bombed, until, at the end of June, I called a halt. This sustained attack brought us headlines all over the world, but I was not entirely satisfied. I summed up the situation and outlined my plan for future operations in the following document:

EOKA.   ORDER   28th June 1955.

The second period of our operations has been brought to a conclusion. The material results were less than I expected. Each area commander will summon his group leaders for a session of self-criticism to discover the mistakes they made and to take steps to see they are not repeated. I noticed in some groups a lack of fire and impetus and that is why the results are unsatisfactory.

If, however, the material results were disappointing, they were balanced by most rewarding consequences on the international level and especially on British public opinion.

Our activity showed the world a focal point of agitation and resentment against the British administration in Cyprus which cannot be wiped out no matter what measures the Government takes – a focal point which has self-determination as its creed. This admission by international personalities does honour to our efforts and is giving rise to warm advocacy of self-determination for Cyprus overseas. As a result the British Government is retreating from its policy of 'Never'. I do not know whether or not the British will now be willing to discuss the Cyprus question before the time-limit for a new Greek appeal to the United Nations expires, but I know it is our duty to be ready to face the worst and be ready to resume the fight. . . .

Below I give general instructions, so that everyone will be prepared, and before the action starts I shall meet area commanders to make my intentions clear.

The aim of our next offensive will be to terrorise the police and to paralyse the administration, both in the towns and the countryside. If this aim is achieved, the results will be threefold:

Disillusionment will spread through the Police Force so rapidly that most of them, if they do not actually help us, will turn a blind eye to our activities.

Active intervention of the Army in security, which will stretch the troops and tire them out. The falling morale of the Army will also influence its leaders.

In the face of our strength and persistence and the trouble they cause, it is very probable that the United Nations, through member countries who take an interest in Cyprus affairs, will seek to bring about a solution.

The results we want will be obtained by:

1. Murderous attacks against policemen who are out of sympathy with our aims or who try to hunt us down.
2. Ambushes against police patrols in towns or raids on country police stations.
3. Obstructing free movement of the police across the island by laying ambushes (against individuals or groups).

Further instructions, written and verbal, will determine the methods and means by which these tactics will be pursued.

What I must emphasise at this time is that nothing important can be achieved unless every one of us is inspired by a spirit of self-sacrifice and the contempt for danger which a great cause should instil. Before anything else, therefore, the meaning of our struggle and what we expect from our men must be made plain to them. Boldness and impetuosity will bring us victory.

The Leader,
Dighenis.

British newspapers were, at last, taking notice of Cyprus, and the reactionaries were calling for a military governor. The Army and Police chiefs made no secret of their ignorance and confusion about EOKA: when they met under General Keightley at Wolseley Barracks they admitted themselves baffled, and Commissioner of Police Robins said publicly: 'We know nothing about EOKA.' Serious measures were taken for the first time: a 'Mobile Reserve' for the police was announced; new laws for curfews and detention without trial were passed; the courts imposed fierce sentences. But the morale of the people grew steadily stronger, and the answer to British terrorism was given by Christofis Pantelis, brother of the first EOKA man killed in the struggle, when with others of the Larnaca groups, he was given a long prison sentence. He cried to the judge: 'I have merely done my duty as a Greek fighting for freedom.'

The British Government, in their anxiety, looked for support from Turkey, which was encouraged to interfere on behalf of the small Turkish minority (eighteen per cent of the population) in Cyprus. The British Prime Minister, Sir Anthony Eden, who in 1953 had refused to discuss the Cyprus question with Greece, invited both Greece and Turkey to a 'tripartite conference' in London. This was the first move in Britain's long-drawn campaign to prove that Cyprus was an international problem, and that world peace would be threatened if the island was not kept as a base. This pretence was maintained in the face of overwhelming evidence from British and foreign experts.[1] Since the Greek Government were weakly agreeing to this meeting and falling into the British trap Makarios flew to Athens on 11 July 1955 to demand that Greece make a new appeal to the United Nations; he said he would agree to the London talks only if self-determination was guaranteed. Before leaving Nicosia, he sent me this message:

I congratulate you. EOKA has contributed infinitely more to the Cyprus struggle than 75 years of paper war. The name of Dighenis is an enigma to the British. And it is a legend as well. Already it has passed into the pages of the liberation movement's history.

*

My next big attack was planned to coincide with the United Nations debate in the autumn of 1955. Meanwhile, my chief objective would be to paralyse the police, so that the army would be drawn deeper into the terrain of my choosing and their strength dissipated; at present they were concentrating on guarding government buildings and on riot duty. My town groups would execute police who were too zealous on the British behalf, while my countryside groups would attack police stations, kill isolated policemen

[1] Nearly all military authorities agree that Cyprus would be of little use as a base in war. Here are two typical opinions:

'I have never heard, during meetings of Western military commanders, discussion of the use of Cyprus in the event of operations in the Eastern Mediterranean. The island was ignored by the belligerents in both world wars. . . . There are no plans to use it as a NATO base in future.' – General Hans Spiedel, NATO Commander, 'Kathimerini' December 1956.

'[Cyprus] has none, or practically none, of the requisites of an efficient base for the deployment and subsequent employment in military operations of either sea, land or air forces. It lacks almost every facility which a Commander in war would expect to find in a base of operations.' – Field-Marshal Sir Claude Auchinleck, *Sunday Times.*

and ambush police patrols, which were already being stiffened by soldiers. As a first step I issued this leaflet:

TO THE POLICE: I have warned you and I shall carry out my warning to the letter. Darker days await the tyrants of Cyprus, heavier punishments the traitors. . . . Do not try to block our path or you will stain it with your blood. I have given orders that:

Anyone who tries to stop the Cypriot patriots will be

EXECUTED.

Anyone who tries to arrest or search Cypriot patriots will be

SHOT.

YOU HAVE NOTHING TO FEAR SO LONG AS YOU DO NOT
GET IN OUR WAY.

EOKA,
The Leader,
Dighenis.

To stretch the British forces further, action would start in the mountains. I decided that I must move out of Nicosia and put myself at the head of the mountain guerrillas, who needed training, organisation and a taste of seasoned leadership. They must learn war by waging war. It was essential that I should suffer the same hardships as my men, and this was the only way to do it. A leader cannot sit back in safety and comfort: when he offers his life to the cause it creates faith and courage in his followers and the most improbable feats can be achieved when they are led with dash and daring. I knew my death would mean the end of the campaign, for there was no one to take my place; but with the stakes so high I had to risk everything.

So, on 6 July 1955, I moved into the great range of mountains that covers almost the entire western half of the island, rising slowly from the fertile Solea and Marathassa valleys to the Pitsillia vineyards and the pine forests of Troodos, where the Government had its summer quarters. The range is dominated by Mt Olympus, 6,400 feet high: from its peak the sea is visible on both sides of the island; it glimmers in the north across the thickly wooded Tyrillia and in the south over the Limassol hills, while westward the Paphos forest stretches as far as the eye can see. I lived first in the most prosperous village of the Marathassa valley, Kakopetria, where we stayed in a house owned by John Katsoullis, a schoolteacher who had served as a reserve officer in the Greek army. It was a small, isolated building overlooking the jumble of jutting balconies and tin roofs: here I was free from observation and could work in safety.

I began by visiting Renos Kyriakides, whose group at Kyperounda was the strongest and best armed. I showed him a bend in the road to Handria where an ambush could be laid for the army trucks which passed regularly and explained how the roads could be blocked at key points to prevent reinforcements arriving, while the attackers escaped. There were many good ambush sites in this rugged country, and I set to work to find the best.

While staying at Kyperounda I had another encounter with the army, who were, as usual, slow off the mark. On 30 July 1955 three trucks full of soldiers drove into the village at first light, while we slept in the house of a young woman called Thekla. Quickly we gathered our belongings and guns together and loaded them on to a donkey: then, with Thekla goading the animal on, we left the village under the eyes of the troops, who thought we were peasants off the fields. We took to the mountain and were soon out of danger. Later I returned to Kakopetria to complete my preparations. Recruiting continued and caches for food and arms were built. Three large food dumps were established, each containing sufficient dried and tinned food to last fifty men for a fortnight.

Archbishop Makarios remained blind to the value of guerrilla warfare, and in Kakopetria I found another letter expressing his doubts waiting for me. I sent a reply saying that I eventually intended to fight in both town and mountain and I wrote in my diary that night:

August 1, 1955: The Archbishop's attitude is strange. Is he worried about the financial side of things; is he afraid of losses; or of responsibility for bloodshed? Which of these things? Perhaps it is a matter of pride since he spoke against guerrilla action from the start and did not want to bring in arms necessary for this kind of war. Whatever the reason, I shall go forward.

The problem of smuggling arms into the island was as intractable as ever and I received no help from those in power. Despite much hard work on my part it was not until August 1955 that I was able to import a first load of guns: they entered through the port of Limassol in a suitcase, with the connivance of EOKA members in the customs service. A small but steady flow of arms and ammunition was maintained from this time onwards. British intelligence went to immense trouble to guard the coasts and watch the ports, but we always found a loophole in the net; and if they eventually discovered our system, we simply created another. The intelligence service may be surprised to learn that I never brought a single large cargo of guns into Cyprus until the very end of the struggle, either from Egypt, as was often said, or from anywhere else: we relied entirely on these small gaps in the security net for our supplies. Explosives were never a great problem after the first few weeks, for we could rely on local sources, such as the mines at Amiandos, where teams of workmen smuggled out hundreds of sticks every month in their lunch baskets.

Our drive against the police in the towns was making progress after a slow start due to the total inexperience of the execution groups. Sergeants and constables had been killed in the streets of Nicosia and Famagusta and others had been wounded. Village police stations had been raided by guerrillas and their arsenals seized. Resignations began pouring into Force Headquarters and those who continued to work for the British hardly dared to show their faces: even men living inside police stations did not come out until after dark.

At the end of August 1955 we struck the fatal blow against police morale with the public execution of P.C. Michael Poullis, of the Special Branch, who had been spying on the Nicosia groups and interfering with their work: two attempts had already been made on his life but he chose to ignore our warnings. His movements were watched, and on 28 August he was detailed for duty at a Communist meeting in Ledra Street, Nicosia. As the meeting broke up and the street filled with people Poullis stood on the pavement with a Turkish constable. Among the crowd, watching him, was a three-man execution team led by Michael Karaolis, a twenty-two-year-old Government clerk. Suddenly, Poullis left the Turk, crossed the road and stood alone. Karaolis saw his chance: in full view of hundreds of Communists and several other policemen, he walked up to Poullis and shot him through the heart, and before anyone could react he escaped with his group. Unluckily, he had left a bicycle at the scene and it was later traced to him. I ordered that he should join Afxentiou's guerrillas in the Kyrenia mountains; but he was stopped at a road block on leaving Nicosia and arrested. Later he was tried and sentenced to death. This killing of a member of the Special Branch in broad daylight in the centre of the capital shattered opposition to EOKA among the Greek police.

The British were highly alarmed and on the day of the execution the Cyprus Colonial Secretary, J. Sykes, appealed over the radio to the public to give information about EOKA. He said:

A fortnight ago Miki Zavros (a special constable) was shot down from behind by a pair of callous murderers. Before that Sgt Demosthenous was brutally assassinated. Sgt Costopolos died of wounds received in a cowardly ambush. Tonight it is the home, wife and family of Constable Poullis which is grieving for a good and honest man murdered by the evil agents of political terrorism . . . etc., etc., etc.

This was the start of a violent propaganda campaign conducted over the next four years against our technique of surprise attack from behind. The British, who arm their commandoes with knives and instruct them to kill in just this way – from the rear – protested vociferously when such tactics were applied to themselves. It may be argued that these things are only permissible in war. This is nonsense. I was fighting a war in Cyprus against the British, and if they did not recognise the fact from the start they were forced to at the end. The truth is that our form of war, in which a few hundred fell in four years, was far more selective than most, and I speak as one who has seen battlefields covered with dead. We did not strike, like the bomber, at random. We shot only British servicemen who would have killed us if they could have fired first, and civilians who were traitors or intelligence agents. To shoot down your enemies in the street may be unprecedented, but I was looking for results, not precedents. How did Napoleon win his victories? He took his opponents in the flank or the rear; and what is right on the grand scale is not wrong when the scale is reduced and the odds against you are a hundred to one. No one complained of cowardice when we ambushed trucks or killed soldiers from concealed positions in the mountains: but, in principle, there is no difference between mountain guerrilla attacks and street killings by the brave boys who formed our close-range execution teams. These young men, indeed, ran the greatest risk of all, and did not care who called them 'thug' or 'coward'. They knew what they were fighting for. All war is cruel and the only way to win against superior forces is by ruse and trickery; you can no more afford to make a difference between striking in front or from behind than you can between employing rifles and howitzers. The British may criticise me as much as they like for making war in Cyprus, but I was not obliged to ask their permission to do so; nor can they now deny that I made it in the most successful way. For my part, I always drew the line at unnecessary cruelty.

*

During the next few weeks we delivered a series of blows at the British which eventually led them to replace Sir Robert Armitage, the civilian Governor, with a professional soldier. The army in Cyprus had been reinforced, by regiments from Suez and by commandoes from Malta, and there were constant searches and curfews; never before had the people seen so many and such hostile troops. The Government's actions, ill-treating and imprisoning men without trial, hauling down Greek flags, arresting and beating schoolboy rioters, had brought them new un-popularity. The youth of Cyprus, in its nationalist ecstasy, defied clubs, tear gas and bullets. During a huge demonstration in Metaxas Square, the centre of Nicosia, in September 1955, army trucks were stoned, overturned and set ablaze; the doors of the British Institute were broken open and the building burned to the ground.

The tripartite conference, which was held at the end of the month, only aggravated the situation. It was a cynical example of Anglo-Turkish collusion, acknowledging once more the rights in Cyprus which Turkey had abandoned in the 1923 Treaty of Lausanne. The failure of the conference was inevitable and it was the cause of the final destruction of good relations between Greece and Turkey. To emphasise that they meant business over Cyprus, the Turks engineered a bloodthirsty pogrom against the Greek minorities in Turkey. As a pretext for this they exploded a bomb in the Turkish Consulate at Salonika; immediately a Turkish mob raged through the streets of Constantinople and Smyrna, destroying everything Greek. Of eighty-three Orthodox churches, only six were spared; 2,500 Greek homes were wrecked, burnt or looted; two bishops and many priests were among those murdered. These dreadful events brought no protest from Britain, or from Greece's ally, America. A disgraceful stain on civilisation was glossed over for the sake of keeping the Turks quiet. The Americans wanted no trouble with a country which they had filled with rocket bases.

The Anglo-American front also operated against us at the United Nations where, on 23 September 1955, the Greek appeal over Cyprus was again rejected. There were protest demonstrations and a twenty-four-hour general strike in the island.

On the night the United Nations appeal was turned down the British suffered another blow when sixteen of my best men escaped from Kyrenia Castle, where they were held with eighty other detainees. The castle is an immense, rectangular building with towers at each corner and walls many feet thick around a central courtyard. It is enclosed on two sides by the sea, and on a third by the little harbour of Kyrenia. The north tower, which housed the prisoners, was built in Crusader times, and its rooms are lit by arrow slits looking out across the sea to Turkey, forty miles away. Army guards patrolled the parapets, but the welfare of the detainees was left in the hands of four Cypriot sergeant warders and a staff of twelve. Among those who worked on the escape plan were Markos Drakos, Christos Eleftheriou, Lambros Kafkallides, Mikis Firylas and Evangelos Evangelakis of Nicosia; Lefkios Rhodosthenous of Limassol; and Michael Rossides of Larnaca, whose father smuggled the plan out of the castle and sent it to me for approval.

The detainees were held in two large rooms, one above the other, and on the night of the escape those in the upper room created a noisy disturbance, banging their tin mugs on the table and singing the Greek national anthem. The sergeant warders had been warned to keep out of the way, and the others on duty went upstairs to see what the trouble was about. Meanwhile the escapers were smashing their way out: they had smuggled into their cell two big iron cannon balls from the courtyard and with these they broke a hole in a bricked-up medieval gun port, hurling them again and again at the wall until the hole was big enough for a man to get through. Eight bedsheets were knotted together and thrown down the wall. One after the other sixteen men swarmed down the improvised rope to the beach below. Drakos, the last to leave, timed each man with his watch: they had calculated that it took a certain number of seconds for the sentry to make a circuit of the castle walls, and each escaper climbed down when the guard was at the farthest point from the north tower. Finally Drakos swung himself down to the beach. As he looked back and saw the outline of the sentry's head against the sky. He called out, 'Good night!' and the soldier, thinking perhaps that it was a policeman from the police station just around the corner, shouted back: 'Good night!'

Most of the escapers later became group leaders with key positions in the Organisation. Drakos led five men to the mountains, where they were given food and shelter; later they formed the nucleus of the guerrilla group based on Kykko Monastery. Evangelakis and two others reached Nicosia by separate routes, despite a widespread search for them in the Kyrenia mountains by hundreds of commandoes.

This was the last humiliation that the Armitage regime was allowed to suffer: two days later, on 25 September 1955, it was announced in London that a new Governor had been appointed and would arrive in Cyprus immediately. My opponent was to be Field-Marshal Sir John Harding, GCB, CBE, DSO, MC, who had commanded British troops in North Africa, Italy, Germany and the Far East and had just relinquished the post of Chief of the Imperial General Staff. He was, in fact, the leading British soldier of his day, and no higher compliment could have been paid us than to send against our tiny forces a man with so great a reputation and so brilliant a career.

I had planned to launch my next offensive at once if the United Nations decision went against us, but the advent of Harding created a new political situation – according to the politicians – and, in conformity with suggestions made to me, I postponed the attack for the time being. Whatever the changes to be made in British policy, it seemed obvious to me that they would not be very pleasant for us. Harding's arrival on the scene would mean an intensification of the repressive measures taken up to now: the mailed fist would rule in Cyprus. My forebodings were confirmed when Harding, on taking over, said that he would draw on the experience gained in the struggles over Malaya and Kenya; he hoped that EOKA would be quickly crushed so that he could hand over to a civilian.

I must point out here that the British, in misunderstanding the Cypriots so completely, contributed generously to their own defeat. I laughed aloud when I read that General A or Brigadier B had come to Cyprus to put into operation the methods which had won him fame elsewhere. They could not understand that the Cyprus struggle was unique in motive, psychology and circumstance, and involved not a handful of insurrectionists but the whole people.

Even after they had overcome their initial surprise at the start of our campaign, the British showed no sign of clear thought, or of a unified plan; whereas we, with a general strategy carefully thought out in advance, could change our methods to suit circumstances, but always had a clear line to follow. Our policy can be put in five words: attack, alertness, flexibility, secrecy, speed. Lacking a plan, the British were thrown on to the defensive. The police were knocked out of the fight and the army did not know what to do. Their reaction to raids on police stations provides a perfect example of this defensive thinking. An armed sentry would walk round and round the building all night; weapons were kept loaded and if the police had to close the station temporarily they took their arms with them. The British apparently thought they could trick us by sending military reinforcements on certain nights of the week, so that we would never know when the army were there; of course we always did know and always attacked on the nights they were absent. After a raid, troops would be sent out to patrol the countryside. I watched a typical example for several days at Kyperounda: it followed the same route, at the same speed and at the same hour, simply offering itself as a target.

The British answer to our methods was to flood the island with troops. It was the wrong answer. Numbers have little meaning in guerrilla warfare. From the guerrillas' point of view, it is positively dangerous to increase the size of groups beyond a certain point. I call this the 'saturation point'. It is determined by the nature of the terrain, the skill of the fighters, their requirements in food and supplies, the tactics employed and the need to keep down casualties. Any given area can usefully absorb a certain number of men; in mountainous country, where peaks and ravines are dead ground, the figure is only a fraction of the numbers required elsewhere. I myself, when I joined the *andartes* in the mountains, always felt uneasy if there were more than half a dozen of us together. Even in the plains the saturation point is lower than one might suppose: for example, to use more than five or six men for a village attack would serve no purpose, for the more numerous the attackers, the more difficult it is for them to escape after the action. On the same principle, villages where we were strong pretended inertia, on my orders, until it was appropriate for them to strike, while others, where our forces were weaker, continued to attack repeatedly, simply to deceive the enemy. If this led to arrests, even of a whole group, it was not important, for there was always a complete reserve group waiting to fill their places. Thus I never disclosed my full strength to the enemy, but after each sudden eruption of violence left an empty battlefield. When the British tried to strike back, they found nothing to strike at. This was the secret of my success throughout four years of hard fighting, and my principles did not change when Harding came on the scene, with greater power and a better grasp of strategy; I simply adapted them to meet the new challenge.

I do not mean to imply that I would not have welcomed stronger forces when I began my campaign in 1955. At that time the British garrison amounted to about 4,000 men, mainly raw conscripts, and with 500 trained and properly armed men I could have driven them into the sea with a series of rapid blows, delivered where least expected. But my resources were meagre and I could not hope to win a military victory; it was rather a question of raising a force and keeping it in being no matter what the enemy did to destroy it. This, and more, was achieved in the first six months. Our intention was to focus the eyes of the world on Cyprus and force the British to fulfil their promises. I was entitled to assume that our military successes would be exploited internationally by Makarios, who was running political affairs and whose task it was to win support for us in Britain, America and the United Nations. I was also entitled to assume that any patriotic Government in Greece, once we had proved ourselves a serious revolutionary movement, would have the courage to put some pressure on America instead of prostrating themselves before the sign of the dollar.

Unhappily, these expectations were to be disappointed, although EOKA, after four years of all-out war with the British was more powerful than ever before and ready to fight on indefinitely. It is no exaggeration to say that if I had been solely responsible for handling the Cyprus question a solution would have been found at once, even if it involved some dramatic developments to begin with.

CHAPTER FOUR

The Guerrillas

October 1955–March 1956

FIELD-MARSHAL HARDING put his cards on the table at once, with typical forthrightness. First, in his political role of Governor, he met Makarios and told him that the Cypriot claim would only be considered in the light of Britain's defence obligations and needs in the Middle East. Some brief negotiations took place and the Archbishop's proposals were rejected. Within a week the way was open for Harding to resume his military role: he filled in the blank cheque that the Cabinet had given him on his appointment and an avalanche of reinforcements began to pour into Cyprus. I was surprised at the overconfidence with which he addressed himself to his task, and at the autocratic temper he displayed; for a man reputed to have a subtle mind and a strong character he appeared to be remarkably boastful. I appreciated that we would hear a great deal about the defeat and destruction of the Organisation from him, but the first operations which accompanied the propaganda were very clumsy. In one of these, several thousand troops, mainly commandoes were deployed in a huge man-hunt for our groups on the Kyrenia Mountains, where we had been most active.

Gregoris Afxentiou was in command there. On the day after Harding's arrival in the island he had raided Lefkonico Police Station and seized the entire stock of the armoury. The attack had been carefully planned well in advance, but it must have appeared as a deliberate challenge to the new Governor. The building was first reconnoitred by Photis Papaphotis, of the Kyrenia guerrillas, who, as son of the mukhtar (headman) of Akanthou, had access to police station and government offices: he studied the layout and reported back to Afxentiou at his headquarters in the Mavron Oros (Black Mountains) area. A few days later Afxentiou took six men, including his deputy Tassos Sofocleus, and Papaphotis, to Lefkonico. They drove first to the High School, where they put on masks, then, with guns in their hands, walked in broad daylight through the streets to the Police Station. The policeman on duty at the gate dropped his gun and ran on seeing them and those inside offered little more resistance: one constable tried to pick up the telephone, but dropped it on an order from

Afxentiou. The guerrillas locked everyone in a cell, including two government officials who were visiting the station, then smashed the armoury
door and carried off nine rifles, two greeners, ammunition and the station
radio in their car.

It was raids and ambushes like this that led Harding to choose Afxentiou's
area for his first big counter-attack, and like almost every operation
that followed in later years, it was used on information supplied by
a traitor. The group, acting on my standing orders for the procedure to
be followed when threatened with encirclement, escaped from the net;
but it was a narrow escape. The whole affair was largely Afxentiou's
own fault. Disregarding my warnings, he had enlisted a man of bad
character, who, after living with the group for a period, grew tired of the
rigorous mountain life and slipped away one night to Nicosia. He quickly
turned informer and betrayed the group's hideouts and habits to the police,
for which he was well paid. Luckily Afxentiou received advance warning
from our agents in the Nicosia police and he was able to move the group
out of the danger area shortly before the search began; even so, weapons,
explosives and stores were captured.

Afxentiou was one of my best men, but I had to show that orders must
be obeyed and that I made no exceptions in matters of discipline. I removed
him from command and made his deputy, Tassos Sofocleus, group leader
in his place. It is characteristic of Afxentiou that he told his men that I was
quite right to make an example of him; he held no grudge against Sofocleus,
but, on the contrary, did everything he could to make his position easier.
I have always found that punishment does not humiliate the good soldier,
if no dishonour is involved: he accepts it as an exercise in correct command.

With the United Nations debate behind us and Harding's policy clear,
there was no longer any reason to delay my new attack, which I called
'Operation Forward to Victory'. On the day negotiations between Makarios
and Harding broke down, 9 October 1955, I ordered the first stage to begin:
this consisted of attacks on enemy agents and unfriendly policemen, combined with raids on village police stations, which would dislocate the
intelligence service and draw out the Army. In a raid on Mitsero mine we
got away with 1,500 sticks of dynamite, 600 detonators and 3,000 yards of
fuse. Even more successful was a raid on military warehouses at Famagusta harbour, where we made our biggest haul of arms so far. Pavlos
Pavlakis, Famagusta commander, had been tipped off by his agent in the
docks that guns were coming in from Suez in boxes marked 'clothes',
'personal effects', etc. They were stored in a badly guarded transit dump
just beyond the harbour area. Pavlakis sent a group of a dozen men under

George Matsis to get them. They bound and gagged the guard, then loaded the boxes into their truck under the direction of a port employee. Before they left Matsis scrawled this notice for the British:

The value of the arms received will be paid by Dighenis at the end of the struggle,

EOKA.

When the cases were opened we found we had twenty-two assorted brens, stens, mortars and bazookas, besides other army stores.

Harding retaliated by banning any kind of demonstration on 28 October, the national holiday marking Greece's refusal to surrender to the Axis in 1940. I ordered the ban to be defied and there were bloody clashes all over Cyprus: public feeling was greatly inflamed when the British chose 28 October to announce sentence of death on Michael Karaolis, the first hero of the revolution. Troops opened fire on a crowd, wounding three men, and more than a thousand arrests were made after street battles in the main towns. It was clear that public morale was high, while the Army were disheartened and the Police had virtually vanished from the scene. My agents informed me that there had been a mutiny at Polemidia, where 600 commandoes were confined to camp; troops at Xeros also refused to go into action and Harding had to visit them in person to hear their complaints.

We had now achieved the right conditions for an all-out assault: the British forces were tied up in the towns by youth demonstrations and sabotage and we were free to attack in the open countryside and the mountains. These were the forces at my disposal:

Strong sabotage and combat groups in Nicosia, Famagusta, Limassol; smaller groups in Kyrenia, Larnaca, Morphou.
Guerrilla groups in the Pentadactylos (Kyrenia range).
Guerrilla groups in the Troodos range: of these the strongest was in the Pitsillia area. There was another at Kykko, formed from the men who had escaped from Kyrenia Castle, which was particularly well-armed.

The main phase of 'Operation Forward to Victory' opened on 18 November 1955. More than fifty bombs were thrown in thirty separate attacks all over the island on that day. One of the most effective attacks was carried out in the heart of Kykko Camp, a large military compound in Nicosia where lines of Nissen huts stood in rows behind barbed wire. Security measures were slack and more than 150 Cypriots worked inside the camp area, in addition to delivery men who went in and out during the day. One of our men carried an 8 lb time bomb past the guards in the saddlebag of a bicycle, which he left leaning against the outside wall of the Warrant Officers' and Sergeants' Mess. It exploded at 3 am, fatally wounding two sergeants: a gaping hole was torn in the building and the roof was blown off. As the official military spokesman announced next day, this incident made ' a very severe impression on the Army as a whole'. Another bomb, deposited in the letter box of the General Post Office, brought half the building crashing down into the street. Still others were flung into English bars, such as the 'Jolly Roger', which was attacked several times until it closed down; the homes of senior British officers and army posts at Limassol and Larnaca were also attacked. By the end of the week several hundred acts of sabotage, shootings, ambushes and raids had been carried out, and the British admitted to five dead and dozens wounded. (The actual figures were much higher.)

Many of these attacks were in the British bases: here, we always made a particularly careful study of the enemy's habits. Our men would find a small section of the camp perimeter which normally escaped vigilance, or which was left unwatched for a few minutes while the guards were changed; they learned the unalterable routine of security and found the weakest joint in the British armour. Explosives were often smuggled into the bases weeks ahead of an attack; containers and time mechanisms would follow later, and the bomb would be made actually on the base. So we could always strike at the right time and the right place, and at short notice.

At the same time we began our first major guerrilla operations in the mountains. Renos Kyriakides had already prepared hideouts and secret arms caches, the latter made from large oil drums built into the mountainside, and in October 1955 I ordered him to set up a mountain stronghold to serve as my headquarters. A massive ridge overlooking the great Adelphi Forest was chosen, with the villages of Spilia and Kourdhali below us, in the south. Near the crest of this ridge, amid dense undergrowth and giant rocks, Kyriakides and his men built seven dug-outs, each able to hold four or five men; these were roofed over with sheets of corrugated iron, brought up from the village on donkeys; earth was spread over the top and bushes arranged to conceal the tiny entrance. The group worked with pick and shovel by night, and returned to Kourdhali by day. Kyriakides had twenty men under his command: an enthusiastic, hardworking band who had little to fear either from the police, who had learned to keep their distance, or the Army, who hardly ever moved off the main roads. It was possible to get in some practice with automatic weapons, using stones for targets, and though hundreds of villagers must have heard the sound of firing, there was no treachery. The work was completed by

E

the middle of November and the group christened their new base 'The Castle'.

I ordered another attack on the Mitsero mine, which was guarded by troops after our previous raids, as a start to the new campaign. Kyriakides led his twelve-man group from Kyperounda at midnight: they opened fire on the guards from prepared positions and in the fifteen minute gun battle that followed several soldiers were killed; only Kyriakides, on our side, was slightly injured. Three nights later the guerrillas attacked again: this time Amiandos mine was the target and only two out of the dozen soldiers in the garrison were unhurt: they escaped injury by hiding under a mine wagon. Soldiers in the Police Station 200 yards away must have heard the firing, but they did not venture out until next morning to collect the bodies of the dead and wounded. After this the Government ordered the mine's stock of dynamite to be moved to safety, and on the way the trucks carrying it were ambushed by Gregoris Loukas's group from Kakopetria. On the same night, near Famagusta, three army vehicles were bombed by Pavlakis' men. Our boldness demoralised the British, who were obliged to stop all Army movements on the roads by night.

My response to this was to order daylight attacks, and to give the guerrillas an example of courage and tenacity I myself led the first big daylight ambush, at the head of the Pitsillia group. I was determined to make this both a model operation and a training exercise for my future leaders: splitting the group into three sections of five men each, I posted two high on the hillside above the Handria road in widely separated positions, under Renos Kyriakides's orders. The third section, under my command, lay in hiding near the roadside at a sharp bend. We waited from early morning until 3 pm: then, at last, we heard the noise of two army lorries. As the first drew level with our positions bombs were thrown and we opened fire. It went off the road and crashed into the ravine, turning over and over. The other truck was also hit but managed to escape towards Handria, with the men inside cowering behind the driver's cab as bullets richocheted off the steel. We saw two soldiers moving below us: both were wounded, but they had been able to climb out of the truck and were escaping towards Kyperounda. One of our men threw a grenade at them as they fled, but I ordered that they should be allowed to go: we did not want prisoners. We then withdrew to the hilltop and waited for nightfall. Three village boys brought us the contents of the crashed truck: two stens, field glasses, first aid kit and gloves. I deliberately chose not to leave the scene directly, to show the men that we were master of the situation; and as we watched a relief party arrived. It had taken them nearly three hours. They made no attempt to search the area, but simply removed the body of a dead soldier and left as dusk fell.

We split into two groups and returned to the Castle that night, Renos Kyriakides leading one section, I the other, completing a seven mile march over very difficult country, through darkness, cold and rain, in six hours. Next day the British took their revenge by killing a harmless old villager riding on a donkey outside Handria: they claimed that the man, a sixty-year-old labourer, father of six children, had failed to stop when challenged.

*

Harding reacted to our intensified attack at once by declaring a State of Emergency on 26 November 1955. From now on he would make his own laws: the punishment for carrying arms was death; for sabotage, life imprisonment. Strikes were declared illegal. The police were given powers of arrest without warrant. The Governor could expel anyone from the island, ban public meetings, seize newspapers or private property. The 'security forces' set about their work in a manner which might have been deliberately designed to drive the population into our arms. On the pretext of searching they burst into people's homes by day and night, made them stand for hours with their hands up, abused and insulted them. Soldiers would empty sacks of grain on the floor of a farmhouse and pour oil, wine or paraffin over it, thus ruining enough food to keep a family for a year; or they would stop a lorry taking produce to market and tip the whole load of fruit and vegetables out on to the road. Anyone who protested had scant hope of getting justice. The police carried blank detention orders which could be quickly filled with the names of recalcitrants: and then only a large bribe to the right official could save a man from months or years in a prison camp. These attempts to frighten the people away from EOKA always had exactly the opposite effect to that intended: the population were merely bound more closely to the Organisation and the young scorned the threat of the gallows. It was a policy that led to unnecessary bloodshed: more than once Harding said that he could not blame his men for 'roughness' when they saw their comrades murdered; but Cypriots also saw their friends and relatives shot down for no reason, often far from the scene of any trouble, and then they sought rough justice of their own. I stopped such things if I knew what was happening, but I could not always know in time.

On the very evening Harding proclaimed a State of Emergency an attempt was made on his life. He was to be guest of honour at the Caledonian Society's annual ball in the great ballroom of the Ledra Palace Hotel. This was a major event in the British social calendar and elaborate security precautions were taken: two policemen were posted in the ballroom the night before and there were guards at all entrances. However, one of our members, a hotel employee, smuggled two hand-grenades into the building and drew up a plan to throw them at the Governor's table after a colleague had switched off the lights at the mains. But at the last moment a message came from Government House that Harding and his party would not be able to attend. Since there were a number of high-ranking officers and Government officials present, the EOKA fighter decided to throw his grenades anyway and five revellers were injured, among them the wife of the British Police Commissioner.

*

At the start of December 1955 I brought Gregoris Afxentiou from the Pentadactylos to my hideout above Spilia: he had purged his offence and I wanted him to take command of the Pitsillia guerrilla force, which I had divided into three groups because of its increased size (about twenty men). Afxentiou had been hunted in every corner of the island for nine months and his face was familiar from police posters everywhere. The dangerous task of moving him from one side of Cyprus to the other, through Nicosia, was undertaken by Kyriakos Matsis, then my central contact. Nearly always, when a wanted man had to be transported some distance, we used a woman as escort; their presence usually averted suspicion and soldiers felt obliged to behave less offensively. Matsis was helped on this occasion by Miss Nitsa Hadji Georghiou, who, when told that they ran the risk of being captured or killed, bravely replied: 'Whoever does not give all for her country, gives nothing.'

Afxentiou was brought from Kyrenia to her house, where Matsis supplied him with a change of clothing. They set off in a Land-Rover with Nitsa carrying bombs in her leather handbag, magazines in her pocket and a sten under her skirt. Matsis passed the time by reciting patriotic poems he had composed himself: one began 'Long live Dighenis, pride of Cyprus!' They agreed that if they were challenged the two men would shoot, while Nitsa would throw her bombs; but they were stopped only once, by a policeman who warned them that a bridge was down in their path. Nitsa leaned forward and masked Afxentiou's face with her long hair and they drove on to Kakopetria in safety. I gave him his new command and briefed him on the organisation of the three groups and the plan to follow in case of encirclement. Within a few days he was in action, dynamiting transformers, cutting power lines and relieving the guards of their guns near Amiandos mines.

Tassos Sofocleus, who had taken Afxentiou's place at the head of the Kyrenia guerrillas, also lost no time in getting to work. A few days after taking over he raided an army camp at Ayios Amvrosios: soon after dark Sofocleus, Photis Papaphotis and twenty-four men surrounded the camp perimeter, then sent a hail of bullets and bombs in among the tents and tin huts. It was fifteen minutes before the Army recovered sufficiently to fire back. The attackers continued the engagement for another fifteen minutes before retiring in good order and on the way back to their hideout they sang a famous patriotic song, 'Old Greece never dies'. Next morning the camp was a scene of devastation. Ambulances called frequently.

Markos Drakos's group, based on Kykko Monastery, was as active as the rest and carried out three ambushes at this time. They were responsible for the deaths of several soldiers in the area around Lefka and Pedhoulas. So our offensive went forward: a raid on Rizokarpasso Police Station, with the whole arsenal removed; an explosion and fire in the Nicosia Commissioner's Office. I intended to give the enemy no breathing space. Harding was furious, and said so to the Press.

There were now nearly thirty guerrillas in the immediate area of my headquarters on the heights above Spilia, divided into three groups under Afxentiou, Renos Kyriakides and Christos Chartas. This was too strong a force for complete safety and I planned to spread the groups over a bigger area at an early opportunity; for the moment, however, there seemed to be no serious threat. Kyriakos Matsis drove up frequently from Nicosia to receive my orders and on one occasion he brought with him a dentist to attend to my teeth, which had been troubling me. As it was raining hard and I had a bad cold, I decided to wait until next day before going down to Spilia to see him and Renos Kyriakides was sent to ask him to wait. It so happened that Afxentiou was absent on a reconnaissance trip; and when Matsis left I allowed Christos Chartas to go with him for a short spell of leave with his family at Polystipos nearby. So, on the night of 10 December 1955, my three chief aides were all away.

Early next morning the lookout reported two army trucks moving into Spilia through a thick mist. I assumed it to be a normal patrol: if it were anything more serious Kyriakides would report from the village. I could also rely on Chartas's group, who were watching the main road from Amiandos to Kakopetria. Nevertheless, it was suspiciously early for the Army to be on the move and I ordered the men to stand to and posted fresh lookouts. At 10 am one of these reported that he had seen, through a gap in the swirling mist, two lorries leaving Spilia: they might be the two that entered the village earlier – and they might not. Then, at about 11 am, a police dog was spotted: the enemy had sent his visiting card in advance! At that moment Afxentiou returned and I sent him with a handful of men to a position directly overlooking Spilia with orders to open fire as soon as the British came within range. Within half an hour he reported suspicious movement in the village; despite the thick fog, which cut visibility down to a dozen yards, more army lorries had been seen.

It was now noon and I no longer had any doubt that the Army, acting on information, was trying to encircle our position along the top of the ridge. The best escape route was to the west, across the mountains to Kakopetria, where the countryside offered good cover. The next report from a lookout was that troops were moving up and had passed our positions, going from north to south. Soon after, we heard a burst of warning shots from Afxentiou's direction – the signal that soldiers were approaching his positions moving from south to north. Afxentiou then withdrew towards me and together we slipped away down the hillside, leaving a gap between the two British forces, as they closed in. As we moved westwards along the route to Kakopetria we heard prolonged firing through the mist: the two enemy patrols were firing on each other. We did not wait to see the result: but an EOKA member who had been arrested and forced to act as a guide later gave me the following account:

The British believed they were surrounded and began to fire wildly in the mist and kill each other. The shooting went on for nearly half an hour. I lay flat behind a pine tree with a soldier who had been leading me on a rope. Words cannot describe what was happening. Not a branch was left on a tree. The soldiers were scattered right and left, wounded and dead. Finally one of them gave a signal and they stopped firing. Their leader had been killed: a bullet had gone through his right eye and come out at the left temple.

We moved on stealthily towards Kakopetria: there was only one main road in our path, and I fully expected to find it patrolled since the Army did not lack fast transport. But to my surprise the road was unguarded and we slipped across it, one by one. The winter dusk was falling as we rested briefly on the other side. Suddenly one of my men saw a soldier with a dog no more than 50 yards away: we had been tracked through the forest by a small patrol. We jumped up and I ordered my party to split into two groups, sending ten men on ahead at the double, while I, with three other guerrillas, brought up the rear. We were so close to the patrol at one stage that Evagoras Papachristoforou whispered in my ear: 'Look out; there's an Englishman two yards away from you.' By now it was dark and impossible to see more than a few feet. We veered off sharply in a new direction and a minute later we heard shots and a voice shouting, 'Hands up!' It was the gallant soldier who, having recovered from his fright at bumping into us, now thought some action was called for. We laughed and went on our way without firing back. The pursuit was over.

Our route led over difficult and precipitous ground and our only guide was the Pole star. In order not to lose each other as we climbed I and my three fighters, Papachristoforou, Harilaos Xenofontos and Lambros Kafkallides, clasped hands; several times we narrowly escaped a fall which would have meant certain death. We crossed the main road again as it twisted along the valley but there were no signs of patrols. The British had not even sent troops towards Kakopetria, which seemed an obvious move in the circumstances, and would have trapped us. And so, at 3 am on 12 December, we reached the heights above Kakopetria where, with only a light raincoat for protection, I lay down in streaming rain to rest until dawn. As soon as it was light I surveyed the horizon. It was quiet everywhere, both in the hills behind us and in the village below. We had scored another success and inflicted defeat and humiliation on the enemy although, indeed, this was due to the Army's lack of skill as much as to our hardiness and cunning.

Consider the facts: our position had been betrayed and attacked by 700 troops, who had not only failed to kill or capture us, but had fallen into a trap and fired on each other. (I heard later that they had suffered at least fifty casualties in that half-hour of chaos on the hillside.) Although they later made contact with us and knew which way we were moving, they failed to bar our escape route. I could only suppose that their casualties had been so severe as to disrupt the unit's organisation and take the commanding officer's mind off his job.

We discovered some time after that our positions had been betrayed by Costas Zavros, a forest guard, and a member of the Fantis family, notorious traitors to our cause, most of whom were liquidated by us after they had carried on their work for some time. Zavros was also executed and a Government cheque for £400 was found on his body.

From our new position above Kakopetria I sent one man into the village to fetch food (we had not eaten for twenty-four hours) and a guide. When he returned at nightfall we moved down the mountainside and passed through the village streets unchallenged, although there was a detachment of 150 troops there at the time. We spent the night at a friendly house, where I learnt that Renos Kyriakides had been arrested while trying to break through the cordon at Spilia. Next evening we set off through the rain to the hides where Gregoris Louka and his group were staying not far from the village.

My task now was to regain contact with my area leaders everywhere and find a fresh command post. I decided to form a new guerrilla group in the area south of Galata, which I would lead personally, and on the evening of 15 December 1955 I left with four men to begin work on a hideout. We stopped first at a house in Kakopetria to pick up a guide; and here we nearly fell victim to treachery again. The family in question all seemed good patriots, but they had a son who worked, unknown to us, in the British bases. He was able to overhear our conversation and informed the police soon after we had left. We arrived in Galata at midnight and departed again at dawn. As we climbed the hillside a convoy of at least fifty trucks carrying 1,000 soldiers passed through the village. Luckily the traitor had not discovered the exact route we were taking and we watched the convoy move on to the next village down the road, Evrykhou, where a rigorous search began. The wretched youth later carried out other acts of treachery and I had him executed. His father told me that he would never forgive him.

Thus we were in danger with every step. Yet it seemed that some divine power was protecting us and giving us new strength. I never felt tired, whatever hardships we underwent. After a battle lasting from dawn until 3 pm I marched for twelve hours, then slept for three under driving rain; for five days more I marched on amid many dangers, but despite my fifty-eight years I felt neither fatigue nor depression.

On the morning of 16 December, after another six-hour march and four hours' sleep, we began work on the new hideout: during the night we lay in the open with only a blanket and a raincoat while it rained continuously from 1 am to 7 am. At dawn, soaked to the skin, we sheltered in a nearby hut and lit a fire to dry ourselves, then carried on with the work. After several more days' work the hide was ready. Throughout this period of unremitting physical labour I was in full charge of the Organisation, issuing orders, studying plans and forming new groups, thanks to the devoted couriers who carried our messages in every part of the island.

Among the reports they brought about our recent actions was one which saddened me, but also made me proud. It related the story of an ambush laid by Markos Drakos's group from Kykko Monastery on the north coast road near the ancient palace of Vouni. The guerrillas had opened fire on an Army Land-Rover as it turned a sharp bend, killing the driver. The vehicle went off the road, but the officer in charge, Major Brian Coombe, was unhurt and fired back: in the long gun battle that followed Haralambos Mouskos was killed and two other fighters, Andreas Zakos and Harilaos Michael, were captured. They had been unable to fire back because their automatics had jammed. Drakos himself was badly wounded in the head but, although blinded by blood, fought until his ammunition was exhausted and then escaped to fight another day. Zakos and Michael were tried and sentenced to death some months later, under the Emergency Regulations.

The intensity and depth of public support for EOKA was clearly shown when Mouskos's body was brought to Nicosia for burial. Crowds lined the route and knelt in the road at every village as the cortège passed through. The Archbishop, who was a cousin of the dead hero, presided at the funeral and vast throngs of people defied the official ban to follow the coffin to the cemetery. The British treated the procession as though it was a riot and fired tear-gas shells which hit the hearse and injured several bystanders.

*

As the year drew to a close I gave new impetus to 'Operation Forward to Victory' by allowing area leaders to choose their own targets and attack in their own time. Our achievements had inspired many fine young men to join us and I wanted to show confidence in my leaders' initiative. To mark the end of 1955 I also issued a leaflet comparing our losses with those of the British. I pointed out that our casualties totalled one killed and three wounded by enemy action; whereas the British had a death roll of over 50 plus 100 or more injured. The figure could only be estimated as the authorities persistently concealed their losses to keep Army morale high, while calming public opinion in Britain. Many of the wounded were secretly transferred to Suez.

A large number of British casualties were caused by our execution groups in the towns: the most active at this period was the Nicosia team headed by Isychios Sofocleus, a youth of dash and spirit, who took command in November 1955. Their first attack was directed at a four-man military patrol in Hippocrates Street, in the centre of the walled town. Sofocleus and three other fighters opened fire on the patrol with automatics, killing one soldier and wounding the rest. The soldiers returned the fire with sten guns, but we suffered no casualties. This daring and unexpected attack drew speculation from British intelligence that the raiders were guerrillas from the mountains or commandoes specially imported from Greece. A week later Sofocleus led a daylight attack on two soldiers in Ledra Street which, at the time, was full of shoppers looking for Christmas presents. One soldier was killed and the other wounded. As the gunmen ran through the twisting streets they were fired at by a patrol and the fighter Alecos Pantazis was wounded and captured; the other men escaped. Next, Sofocleus undertook the execution of a British agent called Savvas Porakos, who ran a Nicosia hotel: bursting into the private room where Porakos was dining with his son-in-law, a British police officer, Superintendent Charles Williams, the group sprayed the room with machine-gun fire. Porakos was killed and Williams, badly wounded, staggered to the front door of the hotel and fired several shots at the assailants, who escaped unharmed. Twelve days later they chose as a target a British officer, Captain J. Lane, who, they had observed, walked every morning from his hotel to a taxi rank where he would take a cab to Army Headquarters at Wolseley Barracks. Two of Sofocleus's group made the attack while a third kept watch. The officer, hit by five bullets at point-blank range, fell in the road, then got up and staggered a few paces before collapsing, dead. The same group were responsible for the first fatal attack on RAF members. This was also carried out in the busy shopping centre around Ledra Street, in broad daylight. Sofocleus and four fighters moved through the streets with sten guns concealed under their gabardine raincoats, passing a military patrol as they went: they then followed their target, three airmen, up the street, overtook them, turned and opened fire. Two died on the spot and the third staggered down the street with four bullet holes in his back and collapsed in a shop. During an exchange of fire one of our group, Renos Demetriou, was wounded. His comrades, however, were able to get him safely to a clinic where he was looked after. Such was the work of the town execution groups.

The British had no answer to this kind of warfare and we were able to strike when and where we liked. Yet, on New Year's Day, Harding broadcast an absurd boast that 'the days of EOKA were numbered'. I was at a loss to know what this could mean, since the Organisation was obviously stronger in all respects than it had ever been. Later, however, I decided that it was inspired by the operation he had planned for next day. Early on 2 January 1956 some 800 soldiers surrounded an area of wooded country near Kakopetria. They spent most of the day searching two square miles of ground and ended by arresting a three-member group which tried to break through the cordon. I thought it likely that Harding had been given news of my presence in this district and my arrest was the great event he was forecasting. I was in fact a few miles south of the operational area, watching the progress of the search through binoculars. I was astonished at the unmethodical way the troops went about their work. The correct course would have been to send small patrols to vantage points in the surrounding countryside: had this been done, contact would certainly have been made with one of my groups. But the enemy was content to rest on his laurels and throw away the opportunity. The British scored two minor successes in January, arresting another three-man group near Limassol and capturing the Limassol area leader, after treachery. As always, a reserve was waiting to step into his shoes.

It was on the very evening these arrests took place that five important members of the Organisation escaped from Camp K, a detention centre near Nicosia, where all prisoners held without trial had been moved after our last mass escape from Kyrenia Castle. This was a collection of corrugated iron huts surrounded by barbed wire and guard towers, in the midst of bare, flat fields half a mile from the main road to Nicosia. A grocer who called regularly with supplies took in a pair of wire-cutters; but he did not trouble to hide them. He simply kept them in his pocket, and when the warder on duty at the gate stooped to examine the boxes of food on the ground, he passed the clippers to a detainee over the warder's bent back.

A few days later the five escapers – among them Antonis Georgiades, who became my personal aide, and Polycarpos Yorgadjis, leader of the Nicosia area – snipped their way through two rows of wire under cover of a noisy demonstration which drew warders to the other side of the camp. This took them into a new compound under construction, where they mixed with the labourers. Since detainees wore their own clothes there was no way to tell a worker from a prisoner and so, borrowing a spade from one man, a lunch-box from another, they passed safely through the main gate. The only difficulty came when everyone boarded the bus and it was discovered that there were five seats too few: a loud argument began, which ended abruptly when one of the detainees said a quiet word to the driver, who shot off to Nicosia with a jerk. There the escapers were picked up by a waiting car which took them on to Kythrea, where a friendly Greek police sergeant was waiting to wave them through a road block on their way to the Kyrenia mountains. I sent Georgiades to raise a guerrilla group at his home village of Milikouri, while Yorgadjis went to join Afxentiou's groups; another escaper, Solon Pittarides, took charge of the Tylliria guerrillas; and a third, Michael Rossides, was made Larnaca area leader.

Harding, recognising his failure to subdue us quickly by force, fell back on political moves. One of his most desperate manoeuvres was the attempt to salvage the Cyprus Communist Party, AKEL, whose opposition to EOKA had sentenced them to political death. The British wanted to keep the Communists alive to counterbalance EOKA and, since AKEL had no martyrs on the battlefield, some were created in the jails. Harding ordered a dramatic

2 am arrest of AKEL officials, closed their newspaper and banned the Party: but out of 2,500 Party members, only eighty-five were arrested, and nearly half of these were harmless fellow travellers. All six members of the Party's politibureau stayed at liberty; their newspaper reappeared under a different title, but with the same staff; and the Communist trade union carried on its work unhindered. The union leader, Andreas Ziartides, was declared a 'wanted man' in Cyprus, but he was able to reach London and live there untroubled by the British police. I have no doubt that AKEL and the authorities together drew up the list of those who could be spared.

Harding's next step was to re-open negotiations with Makarios; but at the same time he brought in more and more troops to emphasise his intention to crush the revolt if his terms were rejected. I warned my area commanders, in an order of 16 January, to prepare for a long fight, to build up both the fighting groups and the youth movement, and to increase the pace and intensity of their activities until the end of the month, when a meeting was to take place between Sir Anthony Eden, the British Premier, and President Eisenhower.

One of the most important weapons in my hands, while these talks were in progress, was the youth movement, which rose to the occasion splendidly. First, I brought the elementary schoolchildren into the struggle with an order on January 29:

See that the Greek flag is flown from all elementary schools and is kept flying. This will certainly mean that these schools will be closed, but it will also show our unshakeable will to fight to the final victory.

Many schools were, indeed, shut down. Soldiers wasted a great deal of their time going round the villages removing flags, which were raised again as soon as they left. There were frequent clashes between armed troops and crowds of small children. Flagstaffs were mined and troops were often injured as they tried to haul down the flags: they then tried to make villagers do the job for them, under threat of prison. Next, I ordered the formation of a schoolgirl's section which would take part in street demonstrations alongside the elementary schoolchildren. Thus we showed the world at large that the whole of Cyprus, from the smallest schoolgirl to the Archbishop himself, was in the battle with EOKA.

*

I myself moved in January 1956 to the mountains around Kykko Monastery to reorganise the groups there, give them new missions and find a better and more secure command post. I set out on foot on 17 January and after a tiring eight-hour march under heavy rain I arrived at Kalopanayotis; from there we went by car to Vassiliki, a wooded, hilly area a mile or so from the monastery, where Markos Drakos had his hideout. This was my main base for the next five months: we were supplied by the monks and given every assistance by the Abbot of Kykko, who is master not only of the richest and most powerful monastery in Cyprus, but of one of the greatest shrines in the Greek Orthodox world. Situated in the heart of the Paphos Forest, the monastery clings to a steep hillside, part of a massive ridge which rises to 3,260 feet. The forest rolls away into the distance, pierced by peak after peak: it is the wildest countryside in the island, inhabited only by circling eagles and solitary forest guards, who watch for fires among the dense slopes of pine, fir and cedar. A man may walk for days without passing a village or meeting another human being. It is bitterly cold here in winter and the hills were covered with snow when I arrived.

One of the most urgent problems facing me at my new headquarters was that of arms. Thanks to the work of a team of chemists, whom I had instructed to study the question, we were learning to make powerful explosives from materials readily available in Cyprus; but supplies of arms from Greece were reduced to a trickle and I was told, by my agents, that the Greek Government was trying to stop the flow completely. Faced with this shortage I devised a plan to seize all the sporting guns in the island in one big operation.

I sent out orders to all area commanders giving detailed instructions for simultaneous raids in every village in Cyprus on the night of 22 January: there were several thousand shotguns registered with the police, so we were sure of a good haul. The day before the operation was due to begin I received a warning message from Afxentiou's group, saying that an order giving details of the raid had fallen into British hands. I did not hesitate: I told all groups to go ahead with the plan, because I did not believe the Army had time to stop us: at the worst they might lay ambushes to capture our men as they returned from the expedition. This, in fact, happened only in Afxentiou's area, where one fighter was wounded and a soldier killed in a brief clash by night. The British, obviously, thought that the order referred only to Afxentiou's groups and had acted accordingly. A competent command should have done better than this: they might have guessed, and taken some precautions, against the chance that the order had been made in other parts of the island as well. The police could have demanded that all guns must be handed in immediately; and this was exactly what they tried to do next day, when it was too late. Our drive was a great success and more than 800 shotguns were seized, with which I improved the armament of the guerrilla groups and also raised special OKT (shotgun) groups. These were used to harry the British by night, attack army camps, create diversions for major guerrilla attacks and execute traitors. I brought the shotguns' range up to 80 yards on the level and 100 yards when firing downhill (as we usually did in ambushes) by manufacturing heavy lead pellets, for which special matrices were made.

The climax of the negotiations between Archbishop Makarios and Field-Marshal Harding was now approaching, after nearly six weeks of proposals, counter-proposals, meetings and deadlocks. Makarios seemed to think there was some chance of reaching an agreement and, although I personally did not believe this, I secretly ordered a suspension of all attacks on 15 February 1956, so that no one could accuse me of barring the way to peace; but I warned the groups to stand by in readiness to resume operations at short notice.

Our goodwill and our desire for a just settlement was thus made clear, but Harding did not respond: searches, curfews and arrests continued and it seemed increasingly plain to me that the vague proposals for a settlement which he was putting forward were nothing but a trap. I confirmed to the Abbot of Kykko, who visited me at Vassiliki, that I had written to the Archbishop saying I would lay down my arms only if the following four conditions were observed:

1. We must have cast-iron guarantees that the British would carry out the terms of any agreement reached.
2. The British troops and police who had filled the island since the start of the struggle must leave.
3. We must have a complete amnesty for all our fighters, in or out of prison and detention camp.
4. Internal security (i.e., control of the police) must in no circumstances be left in the hands of the British during any interim period of self-government.

I had little belief in British sincerity and scant hopes that they would fulfil these conditions. It was for these reasons that I decided to go against Makarios's wishes and give a warning demonstration of our strength before the final round of talks. On the evening of 29 February, an hour before the key meeting between Makarios, Harding and the British Colonial Secretary, Mr Lennox-Boyd, who had flown to Cyprus specially for the occasion, I allowed my men to explode nineteen bombs in Nicosia. As I had foreseen, the British insisted rigidly on their terms and the negotiations were finally broken off that night.

The sequel is well known and there is no need for me to repeat the story here. On 9 March 1956 the Archbishop of Cyprus, together with the Bishop of Kyrenia and two leading church officials, were exiled to the Seychelles Islands in the middle of the Indian Ocean. There is, however, a significant footnote to this piece of history: as the Archbishop and his associates were being taken to their island prison the Greek Government, calling the British their friends and allies, allowed a British plane loaded with war materials most probably destined for Cyprus, to land on Greek soil. In a letter dated 14 March 1956 the Ministry of Foreign Affairs advised the General Air Staff that the aircraft, which was carrying explosives, could land at Athens Airport, and added:

Our point of view is that no matter how strained Anglo-Greek relations may have become, the Cyprus question has not ceased to be a dispute between friendly and allied nations. Our attitude towards Britain over Cyprus does not mean that we should allow ourselves to be drawn into actions in other respects which ignore our general obligations to an ally.

Such was the attitude of the Greek Government towards Britain's scandalous attempt to crush Cypriot freedom by kidnapping the leader with whom it had been negotiating.

CHAPTER FIVE

My Escape in the Mountains

March–August 1956

THE exile of Archbishop Makarios meant that I had now to take on the political as well as the military leadership of the resistance. I did not shrink from this double burden: indeed, the additional reponsibility gave me greater freedom of action and added strength, just as the Archbishop's deportation, far from quenching the fires of revolt, fanned them into flames. I launched a new offensive designed to transform the whole island into a battlefield.   I believed Harding had made the greatest mistake of his career and I took full advantage of it.

We were thus flung into a new phase of the struggle in which no effort would be spared to destroy us. It is interesting to compare the disparity of the forces involved at this stage: my records give figures for our mountain, town and village groups with some exactitude. The following list is compiled from strength reports made by all area commanders in February 1956:[1]

MOUNTAINS: 7 groups, 53 men
Kykko area:
  Vassiliki: Markos Drakos's group (12 men)
  Tylliria: Solon Pittarides's group (5 men)
  Milikouri: Antonis Georgiades's group (5 men)
  Stavros Psokas: Ch. Eleftheriou's group (6 men)
Pitsillia area:
  Makheras: Gregoris Afxentiou's group (10 men)
Paphos area:
  Lysos: Yannakis Droushiotis's group (5 men)
Pentadactylos area:
  Kalogrea; Ayios Amvrosios: Tassos Sofocleus (10 men)

TOWNS: 47 groups, 220 men
Nicosia: 15 groups (80 men)

---

[1] It should be noted that only the mountain guerrillas, plus a few town leaders and administrative staff, couriers, etc., were full-time fighters receiving an allowance from the Organisation. The vast majority of those who fought in the struggle gave their services freely, while earning their living as usual.

Famagusta: 14 groups (76 men)
Limassol: 11 groups (34 men)
Paphos: 3 groups (18 men)
Larnaca: 2 groups (6 men)
Kyrenia: 2 groups (6 men)

BRITISH BASES:
Episkopi and Polemidia: 2 groups

VILLAGES: 75 groups, approximately 750 men
Nicosia area: 11 groups
Famagusta area: 12 groups
Limassol area: 13 groups
Larnaca area: 7 groups
Pitsillia area: 11 groups
Tylliria area: 6 groups
Paphos area: 10 groups
Pentadactylos–Karpassia area: 5 groups

Our total front-line strength was therefore 273 men, sharing between them about 100 guns (those I had sent in the first arms shipment, with a few smuggled in later), backed by 750 villagers armed with shotguns.[1] Against this, Harding could call on an ever-growing army, at that time about 20,000 strong, and a police force of nearly 5,000. This cumbersome body provided a wealth of targets, new and old, in both town and mountain, and with my slender but freshly reorganised forces I felt that I could afford to try a bolder strategy. My purpose was to strike and strike again at the enemy and never to give them a moment of relaxation wherever they might be: only thus could we survive a long fight against such vast odds. We must be everywhere in attack, and nowhere when attacked ourselves.

All over Cyprus and in the bases there were bomb-throwings, ambushes, sabotage and shootings. The island's life and work were brought to a standstill by a week-long general strike, during which no newspapers appeared and only a handful of shops opened to sell food. The British police, imported in large numbers by Harding, patrolled the streets officiously at the head of bands of Turks, described as 'Auxiliary Police', and made their presence felt during the strike. With the capital virtually occupied by the army and police, Isychios Sofocleus, the Nicosia execution team leader, went out, carrying a sub-machine gun under his raincoat to find a target: he had barely turned the first corner, into Hippocrates Street, when he came face to face with two policemen, one British and one Cypriot. The Englishman, Sergeant Gerald Rooney, reached for his gun, but Sofocleus

---

[1] Village groups were armed almost exclusively with shotguns.

F

fired first and Rooney fell dead, his companion lying gravely wounded beside him.

There had been twenty-one such attacks in this small area of Nicosia since the start of 'Operation Forward to Victory' in November 1955. A total curfew was imposed while two battalions of troops manned the rooftops, erected barbed wire barricades and searched every house for arms. The police went round every curfewed home handing paper and envelopes to householders with instructions to write down everything they knew about EOKA. Next day, when the envelopes were opened by the Commissioner of Nicosia every one contained a blank sheet of paper. The Commissioner, furious, mustered the inhabitants in the street and told them that they were to be punished for refusing to help the authorities: then he closed down their shops and houses and evicted them from the district, warning that there would be further evictions if the public continued to refuse their co-operation.

The Cypriot people did refuse and Harding's answer was to inflict collective punishments in a variety of forms: a favourite was the collective fine. Village after village was made to pay sums ranging from a few hundreds to as much as £7,000. The British kept this practice up for six months, until, after fining the Greek citizens of Famagusta and Limassol £40,000 and £35,000 respectively, they realised that the only result of their actions was to turn the people still further against them. But by this time Harding's forces were thinking not of winning support but of breaking public morale. The spirit of revenge infected some of the British so that undisciplined reprisals were sometimes taken on villagers after an EOKA action. Activities of this kind obliged me to issue a leaflet denouncing Britain to the civilised world, and warning that I would be forced to take reprisals of my own if they continued. The sums of money used to bribe people to give information were also increased, but the few paid traitors met with general contempt: one well-known informer, for example, was publicly denounced by his family, who refused to visit him in the place where he was kept under British protection.

We returned blow for blow. Among our attacks was the first successful piece of sabotage at Nicosia Airport, where a policeman working in the immigration department planted a time bomb, on my orders, in the cockpit of a Hermes troop-carrying aircraft. It was totally destroyed. But, by a trick of fate, it was an unsuccessful attack that attracted most attention in the outside world: an attempt on the life of Harding himself.

I had studied several plans made by my group leaders to kill Harding, but none had been put into effect until now, because of the long-drawn negotiations with Makarios. After the deportations I saw no reason for further restraint. The best of these plans had been suggested by a young man called Neofytos Sofocleus, who had joined the staff of Government House some months before and had been made the Governor's personal valet. His idea was to place a time bomb in Harding's bed and I gave my approval; but, knowing that our men were not properly instructed in the exact use of time pencils, I told them to wait for my detailed instructions before proceeding further. A device of this kind is very easily affected by changes of temperature and requires a careful study of the circumstances in which it is to be used. Unfortunately, Sofocleus feared that he was soon to be dismissed from the Governor's service, and the Nicosia group decided to go ahead on their own initiative. A section leader, Yacovos Patatsos, explained the time mechanism to Sofocleus on the principle that if the room temperature remained at a constant 67°F the bomb would explode twenty-four hours after the safety-pin was removed. Patatsos also showed him the bomb, which was flat, book-shaped and less than two inches thick: they agreed to attempt to get it into Government House next day, strapped against Sofocleus's stomach.

It was on a Monday morning that Sofocleus cycled up to the gates of Government House with the bomb, already fitted with a time pencil, flat against his body and well concealed by a raincoat. He passed the guards, who knew him well, without a search and went to bed that night after setting his alarm-clock for 2.30 am. When it woke him he removed the safety-pin from the time pencil: the explosion should now take place at 2.30 am next morning.

While luncheon was in progress next day Sofocleus again strapped on the bomb, went upstairs to Harding's bedroom and began to clean the floor. When he was sure no one was about he quickly slipped the bomb from under his clothing, placed it between Harding's mattresses and left immediately. He walked rapidly down the drive and out through the main gates. Outside a car was waiting to take him to the mountains. But, as I had feared, the group had not taken the possibility of a change in temperature into account. Harding, it appeared later, slept with his bedroom window open and the temperature fell sharply during the March night. The result was that the bomb failed to explode and was still in place when the Governor's batman turned back the mattress next morning to air the bed. The bomb was taken out into the grounds and detonated. Next day the Greek Cypriot staff of Government House were all dismissed amid heavy criticism of Harding's security measures.

It was not long after this that Harding put a reward of £10,000 on my head. I retaliated with an order which, in turn, proclaimed the Governor a man wanted by EOKA, in the following terms:

We proclaim, WITHOUT ANY MATERIAL REWARD the Gauleiter SIR JOHN HARDING, whose execution is the duty of every patriotic Greek. Instead of monetary rewards, which are given by the vulgar to the vulgar, we shall declare the man who executes him a national hero whose name will be written in letters of gold in the Pantheon of Heroes of the Cyprus Struggle.

EOKA,
The Leader,
Dighenis.

The mountain guerrillas were also active. Afxentiou led the way with a major ambush in the Pitsillia: with a large force of fifteen men he waited at an S-bend near Handria village and it was not long before two army lorries offered themselves as a target. As the first truck came into sight all the fighters opened up from both flanks of a gully, catching the soldiers in their crossfire. The second vehicle was also hit and spun round with flames shooting from the engine. Several soldiers are believed to have been killed but, as usual, the British concealed their losses. The guerrillas withdrew according to plan and on returning to base they discovered that Christos Chartas was missing: next day they heard on the radio that he had been killed by a stray bullet in the exchange of fire.

Harding tried to strike back at the mountain groups, but, lacking any comprehensive plan and failing to grasp our methods, he had few successes. His activities were dependent on spasmodic tips from informers, which were often inexact and unreliable and led him to concentrate on narrow zones: as many as fifty truckloads of troops would be poured into one small area, which would be searched for a day; but nearly always we slipped away before the search began and watched its progress from the neighbouring heights, certain that they would not extend the operation beyond its original limits.

From my hideout I watched soldiers leave Pedhoulas daily to scour the mountains of the Paphos Forest. Often they came within rifle range, but we never gave away our hiding place by opening fire. They set out as if on a training march, moving off the road from time to time to rest, while their officers scanned the horizon above our heads with binoculars. I pitied them and the commanders who sent them on such futile missions. One day more than 700 soldiers, supported by helicopters and guided by tracker dogs, searched the Kykko area from dawn until 3 pm and then went home empty-handed. They could hardly have advanced in any direction outside their prescribed circle without running into my headquarters or one of three other groups holed-up nearby; but most of their time was spent in a barren search of the monastery, where they led their dogs into the church and sacrilegiously allowed them to sniff and lick the Holy Altar.

So Harding persisted in his error: he underrated his enemy on the one hand, and overweighted his forces on the other. But one does not use a tank to catch field-mice – a cat will do the job better. The Field-Marshal's only hope of finding us was to play cat and mouse: to use tiny, expertly trained groups, who could work with cunning and patience and strike rapidly when we least expected.

*

When, in May 1956, I heard that Harding had ordered the first hangings to take place, my feelings were bitter indeed; and yet I realised that this was simply a sign of defeat and desperation. The British, having failed to crush us by force, had resorted to judicial murder. The first to die were two young members of the execution groups, Michael Karaolis and Andreas Demetriou, who, after waiting five months in a prison cell were hanged before dawn on 10 May 1956, then hastily buried in a corner of the prison grounds. This small square of earth, ringed by high walls topped with broken glass, was made into one of the most hallowed places in Cyprus by the British, for it was here that they later buried the great heroes of the struggle: Gregoris Afxentiou, Kyriakos Matsis and others. Their intention was to prevent the graves from becoming places of pilgrimage: instead they created a national shrine, and found their enemies were as dangerous in death as they were in life. The quality of the two upright and religious boys who first went to the gallows can be gauged in this letter from Karaolis to his family, the last he wrote:

Comfort my mother and tell her that my last wish is that she should not weep for me, nor allow pain to poison her heart. Give my thanks to my lawyers, who have worked so hard in my defence, including, of course, Mr Pritt. Neither courage nor hope have deserted me and my soul is serene and strong as ever. I ask everyone to forgive any wrong that I may have done, as I forgive all who have wronged me. Goodbye now, and may God grant happiness to everyone. I kiss you again,

Michalakis.
Central Prison, Nicosia.
May 9, 1956.

These executions were condemned by a large part of world public opinion and led to serious disturbances in Greece. The Athens police failed to suppress a huge demonstration protesting against Harding's action and a riot developed in which seven people were killed and 200 injured. The Mayor of Athens formally hammered to splinters a marble plaque dedicated to Queen Elizabeth and Prince Philip while a crowd cheered and applauded and there were many similar scenes in Greece. Public opinion in Britain was also against the hangings and only extremist Tories tried to defend Harding. Their attitude was expressed by the *Sunday Times*, which said in a leading article: 'History shows over and over again that when imperial power shirks its reponsibility nothing but evil follows and the worst sufferers are the people governed.'

My own reaction was to order the execution of two soldiers who had been captured by EOKA some months before. Within twenty-four hours of the hanging of Karaolis and Demetriou these two hostages were shot and secretly buried. Leaflets announcing the reprisals were then distributed in the towns. The British at first refused to admit that the men were dead: but when I issued full details of their names, ranks and captured weapons the denials ceased.

The attack continued on all fronts, with the town bomb-throwing and execution groups in the forefront of the picture. Nicosia fighters attacked a radio outpost at the RAF Station; the Famagusta groups executed an English colonel at Boghaz village; while the Limassol execution team, headed by Michalakis Thrassyvoulides, shot a British security agent in the main street. Among so many bombings and killings it was not always possible to avoid injury to people of other nationalities. There were a large number of United States citizens in Cyprus, for example, and they were not easily differentiated from the British. Inevitably, there were accidents: but they were few, and only once in the entire four year struggle did a mistake of this kind result in death. That was when a United States Vice-Consul, Mr William Boteler, was killed by a bomb thrown into a Nicosia restaurant in 1956. Afterwards, I issued the following leaflet:

A TRAGIC MISTAKE

On Saturday the American Vice-Consul was killed as a result of a bomb explosion, and other American citizens were injured. We know very well that British propaganda is trying to exploit this sad incident, maintaining that the attack was premeditated. We state categorically that it was a tragic mistake. No Greek bears hatred for the American people, whose liberal feelings must, we feel sure, place the majority of them on our side in the righteous struggle. We are deeply grieved at the death of the American diplomat. We advise foreigners living in Cyprus, for their own safety, not to frequent English places of entertainment, since it is not always possible to distinguish them from the English enemies.

EOKA,
The Leader,
Dighenis.

I was also strongly opposed to any action which would affect the Turkish Cypriots, for I knew the British would seize on any chance to increase the division between the two communities. But it was impossible to avoid all action against them: certain Turks in the police worked energetically against the Organisation particularly in Paphos, and the area commander there, Yannakis Droushiotis, decided one must be executed. On the death of this man, a constable, the strength of Anglo-Turkish co-operation was clearly shown.

Early British approaches to the Turkish Government had not met with any great response, but by the middle of 1956 the Turks had been persuaded, or bribed, into an alliance against us. Harding then put all the guns he could in the hands of the Turkish Cypriots. The young men of Volkan (the secret Turkish underground organisation) were very often members of the auxiliary police, and did not hesitate to use their weapons against the Greeks in whatever capacity they were acting: simultaneously they acted as terrorists and policemen. Nothing could have suited the British better.

We had already seen many shocking examples of their work when, in May 1956, after the death of a Turkish policeman (he had tried to chase an EOKA fighter, who turned and shot him dead), the first major Anglo-Turk attack was launched on the defenceless Greek population. As soon as word spread that this policeman was dead the Turkish hordes poured into the Greek quarter of Nicosia raiding, burning, looting, murdering and behaving more like wild beasts than human beings. Then, after a second Turkish policeman was killed by a bomb thrown into a truck, their fury knew no bounds. A funeral procession turned into a wild riot and the mob stormed the nearest Greek building they could find, which happened to be an oxygen-producing factory, smashing the machinery, setting fire to the building and finally beating the elderly caretaker to death in a scene of horror which is described in the coroner's report:

The factory in front of them was Greek. They attacked it first with a shower of stones. They set on fire several of its rooms and the cornfields round it. The deceased after telephoning for help, locked himself in a small room with another Greek. They saw that people outside were pushing to force the door open, whereupon they leaned against it with all their strength, but in spite of their efforts the door was forced in. From this moment onwards no evidence

73

could be found to reveal what happened. Dr Kienadis, who carried out the post-mortem examination, observed about eleven lacerated wounds of various sizes on the head, limbs and thorax and innumerable bruises all over the body; the brain was crushed and substance protruding. The stomach was penetrated at two points and both lungs were lacerated. The coroner's court finds that the deceased was brutally beaten to death with blunt and sharp-pointed instruments in circumstances amounting to murder by unknown and untraced persons from a mob of about 300 to 400 including a score of auxiliary and special constables, who attacked the Kyriakos Factory on the afternoon of 29 May 1956.

The police force, however, was a two-edged weapon, and whatever damage was done by the Turkish portion of it was more than counteracted by my agents on the Greek side. My information about what was going on behind the security curtain improved daily, particularly after May 1956, when a Special Branch sergeant, George Lagoudontis, began to tape-record top-level British conferences in the Operations Room of Police Headquarters. These meetings were held every day at 9 am and were attended by a Brigadier, an Assistant Chief Constable and sundry other officers, who discussed the security measures to be taken that day and in the future. If they required information on some point they would call Lagoudontis on the intercom telephone: this gave him an idea. He smuggled a miniature tape-recorder into the police station and placed it in his desk drawer. From this, one quiet evening when a Greek officer was on duty, he ran a wire through the telephone flex into the next room, where it ended up linked to a tiny microphone concealed by a large wall map of Cyprus. This part of the operation was done with the help of a telephone engineer with whom Lagoudontis had previously drawn up a plan. The instrument could be simply started by slipping a hand into the drawer and pressing a button. The tape lasted seventy-five minutes and the reel could be changed without much difficulty if a conference was prolonged.

Every lunch-hour Lagoudontis would play the recording back and note important points, or he would pass the whole reel to his EOKA contact. One day the voice of the Special Branch chief, Barlow, was heard on the tape talking about three of his informers by name. One was a stool-pigeon who had been put in a cell to eavesdrop on other prisoners. As he left the police station by a back door next day he was shot dead by EOKA fighters. The other two were also executed soon after. Officials suspected a leak. They dismissed another policeman whose desk was near the Operations Room and moved the conference from the first to the ground floor. This time Lagoudontis simply got a sergeant to wedge the recorder itself under a ledge of the conference table, a heavy affair which seated 14 to 16 men. Now there was no danger from incriminating wire, but reels could not be changed while the talk went on. The sergeant would take around paper and pencils just before the conference began and put his hand under the table to press the button. Lagoudontis thus got fewer recordings: it was not always possible to set the instrument going. Soon he was reduced to two or three tapes a week, as security precautions increased, and by the end of the year he could get no more, for a British police sergeant was posted in the Operations Room night and day.

By that time, however, he had other sources of information. He was completely trusted by the British and leading officers would visit his home regularly, to be plied with whisky. One assistant superintendent used to talk freely: so freely, indeed, that Lagoudontis became suspicious and decided on an independent check. He invited the man to a party with other British officers and called in some girls, to dance to the police band, and a Greek cabaret singer: her job was to ask everyone to take off their coats and relax. Lagoudontis personally took the ASP's coat and hung it up in the hall. He slipped the keys from the pocket and quickly took a wax impression, from which a duplicate was later made. From that time on he had free access to his superior officer's private papers and could check that what he said was true.

George Lagoudontis was a fine example of the kind of man produced by the Cyprus police. At the end of the struggle I presented him with a written commendation, which he has framed. It hangs on the wall of his home alongside a similar certificate which he received from the Governor of Cyprus.

*

At the end of May 1956 my agents in the police warned me that Harding was planning a large-scale operation which centred on the area of Kykko Monastery and Kambos, where I was suspected to be living with the guerrilla groups. I decided to thin my forces out over a wider area. Of the five groups near Kykko, I moved one six miles south-west towards Stavros Psokas and another to Pyrgos on the north coast. Then I led two other groups in a non-stop march for twenty-four hours across the mountains to a wild and lonely area deep in the Paphos Forest, known as the Mavron Kremas (Black Chasms), where I set up my command post. Next, I authorised the head of my contact net in Nicosia to issue orders on my behalf for diversionary activity everywhere, should we be cut off temporarily by the British. I was ready for whatever was to come.

We did not have long to wait: a vast man-hunt began in an area of several hundred square miles, stretching from Lefka and the Tylliria in the north to Kykko and Kambos in the heart of the mountains. The searches were different both in manner and extent from any that had gone before and I had to admit that Harding had improved his tactics. First Milikouri was turned inside out and 300 people were taken away for questioning. Then the Tylliria group was encircled and captured, followed by another small group of four men near Kambos. Later, the operations extended south-westwards and the group which I had moved towards Stavros Psokas was arrested: I had myself visited this group only a few days before.

The enemy's plan was now becoming clear: after the area north of Kykko had been cleared up, the operation would be extended throughout the whole Paphos Forest in an attempt to kill me and wipe out every remaining guerrilla band. Harding was avid for victory and meant to throw all his resources into one immense bid to destroy me. Our first need was for an expert guide: it was obvious that we would have to run before these waves of troops as fire-fighters do before a forest fire, slipping through the encircling flames where they are thinnest. I sent for Antonis Georgiades who led a guerrilla group near Milikouri, his native village, and knew every inch of the countryside. He led us deeper into the forest, to a new hideout on a 4,000 foot peak in the area of Dipli. This night march was the most difficult and dangerous of my life: once I slipped and plunged over a precipice. Georgiades thought I was lost, but found me clinging to a bush over a drop of several hundred feet and pulled me back to safety. He himself had narrowly escaped death a few minutes before, saved by his haversack after a fall from a considerable height.

As soon as we reached Dipli I sent orders for diversionary attacks in the towns, in the hope of drawing the Army off. I could not say whether this succeeded, but I did observe a number of gaps in the operational zone, and the searches were not extended into my area for some weeks. Had they been expanded immediately, contact would have been made with my groups and I might well have been killed.

The towns and villages burst into action: dozens of bombs were hurled from the rooftops of Nicosia into police and army trucks which had been lured into the streets by demonstrating schoolchildren. At Famagusta a bomb landed in a packed lorry taking soldiers for a rehearsal of the Queen's Birthday Parade, killing several of them and wounding everyone who survived. It was the Limassol execution group that made what was, perhaps, the most daring diversionary raid of all. Their target was a bar frequented solely by British troops and police, called 'The King's Arms'.

The execution group leader, Michalakis Thrassyvoulides, who worked in a shop near this bar, was well known in the area: nevertheless, he prepared and submitted an attack plan and personally led two fighters, Nicos Sofocleus and Christakis Pantelides, to the scene. On a Saturday night, when the bar was at its busiest, Thrassyvoulides gave his two men revolvers and explained the plan; then, taking his own gun in case of emergencies, he led the way to 'The King's Arms'. Sofocleus and Pantelides burst open the doors and emptied their guns into the crowd of soldiers, killing two, and vanished before anyone could fire back. They ran, led by Thrassyvoulides, along a prearranged escape route, to a house where they hid the guns and then left for the mountains, to hide out during the three-day curfew and search of Limassol that followed their attack.

Meanwhile, in the mountains of the Paphos Forest, the second phase of Harding's great operations had begun. At 2.30 am on 8 June 1956 I was woken by the barking of a dog; in so isolated an area it was almost certainly an army dog, and it sounded, from its yelps, as if it had wind of something. I roused my men, told them to gather their belongings together and moved to the crest of the ridge. Just before dawn I saw a convoy of British trucks moving up the road from Milikouri: once more the enemy had given us notice of his intentions! We set off at once for the heights overlooking a key road junction, from which we could move further south into the Paphos district, or eastwards towards Limassol. We arrived at 10 am, but there was no sign of the enemy: this was as surprising as it was pleasant. It meant not only that the noose had been left open to the south, but that the troops, who must by now have found our abandoned hide at Dipli, were not attempting to cut off our retreat. I sent two scouts to reconnoitre the mountains to the east, which they found occupied by soldiers: they did not seem very alert, since our men had crawled to within a dozen yards of their position without being spotted. On receiving this information I decided to cross the road junction below us and take up a new vantage post on the peak overlooking it from the south. During this move we saw fresh footprints and some new, empty cigarette packets, which showed that the army had recently passed by; but from our new position we saw only two vehicles pass up the road until sunset, when we withdrew into a saddle of the hills to rest. Clearly, no search of any intensity was being conducted in this area: at the most, the British were planting small groups of men in concealed positions, in the hope that we would fall into an ambush. At 10 pm we heard two bursts of fire from the direction of Kykko and I wondered if Markos Drakos's group had failed to get clear of the net.

At first light next day we moved to a point overlooking the ground to the east, between a helicopter strip and an army post: neither showed any signs of activity and throughout the day we observed no movement of troops. So, at dusk, we set off through wooded country to the east, stopping to rest at midnight. The worst danger was past, but we might still run into another enemy line. At 4 am we moved off again in a north-easterly direction and all that morning we trudged on through the trees, tired and thirsty, for we had run out of water. The temperature was over 90°F, the rocks were too hot to touch and the streams which in winter had been icy torrents had now dwindled to threads or dried up completely.

We were very glad to halt when, at 1.30 pm, we reached a small stream in a thickly wooded valley. We rested through the heat of the afternoon for an hour and a half and at 3 pm I ordered the group to fill their water-bottles before we moved on again. Suddenly one of my men, Lambros Kafkallides, shouted a warning: looking up I saw an army patrol coming up the bed of the stream and at the same moment they saw us. To try and defend ourselves would only attract more troops who were on the heights around us in their hundreds. I shouted to the group to break and run for cover. Under heavy automatic fire from the patrol, who were only a dozen yards away, we vanished into the bushes. The bullets passed well over our heads and the soldiers did not press the chase: plainly they were as alarmed as we were. However, when we reached the heights overlooking the stream we saw other patrols converging on the area from every direction. We were beset on all sides, but the thick-leaved oak forest, tangled with dense, almost impenetrable, undergrowth provided excellent cover. My group totalled six men: I split them into three pairs and we buried ourselves among the trees. We could keep a lookout in every direction, but still we were close enough together to pass a warning with a glance or a whisper. All that happened was that a sentry was posted near us, almost within touching distance of the tree I was standing behind, and there he waited for half an hour before moving off. The British must have known that I was in the area because of the articles I had been forced to abandon by the stream – my beret, my Sam Browne belt and various papers. Yet there was no attempt to pursue us, or to make a thorough search; and although several helicopters flew off in the direction of Nicosia, presumably to inform Harding of the incident, none came to look for us. So we waited, motionless and silent for two hours, wondering at the majestic clumsiness of the enemy.

At dusk I softly called my men together and told them we would move off as soon as it was completely dark. We were only a mile from a road running along the valley of the River Platys, which lay directly across our path from north to south, and there was still a small chance that the British had failed to seize it and cut off our retreat. I told my men that we would very probably face another clash with a patrol before the night was out and so we must move in absolute silence: the sound of a falling stone might mean death for us all. Slowly, tortuously, walking in stockinged feet, moving uphill on our hands and knees and downhill on our bottoms, we went forward. It was 1 am by the time we reached the high ground above the road. Imagine our delight when we found it was free of troops! I had never thought we would escape with such ease.

We crossed the road and the river and began to climb again, until at 3.30 am we scaled a peak to the south-east of Kaminaria, a small village where I hoped to get supplies. We had now been without food for thirty hours and without water for eighteen, but I decided to stay where we were throughout the day. To moisten our mouths we chewed the leaves of the rushes among which we were hiding. At sunset we moved cautiously down the hillside towards Kaminaria until we came to a stream just outside the village: there we lay in the bushes and slaked our thirst, while Antonis Georgiades went in search of food. He returned to report that troops had overrun the little place during the day and terrorised the villagers with demands for information about us. The hills around Kaminaria were occupied by soldiers almost to the very point where we had been hiding and they had left the village only a few moments before he entered.

That night and all next day we stayed by the stream. We were all suffering from thirst exhaustion and I remember drinking about fifteen bottles of water as we lay there. Our wait was enlivened by two alarming and rather comic incidents. On the opposite side of the stream a child appeared at the top of the high, nearly vertical bank, calling to a goat which was wandering slowly towards us, chewing as it went. When it was only a few feet away it stopped, raised its head and looked at us with a glassy, contemptuous eye. The little girl began to shout at it, but the animal did not move. It continued to crop the weeds, raising its head now and then to give us a glance. The shepherdess continued to shout and scream, and we feared that she would come down to collect it. Then she would really have something to scream about, and we would have the whole village running up to rescue her. But the goat graciously moved on, just as its owner was about to clamber down the bank.

An hour or so later an elderly woman appeared, this time on our side of the stream, bent double as she hacked at the weeds she was collecting for her livestock. Nearer and nearer she came, while I wondered what to do if she discovered us: we could not let her run off to the village and alarm the troops, who certainly had the whole area under observation; but on the other hand if we kept her with us until nightfall, her family would come looking for her. We lay face down in the bushes while she came steadily closer, hacking away with her knife. But, like the goat, she turned back just as I expected her to step on one of us, and made off the way she had come, mumbling to herself.

At sunset Georgiades and Pavlos Nikitas went into the village to get food for the next stage of our journey, but as they reached the outskirts there was a burst of fire from the bushes at the side of the path. An army patrol had been lying in ambush. The two men ran for their lives and made their way back to our position by a roundabout route empty-handed. It was some hours before they found us again, and when they did I ordered everyone up and out at once. Our first stop was Trooditissa Monastery, five miles to the east, on the slopes of Mt Olympus. Having left my map at the stream when we met the patrol, I had to rely on the Pole star and my sense of geography to find our path, for we had moved away from the countryside familiar to Antonis Georgiades. After this second brush with the army at Kaminaria I feared that the roads in our path would be blocked: but once again the way was clear. Looking back, we saw the beams of searchlights sweeping the area around the Platys river valley, where the army was still hunting for us, and went silently on our way.

We reached Trooditissa at 1 pm next day, 13 June. Here the Abbot gave us food and clothing and I sent one of the monks off to Nicosia with messages for the central contact, explaining that I was safe and well outside the British net and asking for information. However, the monk stopped at a village on the road and heard on the radio that the man he was to meet in Nicosia, Archimandrite Lefkosiatis, had been arrested, and he returned to the Monastery for fresh orders. By that time we had left, but the monk, realising the importance of the message he had been given, went on his own initiative to see the Bishop of Kitium in Limassol, walking the whole thirty miles because the army had banned all transport, only to find the Bishop was out of town. He then went to Nicosia and delivered the letters to the Archbishopric. Several times on the road he was stopped and searched, but nothing was discovered.

We left Trooditissa at nightfall, safely crossing the main road from Platres, the army's mountain headquarters, to Troodos, the Government's summer seat, and in the early hours of the morning we lay down in a wood south of Troodos and slept throughout the day, after posting lookouts. The danger was over and what remained was a laborious route march: we continued to travel east, passing Mesapotamos Monastery at 7.30 pm on 15

June and finally coming to a halt on the hills a mile from Saittas. This was as far as we would go. Next morning I sent Antonis Georgiades and Lambros Kafkallides into the village with orders to contact EOKA leaders in Limassol. This was done and Georgiades returned at 8 pm with Demos HjiMiltis, leader of Limassol town. I told him that he must find us a place to stay and return next day for further orders. I recorded the end of our journey in my diary on the following night:

17 June '56: I have decided to dissolve the group: Pavlos to Limassol, Kafkallides to his village, Agros; Styllis and Yiangos to the Xeros area via Kakopetria. At about 1900 hours HjiMiltis arrived with Lefkios Rhodosthenous. All moved as arranged. Antonis Georgiades, Rhodosthenous and I went by road towards Limassol, through Ayios Mamas to Yerasa, where we halted on the 18th.

On the night of 19 June 1956 two cars arrived to drive us the last ten miles to Limassol, where a hiding place had been prepared for Georgiades and myself. The Limassol men had recruited as driver an imposing policeman called Chief Inspector Costas Efstathiou, better known to his British colleagues as 'Fat Costas'. He was not, of course, told the identity of his passenger. Like most of the police 'Fat Costas' did what he was told by the Organisation and asked no questions. We passed through the streets of Limassol unchallenged, arriving at 1 am outside the house of Dafnis Panayides, the EOKA member who was to hide us.

After twelve days of continuous pursuit by several thousand troops; after we had repeatedly been encircled and twice clashed with enemy patrols, we had finally escaped. Thanks to our thorough communications system I was put in touch with all my area commanders. I ordered them to cease action, reorganise their forces and prepare for a new attack immeddiately I gave the word: thus the people of Cyprus would know that Harding had failed in his great bid to crush us.

*

The British triumphantly announced the results of the operation even before it was over; and on 17 June, while I was waiting at Saittas to move down to Limassol, Brigadier Baker, Harding's Chief of Staff, called a Press conference to announce that articles belonging to me had been found in the Paphos Forest after a clash with EOKA guerrillas. The operation continued, over an area of 400 square miles: a mountain group of seven men had been captured, with six automatics, three rifles and three revolvers. It was officially stated that the first contact with my group had bee.1 made at the chapel of Ayia Arka, when a patrol had been fired on by five men who rushed from the building and escaped in the forest. (This incident never took place.) Next day another patrol had contacted my group by a stream, but they had again escaped. The area had then been surrounded and two men had been shot trying to break through the cordon. (This obviously referred to the clash at Kaminaria.) Then a group of seven men had approached the edge of the net, but had been repulsed by the enemy's fire. (This incident did not take place either.) At dawn tracks had been discovered showing that five men had escaped in a north-westerly direction. (We were moving south-east.) Again, on the morning of 16 June, three men had tried to break out of the net and had been fired on. Meanwhile, leaflets calling on the guerrillas to surrender were being dropped on all villages and an aeroplane was flying over the area, transmitting over a loud-hailer the message: 'The game is up.'

Whoever or whatever the British were firing at on these occasions, it was not EOKA. No guerrillas visited Ayia Arka chapel; and as for the other incidents mentioned, my group was 'out of the net' before it was cast. It seems most probable that the soldiers mistook wild animals moving in the darkness of the forest for human beings and opened fire.

Despite the improvement in his tactics, Harding had failed again. What were the causes of this failure? First, although he had isolated a very large area and poured into it something like 10,000 troops, there were gaps everywhere in the net. It seemed to me obvious that the one way to prevent movement in wooded, mountainous country of this sort was to watch every road, without exception. Vehicles were certainly prohibited from using the roads, but my guerrillas had no intention of driving about in cars. As far as I could see there were no sentries and no patrols on any of the roads which lay in our path, and we were able to cross them safely five times, twice in daylight. At Dipli we were ensnared in a triangle of roads, none of which were guarded; after the incident at the stream we were again caught in an area with roads all round us. It should have been possible to cut us off in a small square of ground. Yet, while leaving these gaps, the British could not believe that we had escaped from the immediate area of the stream and we only once met soldiers – at Kaminaria, where they had concentrated because of the village. After that we were never troubled and I could drive down the main road to Limassol unhindered.

Any objective observer would reach some unflattering conclusions about the British Army in Cyprus, which had now risen to some 25,000 men, including most of the best fighting units, Guards, paratroops and commandoes. The officers lacked initiative and judgement and the other ranks lacked

The battle in the Liopetri barn: the bodies of Papakyriakos and Pittas
can be seen on the extreme left and in the right foreground

Hideout in the village of Omodhos given away by an informer and in which EOKA
guerrillas (among them Polycarpos Yorgadjis, Spanos and Karademas) were captured

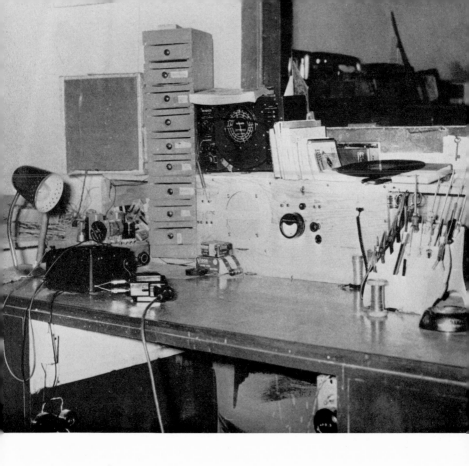

The Organization's electrical workshop for the manufacture of
electrical mines, traps, etc.

training, dash and personal courage. This is a harsh verdict, and I think that this seeming indifference to duty, so unlike what I knew of the British Army, was due in part to the fact that many of them felt that they were fighting for an unjust cause; this view is supported by the fact that frequent instances of military disobedience occurred, and sometimes developed into mutinies.

The army chiefs attempted to console themselves for their defeat by arresting innocent villagers and giving out that they were members of armed groups. It is inexplicable to me that Harding, who certainly did not lack ability, could allow such deceptions to be practised and that his entourage agreed so slavishly with all his miscalculations. The public was fed with a great deal of false news in this way, and though the Cypriots knew the truth well enough, the British people very naturally believed the victorious bulletins of the public relations department, as retailed to them by newspaper correspondents. The gentlemen of the Press are easily deluded and I made use of the fact myself when it became necessary. If, for example, I wished to distract attention from speculation about my own whereabouts, which sometimes came close to the mark, I simply ceased to sign my leaflets 'Dighenis'. At once extraordinary rumours would begin. After my arrival in Limassol from the mountains I issued a few leaflets like this and soon read in the Press that I was dead, dying or had left Cyprus for Greece. It was a trick that worked however many times it was used.

British estimates of our strength were also somewhat strange: according to the Press, who based themselves on information supplied by the army, the 'hard core' of EOKA was somewhere between 50 and 150 men. The trouble was that neither the British nor anyone else knew what was meant by the words 'hard core': sometimes it applied to the mountain guerrillas, sometimes to the front-line fighters of mountain, town and village, but most often it was used quite unthinkingly, as a meaningless propaganda catchphrase. Whatever the estimated strength of EOKA, the public were always assured that it would soon be destroyed. Discussion of our strength in these terms was, in any case, irrelevant for the whole population stood behind the Organisation and for every fighter killed or captured there were an unlimited number of reserves, ready to take up hidden arms. The reserves did some less important work until their time came: they would not know the fighters, or even the others held in reserve, and to avert suspicion I allowed them to show indifference or opposition to the Organisation in public.

I cannot close this critique of Harding's operations without condemning the army's criminal stupidity in setting fire to the stretch of forest where they had contacted me by the stream. The fire began on 16 June, by which time we were well clear of the net, resting at Saittas, twelve miles to the west. Next day it spread to huge dimensions and the authorities announced that twenty-one soldiers had lost their lives and many others had been seriously burned. I learned later that, as usual, they were concealing their losses and the dead numbered more than sixty. The wind had turned suddenly, as often happens at midday during summer in the mountains, and carried the flames among the troops at a speed of thirty miles an hour. Some were burnt as they fled up the mountainside, others when they tried to escape in trucks against the advice of Cypriot forest officers at the scene. They realised their mistake too late and were encircled and enveloped by flames. The explosion of ammunition and petrol tanks, the screams of trapped men and the terrible roar of the burning forest mingled to turn the whole area into a giant inferno. When a British officer in tears begged the Cypriot fire-fighters to help, they choked down their hatred of the tyrant and, heedless of the danger, ran into the flames to carry out the dead and dying. Yet, when the British announced over the radio, quite wrongly, that seven of the charred corpses were those of 'terrorists', soldiers began to dance with joy and British interrogators rounded up all the Cypriots present for questioning, in case an EOKA member had slipped in among them. These villagers were then left a day and a half without water. Such were the thanks they got for their gallantry.

Even after this disaster the army persisted in its policy of setting the forests ablaze. Fires were repeatedly started in the Tylliria and Paphos forests with the intention of flushing our men from their hideouts. (There were, in fact, no guerrilla groups in the mountains by this time: we had all taken refuge in town or village.) Once, when villagers had quelled a fire with great efforts, the army lit it behind them again; and when they began fighting the blaze anew, aircraft fired rockets into the trees to make sure they caught alight. Meanwhile the British Conservator of Forests plaintively appealed to everyone to 'prevent forest fires'.

Harding continued operations in other parts of the island in an attempt to cover up his failure and for the next two months the Pitsillia, the Karpassia and the Paphos areas were ransacked by thousands of troops in a new effort to kill or capture me. All these searches were barren.

★

From the moment of my arrival at Dafnis Panayides's house in Limassol, which became my headquarters for the next two months, I prepared a counter-attack. I started by reorganising the guerrilla bands which had dispersed to avoid Harding's drive. Markos Drakos had nimbly side-stepped the British attack and reached Lefka, near the north coast, after many adventures. I told him now to return to his original position in the Kykko area and reinforced his group with men from the disbanded group of Antonis Georgiades, who was staying with me as a personal aide in Limassol. Three new mountain groups were formed, one in the Tylliria, the others based on the villages of Omodhos and Pakhna. Afxentiou re-mained in command in the Pitsillia and had not been harmed by the opera-tions in his area. Town and village groups were given orders and targets. Supplies of food and arms were issued. My preparations were complete by the end of July 1956; but I had to take into account three important political considerations before beginning my new campaign.

First, the British Government, on American instigation, were talking vaguely of releasing Makarios and negotiating with him, if 'violence' – by which they meant the revolution – came to an end. Secondly, three EOKA fighters, Andreas Zakos, Harilaos Michael and Yacovos Patatsos,[1] were under sentence of death and I did not want to reduce their chances of appeal. Thirdly, Egypt had just nationalised the Suez Canal and British paratroops in Cyprus had been told to stand by for new orders. If the British attacked Egypt the depletion of their forces in Cyprus would give us an opportunity to strike harder than ever before: here was an unlooked for piece of luck that I could make good use of. For the time being, we would await develop-ments and I restricted our activities to a few executions.

However, I could not fail to act if the British decided to execute our three men. I therefore ordered hostages to be taken, but although several plans were made and put into effect a series of accidents dogged all our efforts. The idea was first tried by Nitsa Hadji Georghiou, one of our boldest girls, and Kyriakos Matsis, whom she visited in Camp K. On Matsis's suggestion Nitsa drove to Paphos to discuss the matter with Droushiotis, the area leader, and a plan was prepared. Nitsa and two other girls would persuade some soldiers to take them for a drive to the 'Baths of Aphrodite', a famous beauty spot in Paphos district. They were to stop for a drink at a café on the road where Droushiotis and his men would be waiting. The girls would attempt to put a drug into whatever the soldiers drank, to make them sleepy and more easily captured. Nitsa had cultivated a number of friends in the Services, for the sake of the information they let slip, but

---

[1] Zakos and Michael were sentenced to death for their part in the ambush of Major Coombe seven months before; Patatsos, for the execution of a Turkish policeman.

she thought it better to find strangers for this assignment. She soon struck up a friendship with a soldier who promised to bring a friend or two, if partners could be found for them: everything was arranged – but at the last moment the whole area was put under curfew and the plan collapsed.

Next, Nitsa worked out a plan to lure a British serviceman to her house, where he would be overcome and carried off by waiting EOKA men. This was more easily arranged, and within a few days she had met and invited home an RAF sergeant. When he arrived they went into the bedroom together and on a signal from Nitsa two of our men rushed out of their hiding place in the bathroom; but the sergeant tried to resist and they were forced to shoot him after a brief struggle. It was impossible to remove the body in this crowded residential area and the airman's car, parked outside, had been seen by many people. Nitsa decided to go to the police, explaining that two unknown men in masks had followed the RAF man to her house and shot him. Nothing could be proved against her and throughout her interrogation she stuck to her story. The Government were afraid to put her on trial, in case she revealed that senior officers had been among her visitors and had frequently given her useful information. So she was detained at the Nicosia prison in miserable conditions.

A final attempt to seize a hostage was made by the Kyrenia group under Tassos Sofocleus, who chose a man called John Cremer, a retired civil servant thought to be working for Intelligence. Cremer paid regular visits to a Turkish village for an unknown purpose, going on foot by a little-used path: a four-man group lay in wait for him one afternoon with revolvers. Cremer did not try to resist as he was bound, gagged, blindfolded and taken off to a nearby village. Here he was kept for three days, properly fed and well treated, while I issued a leaflet warning that unless the three fighters were reprieved he would be executed at noon on 4 August 1956. On 3 August a Government spokesman said that the 'course of justice would not be affected one way or another by such threats'; and next day Zakos publicly appealed from the condemned cell for Cremer's release. He told his lawyer that Cremer was responsible 'neither for the actions of myself, nor my comrades, nor for the Government's decision in our case. I hope he will be freed unconditionally.' Zakos's comrades agreed, and in view of this moving appeal and because Cremer was an elderly man I ordered his release. His captors drove him to a lonely spot on a main road and telephoned the police, who came and fetched him.

Harding ordered the execution of Zakos, Michael and Patatsos five days later. At once I struck back with sabotage in military bases all over the island: these attacks were intended to put me in a position of strength for my next move, which could be decisive for the future of the struggle.

The possibility of a cease-fire had recently been under discussion between myself and the Greek Government, with whom I corresponded through the Greek Consulate in Nicosia. A peace offer from our side would expose the British claim that EOKA activity was the only obstacle in the path of new negotiations. The disadvantages were that the British might not reciprocate, which would leave us open to attack without being able to reply; and there was also the probability that they would exploit the proposal as a sign of weakness. Our current sabotage campaign, however, reduced the chances of that.

After careful thought I decided that it was my duty as a soldier to make a generous gesture. By creating an atmosphere of peace I would leave the field clear for diplomacy to find a political solution to our troubles; it could be achieved if the British acted sincerely. I therefore issued, on 16 August 1956, a proclamation which said:

I am ready to suspend operations and await the response of Britain to the demands of the Cypriot people as set out for discussion by the Ethnarch, Archbishop Makarios. As proof of my unshakeable will to press forward to that happy end, the completion of the work undertaken by Ethnarch Makarios, and to provide him with an opportunity to solve our national question,

I ORDER
FROM TODAY, THE SUSPENSION OF OPERATIONS
BY ALL SECTORS UNDER ME.

EOKA declares, meanwhile, that it will stand on guard, ready for new sacrifices, knowing that it has all the moral and material backing necessary.

EOKA,
The Leader,
Dighenis.

Since I had good reason to suspect the leaders of 'Perfide Albion', I warned all my area commanders not to lower their guard: they must remain on the alert, while refraining from any action that might be interpreted as a breach of the cease-fire. Any transgressions would be severely punished, even by sentence of death, if I thought it necessary.

My proclamation was transmitted by Cyprus Radio and the BBC, and within a few hours Harding called a meeting of his advisers to consider their reply.

CHAPTER SIX

The British Choose War

August 1956–March 1957

SEVEN days of silence followed my offer of a cease-fire: seven days in which the British did nothing, apart from issuing a list of casualties since the start of the revolution – as if to suggest it was all over. It was announced that the Government was considering its reply. My proclamation had meanwhile aroused world-wide interest and there were many favourable comments from neutral states; hopes were expressed that a lasting peace was in sight.

The British Conservatives did not approve of this and their annoyance increased as day followed day without a single 'incident' and it became clear that I both could and would keep my word. Tory newspapers now began to present my proposal as a trick to gain time for the reorganisation and rebuilding of EOKA, and agreed among themselves that Harding's summer operations had dealt the death blow to the movement. Cypriots, it was claimed, were at last turning against us and giving information to the police. These inspired reports proved, in the months that followed, to be sadly wide of the mark; they also led me to expect the worst and I sent out orders warning all groups to guard against a surprise attack.

At last, on the evening of 22 August 1956, Harding released his bomb-shell and revealed the British Government's dismal plot: there was no answer to my offer; instead, we were invited to surrender and the terms under which we could do this were broadcast over the radio. When I heard the news on our little set in the underground hide at Limassol I told Georgiades that, at least, we did not have to spend time considering a reply. I made my decision in the space of time it takes to utter the word 'NO!', and I picked up my pen at once to write our answer. My proclamation was circulated with lightning speed and the British were astonished to find a leaflet rejecting Harding's ultimatum on the streets of every town and village by midday on 23 August. It said:

VICTORS DO NOT SURRENDER

When the invader asked the Greek nation to surrender its arms at Thermo-pylae, he was told, COME AND GET THEM, if you dare. As military leader of the fighting Cyprus people I reply to this demand for surrender, COME AND GET THEM, IF YOU DARE. The struggle can never cease until a final solution is found. The British demand shows insincerity and malice. However, in order to manifest my goodwill once more, and to try to avert further bloodshed, I notify you that if this treacherous demand for surrender is not withdrawn by midnight on the 27th instant, and if negotiations do not begin on the terms laid down by Archbishop Makarios, then I shall cease to be bound by the cease-fire, which I declared on my own initiative, and I will resume liberty of action.

EOKA,
The Leader,
Dighenis.

On this defiant chord I issued orders for immediate action and instructed the whole Organisation to prepare for a long campaign, since it was now obvious that there would be no early end to the struggle. The British ultimatum was due to expire on 12 September 1956, and in the meantime I set in motion propaganda to reassure the Cypriot people. My youth leader in Nicosia, Renos Lyssiotis, had boys at work painting sheets with such slogans as 'ALL FIGHTERS ARE AT THEIR POSTS', which appeared as if by magic, hanging from the walls of the Sports Stadium. Every time something of the sort happened, crowds gathered to applaud and cheer. One of Lyssiotis's girl couriers told him proudly that only a donkey would be stupid enough to surrender, and this gave him an amusing inspiration. He set the boys loading a mule with wooden swords and popguns, then turned it loose in the main street of the capital, where it obligingly wandered up and down for several hours carrying a placard which read, 'My Marshal, I Surrender'. Even the soldiers laughed as it went by. Not one of the hundreds of fighters scattered through the island surrendered and the subject quickly became a national joke.

Faced with such unity and determination, Harding claimed that our offer had been no more than an excuse to gain a breathing spell and that, in any case, we could not be trusted to keep the peace. These attempts to turn international opinion against us culminated in the publication of the famous 'Grivas diaries' which, it was hoped, would damage the Greek Government and Makarios by proving their connection with EOKA.

It was true that part of my files had fallen into British hands through treachery. Shortly before the start of the revolution, on 1 April 1955, I gave a section of the diary I was keeping to Gregoris Louka, my bodyguard, for safe-keeping. Louka, a completely trustworthy man and first cousin to Afxentiou, took the papers to his village, Lyssi, where he and his brother sealed them in glass jars and buried them in a field. During these early months of the struggle I stayed in the house of a man called Pascalis, who knew I had given my diary to Louka and guessed where the documents were hidden. This man later turned British agent and revealed everything he knew, with the result that the British Government was able to publish extracts from my private papers on 26 August 1956 – one day before the end of our cease-fire. I do not think that any further evidence is required to show that the British did not want a settlement, but simply wished to impose their own point of view. Harding's chief interest now was to vindicate his policy: only my death and the destruction of EOKA could salvage his military reputation. He took advantage of the fact that the Bishop of Kitium and the Secretary-General of the Ethnarchy, Mr Nicos Kranidiotis, were mentioned in the diaries to put them both under house arrest; thus the sole responsibility for the conduct of the revolution, both in the military and political spheres, came into my hands.

Naturally, these revelations of EOKA secrets had a bad effect in the island, and I wrote that night:

27 Aug. '56: The first impression is deplorable. The morale of the people has suffered a shock. To raise it again I have given orders to area commanders to consider it as if it were a matter of no consequence. I have put out leaflets saying that the whole story of my journal has been fabricated by the British in order to distract world attention from the situation in Cyprus which they themselves have created.

There was no doubt in my mind, after the insulting demand for surrender and the publication of my diary, that Harding wanted to provoke us into a fight to the finish. He got more than he bargained for in the months that followed. Two hours after midnight on 28 August, the cease-fire was shattered by a bomb explosion at the home of a British officer in Nicosia; next day the execution groups went into action, shooting down a British officer in the street.

I set up at this time a 'Political Committee for the Cyprus Struggle' (PEKA) which did good work rebutting British claims and arguments. Harding paid us the compliment of starting his own leaflet campaign, in imitation of our methods, but this merely added to the road-sweepers' labours. Although he could see his leaflets lying unread in the gutters by the thousand, and although it was obvious that they were having the opposite effect to that desired, Harding persisted day after day with the same propaganda line: he could not understand that by reviling EOKA as cowards and murderers, he was insulting the whole Cypriot people. The

Government were finally reduced to issuing forged leaflets attacking EOKA, yet bearing the Organisation's signature at the foot. They could find no other way to make people read their opinions. What greater confession of failure could there be than this?

The behaviour of the British put me in no mood to listen to suggestions which were made at that time by the Greek Consul-General and the Bishop of Kitium (who, although guarded by police at his palace, could still smuggle messages in and out) that I should call another cease-fire, after a period of action. They thought that we should respond to some vague talk of negotiations by the British. I rejected the idea bluntly in a letter to the Consul on 1 September 1956:

. . . It is impossible for me to make a new gesture of this kind to a cunning and dishonourable enemy who would take it to be a sign of new weakness on our part. Moreover, I am afraid that the moral effect of such a move would be to shake our whole internal front. I must confess I did not expect to be confronted with a suggestion of this kind at a time when the dishonourable surrender offer is still in force. National dignity, my personal honour and my knowledge of our strength oblige me to reject the idea. I am astounded that it was ever made. Should negotiations begin however, we can reduce our activities gradually until we reach a state of undeclared cease-fire.

The British Government, under the glare of world-wide publicity, could not entirely abandon the search for a political solution, and on 14 September 1956 (the day the surrender offer expired), the terms of reference under which Lord Radcliffe, the British jurist, was to prepare 'a liberal Constitution' providing 'a wide measure' of self-government were announced. They fulfilled none of my conditions and it was clear to me that the constitution was to be drawn up on the basis of an Anglo-Turkish conspiracy. To counter this conspiracy we needed a forceful and completely united policy in Greece and so, that same day, I circulated a proclamation addressed to the Greek Government and all Greek political parties, proposing that a single national front should be formed to deal with Cyprus affairs. To my astonishment, the Foreign Minister, Mr Averoff, publicly replied that the Greek Government alone bore responsibility for the country's foreign policy and it was absurd for Cypriots to think they could determine what that policy would be. In other words, he regarded national interests as the monopoly of the ruling party. The Cyprus Government exploited this rebuff to the full and I was indignant that our enemies had been given such a chance to sow division. It was not my first disagreement with Mr Averoff since he had taken over the Greek Foreign Ministry in May 1956: a few weeks before he had objected to one of my proclamations, which had been taken in Athens as an attack on his Government. I had then explained my position clearly in a letter[1] in which I said:

I am a soldier and as such I am not interested in politics. No attempt should be made to interpret my actions politically. The Cypriot people expect the Greek Government to take a firmer stand against the Anglo-Turkish partnership and the vacillations of the United States. If the Battle for Cyprus is lost, so too will be the prestige of Greece.

Yet Averoff had decided to take offence at my simple call for Greek unity, and to make his objections public. I drew up another proclamation, pointing out that the blood of Cypriots was not so cheap that they had no right to express an opinion concerning the cause they were fighting for: however, when I saw the damage done by Averoff's over-hasty words, I held my hand and said nothing. If we were to quarrel it would not be through any fault of mine.

The affair served to warn me that I must follow political developments more closely, now that I was solely responsible in Cyprus; for the first time I began to realise the irresolution of the Greek Government and the danger that they would be drawn into making concessions.

*

Our first activities after the cease-fire were on a limited scale: I had ordered the area commanders to keep something in reserve in case, as seemed likely, the British attacked Egypt and provided us with a chance for a major onslaught in Cyprus. I thus chose targets which could be attacked with few losses to our side, and Harding was misled into thinking that we were throwing everything into the new offensive. He did not imagine that, active as we were, our real strength was being reserved until the army had its hands full elsewhere.

We led off with such a spectacular series of coups that it was quite natural for Harding to be deceived. The first of these was our rescue of Polycarpos Yorgadjis, a former Nicosia commander who was held at the central prison. In this feat the courageous Nitsa Hadji Georghiou, who had been detained at the prison since the failure of her attempt to seize a British hostage for EOKA, once more showed initiative. A high wall divided the men's quarters from the women's, but a means of communication had been found: Nitsa, who worked in the kitchen, complained of mice and

---

[1] Averoff wrote to me under the code name 'Isaac' and, for security reasons, usually referred to himself in the third person in his letters. Our correspondence went through the Greek Consulate in Nicosia and the 'postman' was an Ethnarchy secretary who had a valid excuse to call there regularly.

was given a cat with which to catch them; when she went into the prison yard and called it three times, the men knew it was safe to throw a message over the wall, wrapped round a stone. By this means Yorgadjis warned the girl that he had convinced the prison authorities that he was ill and was going to hospital for an X-ray next day. The message was taken out by a Greek warder a few hours later and four armed men were concentrated in a house in Nicosia. Another member of the Organisation, working at the hospital, watched all movements there: if he considered that the operation was possible he was to inform the others at once.

When Yorgadjis arrived at the hospital next day our man there told the waiting group that he was guarded by soldiers, one of whom carried a Sterling automatic. It looked like an easy job. As Yorgadjis and his guards came downstairs from the X-ray examination room, the four fighters were waiting in the main entrance hall. They shot down the guard with the Sterling but as he fell he pressed the trigger and sprayed the hall with a full magazine of bullets, killing two of our members and a male nurse, and wounding several other people. There was a short, sharp exchange of fire with the other guards, during which Yorgadjis escaped by a back door, tearing himself free from his handcuffs. Then the two surviving fighters made off, taking with them the dead guard's Sterling. Yorgadjis took refuge in a house nearby and was later moved to an EOKA hideout, from which he wrote to me:

Leader,
I have just arrived at Gavriel's house, very much distressed at the unhappy results of today's events. My escape can only be considered miraculous. The handcuffs seemed to fall by themselves from my wrists, and through a stream of bullets I ran out of the hospital without meeting our men. I had been taken there by six guards: the attempt should not have been made. I await your orders as to where and how I shall offer my services,

Klimis (Cicero).

I placed him in charge of a mountain guerrilla group. We had lost two gallant young men, Kyriakos Kolokassi and his cousin Ionas Nicolaou, both aged 23; but the moral effect of this daring raid was electrifying and it was increased by the events that followed.

One week later two more of my most valued men escaped, this time from Pyla detention camp. Pavlos Pavlakis and Antonios Papadopoulos, two Famagusta leaders, had both taken part in many successful operations before their arrest: both spoke good English and their friendly personalities had gained them excellent reputations with the camp officials. Pavlakis, in particular, was liked by his jailers, who had made him a compound leader. One day the deputy commandant of the camp visited Pavlakis's hut and admired a fretwork frame made for a religious picture in the camp workshop. Pavlakis offered to make him one like it and the officer thanked him profusely: he did not know that the frame he had admired was constructed specially for the purpose of carrying messages out of camp. That afternoon Pavlakis gave it to a visitor while a guard stood over them. Inside was a warning that they intended to escape next day and a request for a car to be waiting.

Soon after reveille, at 5.30 am, the two detainees went to a lavatory in an outer corner of the compound and changed into army battledress, which they had camouflaged with clay, grass and twigs. They rubbed earth into their hands and faces and began to crawl laboriously, one after the other, towards the barbed wire fence 20 yards away, running between two high watchtowers. Pavlakis led the way: Papadopoulos, directly behind, kept a hand on Pavlakis's ankle: one kick meant 'all clear'; two meant danger. Pavlakis watched the guard on their right, Papadopoulos the one on the left. The towers were a good distance apart and the two escapers would not be noticed as long as they kept still; and so they could move only during spells when both sentries were looking away. With many stops and starts they edged through the 'killing area', where detainees could be shot on sight, until they reached the long coils of wire which guarded the first of two fences round the camp perimeter. Slowly Pavlakis snipped a hole through with his wire-cutters and they crawled under a bush of springy Dannaert wire into a narrow catwalk. Their next objective was a section of the perimeter 300 yards away, out of sight to everyone but the guard in the right-hand tower. It took them seventy-five minutes of painful crawling to get there: so exhausted was Pavlakis that his cramped muscles could not sever the last strands of wire and he had to use both hands on the cutters before they parted.

It was now nearly 7 am – time for the guards in the watchtower to change. The morning sun was up, but still the escapers waited. They were lucky: normally the night sentry stayed in the tower while his relief climbed up to meet him; today he had gone down first, leaving the tower vacant for a few seconds. By the time the guard had clambered up the steel ladder there was nothing unusual to be seen: just two men walking away near the corner of the camp, probably farmers. No one, certainly, could have cut through the wire in the time it took to mount the tower. Pavlakis and Papadopoulos reached the waiting car a mile away and were not missed in camp until the 11.30 am roll-call: even then it was thought that they were working in another compound. Pavlakis at once took over his duties as Famagusta leader again, while Papadopoulos joined Afxentiou's group in the Pitsillia mountains.

The next slap in the face for Harding was provided by the Kyrenia groups under Tassos Sofocleus. The town group, consisting almost entirely of schoolboys from the Gymnasium, led by the young caretaker, Dinos Haralambos, raided Kyrenia police station, which had an apparently impregnable position under the walls of the Crusader castle, where 250 troops were housed. I approved their plan, with some suggestions and alterations, and wished them good luck. At 3 o'clock on the morning of 8 September 1956, twelve men armed with a sten, four revolvers, three shotguns and fifteen home-made grenades, rushed the building. A Turkish policeman fired, wounding two of our men, but the attack was pressed home and the guards surrendered. The raiders burst into the armoury and seized two Sterlings, three revolvers and several hundred rounds of ammunition, then withdrew under heavy fire from soldiers on the castle walls. While three EOKA fighters repulsed an army attack on the west of the station, four others held off a platoon approaching from the south. The troops were forced back into cover behind the walls, while we escaped in cars with the guns.

A fortnight later Tassos Sofocleus, one of my most courageous and able lieutenants, personally led the Kyrenia mountain guerrillas in a major ambush on the main Nicosia–Kyrenia road. He chose a site that I had myself inspected a year before when I was looking for a place to ambush the British Commander-in-Chief. It was a very dangerous operation, for the Kyrenia–Nicosia road was one of the busiest in the island and troops were stationed at both ends of the pass over the mountains. Sofocleus, carrying a Thompson submachine-gun, led his ten guerrillas from the hideout in the early morning and reached the chosen position towards nightfall. This was at a double hairpin bend north of the pass, on the hillside running down towards Kyrenia and the sea. Shortly before 10 pm a target appeared: two army trucks, moving fast from their base to Kyrenia. They slowed to a crawl to navigate the first corner, and as the second truck began to turn, Sofocleus and three men opened fire from the high ground, killing a solider; then, as the two lorries reached the second bend a group of six under eighteen-year-old Vassos Petronas sent in a stream of Bren fire and a burst of shrapnel from a home-made mortar. The leading vehicle went off the road and crashed into the ditch, where it ended on its back, lights blazing, with a passenger trapped beneath it. The other rolled on downhill towards the army camp in Kyrenia – but as it went the door of the cab swung open and the soldier sitting beside the driver fell out on to the road, dead. He had been killed by the first burst, and the weight of his body had forced down the door handle; several other soldiers were wounded.

The group withdrew immediately up the steep side of the pass to the village of Bellapais. The British were infuriated by the audacity of this attack and within two days they had mounted the largest manhunt the Kyrenia range had ever seen, which they called Operation Sparrowhawk; during the next two weeks, 3,000 troops searched every village in the hills and along the coast. They discovered the whereabouts of Tassos Sofocleus's headquarters and, after a long search, he was captured with five of his men.

This vast and costly operation had no serious effect on the functioning of the Kyrenia groups: within the month I had replaced Sofocleus by an equally efficient leader, Kyriakos Matsis, who had just escaped from detention.

Of all our hundreds of attacks at this period, the one which most deeply outraged the British took place on the football field of Lefkonico High School. Soldiers from a nearby army camp used the ground regularly. Their movements were observed by two young EOKA members, Georghios Ellinas and Petros Krambis, who noted that at the end of the game they always washed at a tap on the edge of the field. Over the next three nights, Ellinas, Krambis and two other pupils dug a 400-yard-long trench from the tap to an olive grove, in which they laid their electric cable. On the third night they buried a large bomb in front of the tap and attached the other end of the wire to a battery behind an olive tree. Next day, with a crowd of other pupils, they watched a game between two army teams. As it ended they ran to the battery, while a teacher shepherded the children away. Two girls stayed near enough to see the soldiers gather round the tap, then waved their handkerchiefs as a signal to the waiting boys.

The explosion blew a large crater directly under the men's feet, killing two of them and wounding five others. Within the hour the rest of the regiment had arrived: furiously they rushed through the village beating and kicking everyone they met, smashing windows and ransacking shops for anything worth stealing. Then they arrested every man they could find and herded them all into the village square. There they were made to stand against the wall with their hands up, while they were kicked or punched or struck with rifle-butts. Shots were fired at random and two men had narrow escapes. The doors of private houses were smashed down, money was stolen and villagers made to hand over their watches. There was a great outcry in the island at this vandalism, in which many right-thinking English people joined: one English housewife, Mrs Betty Davey, who lived in Lefkonico, said she was ashamed at what she saw of the troops' behaviour. The authorities were unrepentant and, although they instituted an official 'inquiry', took great pains to cover the affair up and divert attention from it. Harding himself kept a photo of a British casualty, taken on the spot, in his desk drawer and showed it to visitors who raised the question of Lefkonico. I was filled with contempt at this trick; it was, to say the least, unbecoming to a man of his rank and achievement.

Many other explosions rocked the military bases at Episkopi, Akrotiri and Dhekelia. Our most devastating piece of sabotage, at the RAF Station, Akrotiri, was completely concealed by the British at the time and has not, until this day, been made public. There was good reason for this, since we had wrecked the main runway only a few days before the Anglo-French attack on Suez was due to begin. The operation was planned and carried through by one man, a Greek civilian worker at the base. After carrying four time-bombs, hidden in a basket of grapes, into the camp, he concealed them in a storm-drain which ran across the runway. Next he carried the bombs, slung round his neck, for several hundred yards into the drain, crawling on his hands and knees: the job took him six hours to complete, for guards passed over his head every few minutes and he was forced to lie still in case they heard his movements. Finally the bombs were in position and the saboteur emerged and hid until dawn, when he mixed with the other workers. At midnight two great transverse gashes were blown in the runway, putting it out of action for two weeks.

Meanwhile the execution groups had made the towns so dangerous that soldiers were forbidden to enter them unless on duty and military transport was kept off the road as much as possible to avoid our ambushes.

Throughout this period I was directing operations from the house of Dafnis Panayides, the Limassol businessman who had provided us with a refuge after our escape from the mountains. But Panayides had done a great deal of work for EOKA in the past and his home and surrounding land were being subjected to increasingly frequent searches. I decided the time had come to move on. Naturally the problem of a new hideout had been studied well in advance of the move and the Limassol leaders had chosen the man who was to be my host. He was a young clerk of the Ottoman Bank called Marios Christodoulides, who was married and had a nine-month-old daughter. Their house, not far from that of the Panayides, was a small, very ordinary building one hundred yards from the main Limassol by-pass, set in a field by itself. A special underground hide had been constructed which extended beneath the kitchen, under the wall of the house and into the garden, where it was roofed over with a cement slab, topped by an innocent-looking poultry run. The hide was just large enough to hold two six-foot camp beds, with a desk and chair between them; it had electric light and a fan for ventilation and our submachine-guns hung on the wall. Georgiades and I spent most of our time upstairs in the living-room, where we worked behind closed shutters from dawn until late at night, issuing orders, studying reports and dealing with a mass of administrative detail. My presence here was known only to a few completely trustworthy people: Marios and his wife Elli; Maroulla and Dafnis Panayides, who brought my correspondence; Demos HjiMiltis, Limassol town commander and his fiancée Nina Droushiotou, who acted as my special courier; and to Manolis Savvides and Andreas Papadopoulos, Limassol group leaders who had built the hide.

The room I worked in was hidden from the road by trees and this sometimes allowed soldiers to pass within a few yards of my window without my being seen. At night I occasionally heard the heavy footsteps of a patrol crossing the roof of my hideout as they walked through the yard. It was essential to have an unmistakeable, yet unsuspicious, warning signal: a good watchdog was the answer. One day Marios returned from a visit to his home village with a black mongrel of advanced years who had been christened Irma by her previous master. She was tied to a tree in front of the house and soon proved to be everything that a watchdog should. She stayed at her post at all hours of the day and night and barked furiously at anyone and anything that came down the path to the house; even other dogs could not pass without a tirade from Irma and she regarded males with particular contempt. We came to learn that she did not make the same noise for everyone who approached: for cats, for dogs, for children, for Cypriots and for Englishmen, Irma provided several distinct welcomes. When a soldier appeared her yelps were at their shrillest and she seemed to have an instinctive awareness of danger, so that we knew, without looking up, exactly who or what was coming. And when we left her untied she lay quietly at the foot of her tree, more faithful than any soldier. Irma acted as my bodyguard for eighteen months, and then died peacefully of old age. We tried to replace her with other dogs, but they would leave their post, or fail to bark, or fall asleep, and not one of all those we found had a half of her patience, intelligence or loyalty.

*

It was clear to me that events were approaching a climax: the Anglo-French military build-up in the island was immense and the political

British soldiers searching Greek civilians in Nicosia

Combing a region for hidden arms

The interior of an EOKA guerrilla hideout near Kakopetria

Greek Cypriot guerrillas

horizon dark with storm-clouds. A phase of intense diplomatic activity over Cyprus had begun in London, Athens and New York: the Radcliffe Constitution would soon be made public and a fresh debate in the United Nations would follow. At this crucial stage I had to deal firmly with the manoeuvrings of British politicians and the vacillations of the Greek Government.

When a Labour Member of Parliament with interests in Greece, Mr Francis Noel-Baker, publicly appealed to me for another cease-fire I replied in a leaflet that I was not inclined to repeat an offer which had been rejected in such an underhand fashion, and that there was, in any case, no common ground for understanding so long as Britain maintained her present policy. A month later, in October 1956, Noel-Baker visited the island himself and sent me the following letter:

Dear Colonel,

I very much regret that you are the only prominent person closely associated with the situation in Cyprus whom – so far as I know – I have not yet been able to meet. This is especially unfortunate because you are, at this moment, one of the very few people in a position to take an initiative and make a positive contribution towards an honourable and peaceful settlement.

It may be said that this is an inappropriate time for you to make the bold and realistic gesture that is needed. You may also have in mind the tragic failure of the last truce. My reply is that I can see no time in the near future which will, with certainty, be less inappropriate; and, in any case, it is hardly 'inappropriate' to attempt to save human lives. Further, it appeared to many people that you were misled and outmanoeuvred in mid-August.

It is the unanimous and most emphatic view of all the leaders of my own party in England, of many other leading figures there and in other countries, as well as of those political friends whom I have consulted privately in Athens, that the best chance of making a fresh start, leading – among other happy results – to early release of the Archbishop, is a period without military operations long enough to permit all the many and powerful forces of reason and justice to be effective.

I have reason to be convinced that this cannot fail.

I am etc.,
Francis Noel-Baker.

I was indignant to learn that I had been 'misled and outmanoeuvred' in rejecting Harding's surrender terms. By now I was convinced that this Labour MP was playing the Tory game, and I did not reply to his letter or give it any further thought.

Four days later, however, the same suggestion was made to me by the

Greek Consul, Mr Vlachos, who sent me his opinion that it would be politically advantageous to declare a cease-fire immediately after the inscription of Cyprus on the United Nations agenda. I did not agree. EOKA was stronger than ever and I knew the British would only use our gesture as a pretext to avoid an international debate: they would argue that, since the way was now open to direct negotiations, there was no need to bring the quarrel before the United Nations. Again, Harding would continue his operations whatever we did, and we would simply lay ourselves open to his attacks. I did not exclude the possibility of another cease-fire, but it must be considered in the light of the situation created by the United Nations decision, and at a time favourable to us. Events soon proved me right: a few days later we plunged into the most violent month of the revolution.

CHAPTER SEVEN

Harding: The Final Duel

THE ill-fated Anglo-French attack on Egypt commenced on 31 October 1956, and at last I had the opportunity for a full-scale campaign: my strategy in holding something in reserve for so long now paid good dividends. Large numbers of Harding's best troops were drawn off and the whole military situation was thrown into the melting pot. The British ever after referred to November 1956 as 'Black November', and recorded 416 'acts of violence' by EOKA, the highest figure for any single month since April 1955.

The attack began on 2 November, when bomb teams made twenty-one separate raids in every part of the island: meanwhile guerrillas ambushed trucks at Limassol, saboteurs dynamited harbour installations at Famagusta and Larnaca, and the execution groups struck in Nicosia. The mountain guerrillas went into action for the first time in many weeks: George Matsis's group raided Alona police station in the Pitsillia, then ambushed the lorries carrying military patrols to the scene. Several soldiers were killed.

An important weapon in this new onslaught was the electrically detonated mine, which we had recently begun to use on a wide scale for the first time. We planted these killers not only in the roads, but in trees, in walls, under bridges and anywhere else they might cause damage. Their great advantage was that they could be fired from a distance by means of a battery and electric wire: the enemy had little chance to hit back before our men escaped. The mines were prepared by men with no formal training in the arts of war, electricians, chemists and ironsmiths; amateurs all, yet their products very rarely failed, and British troops were blasted off the roads by night and day, often killed in batches of three or four at a time.

One such mine was used with devastating effect in the Paphos district: it was the height of the grape season and the roads were covered with crushed fruit and vine leaves. A group led by Savvas Papaefstathiou carefully raised this muck with a spade and planted their mine beneath it. They did not have long to wait. An army truck came grinding up the hill, rounded a bend and passed directly over the small hump in the road. Simultaneously the mine was detonated, blowing the truck apart and killing three soldiers. Pieces of mangled metal and flesh were found 200 yards from the spot. It was an appalling sight, and the moral effect on the troops who witnessed this, and dozens of similar incidents, was tremendous – much more important to me than the casualties themselves.

Another effective device, but one which we could use only rarely, was the parcel bomb. Many plans were drawn up to kill Douglas Williamson, a civil servant who worked hand in hand with the army at Platres, the British mountain headquarters. Williamson knew that his work against the Organisation had made him an important target and he took great care never to expose himself to any unnecessary danger. It was decided to send him a parcel bomb, disguised as a book, which would explode on being opened. The work was carried out with great care and expertise by a Limassol town group and Williamson was killed as he sat in his office at Platres. Elaborate precautions were taken by Britons opening their mail thereafter and the chances of a similar success were so small that the attempt was never made again.

A high point of the November attack was the full-scale ambush mounted by Markos Drakos and his group of twelve men on the mountain road between Lefka and Pedhoulas. The guerrillas took up their positions overnight and found a target soon after daybreak, when the lookout signalled the approach of three lorries loaded with soldiers moving down to the coast. As the first vehicle appeared round the bend, Drakos's men sent a hail of automatic fire down the hillside, wounding its driver and an officer sitting beside him. Both this and the second truck went off the road, out of action, but the soldiers climbed out and returned our fire, while the third lorry speeded on past them to a safer position: here the soldiers dismounted and began to shell the EOKA men with mortars. In the engagement which was fought out over the next twenty minutes our Bren gunner killed the sergeant firing the mortar with a shot from over 500 yards. The group then withdrew, leaving one dead and four wounded soldiers behind them. We had no losses. Army dogs and human trackers were brought to the scene, but they proved, as usual, useless.

After the collapse of the Suez operation, British troops poured back into Cyprus and I reduced my pressure, leaving it mainly to the execution groups in the towns to keep up a war of nerves: so many street killings took place in the centre of the capital that the London newspapers took to calling it 'Murder Mile'. The Nicosia team led by Nicos Sampson did much courageous work at this time. They were responsible for more than twenty killings in their area between the months of August 1956 and January 1957. Most daring of all was the attack on three British police sergeants on Ledra Street, Nicosia's main shopping centre, carried out by Sampson, Athos Petrides and Andis Tseriotis: in broad daylight, in the crowded thoroughfare, they engaged the three policemen in a gunfight, killing two and seriously wounding a third.

At Limassol Michalakis Thrassyvoulides's group was equally active, executing three soldiers and a British special constable during November. The latter was an officious man, well known in the town for his work against the Organisation, who had actually arrested and searched Thrassyvoulides himself on one occasion without, of course, knowing that he had the town's execution team leader in his hands. Thrassyvoulides swore to kill him and sent in a report on his activities and movements. The area commander gave permission for the killing and the constable was watched and followed. The spot chosen was Makedonos Street, through which the man passed daily. Thrassyvoulides posted two fighters in a narrow lane, while he kept watch for the target. Everything went according to plan. The constable was shot in his car and killed outright and our group escaped unharmed despite the large number of patrols in the streets. Attacks of this kind in Limassol were, of course, a threat to my security, since my house was only a mile from the centre of town, but I decided there was an equal risk attached to keeping the area too quiet, which might arouse British suspicions.

Such was the helplessness of the British Government in the face of these tactics that they tried, with some success, to draw the Labour Party into a conspiracy to tie our hands. The Cyprus question was placed on the United Nations agenda on 12 November 1956, and two days later a fresh appeal for a cease-fire, on behalf of the Labour Party and people from other parties in Britain, was made to me by Mr Philip Noel-Baker, MP (father of Francis Noel-Baker), who was later awarded the Nobel Peace Prize. I ignored this appeal because I was certain that these overzealous mediators had an understanding with the Tories: it is significant that, from this time on, Labour politicians visiting Cyprus always advised us to put an end to 'violence' and open the way to a settlement.

At all events, Harding made nonsense of such pleas when, at the end of November, he flew to London and declared in a broadcast that there was no question of negotiating with Makarios, because British policy was unchanged. In the face of this firmness, the Greek Government turned to appeasement and Karamanlis, the Prime Minister, refused a parliamentary request that a unanimous proclamation demanding self-determination for Cyprus be issued. This drew from me a letter of protest: I wrote to the Bishop of Kitium on 3 December 1956:

The Greek Government's attitude disappoints me, particularly the empty speech of the Prime Minister. If the Government want any sort of agreement, regardless of whether it is in accordance with our desires, then I think the sooner they fall from power the better. I cannot allow our struggles and sacrifices to be rewarded with a mockery of a Constitution. . . . I can hold on for a long time: our fighters are well organised and determined.

I referred in this letter to the Radcliffe Constitution, which was wholly unacceptable to me. I had already explained my views to the Greek Consul and he had passed them on to the Greek Government, who soon after rejected this latest British fraud.

It was while explaining his Constitution to the House of Commons that Mr Lennox Boyd, the Colonial Secretary, first threatened that unless it was accepted he might partition the island between the Greek and Turkish populations. This ridiculous suggestion was seized on avidly by Ankara, and a violent partition campaign was launched in Turkey: every encouragement was given to Turkish Cypriots to make trouble and they did so to the full. The ranks of the auxiliary and mobile police contained many young Turks of Volkan, which had grown to an organisation of some power. They became a scourge of Cyprus, maltreating Greek prisoners, sheltering traitors, looting homes and shops in their 'searches'. Most of them were illiterate and many had criminal records, which continued to lengthen even after their enrolment in the force. Other young Turks went to Turkey for guerrilla training, while Turkish officers came to Cyprus to organise Volkan and start bomb factories; explosions frequently occurred in Turkish houses where bombs were being made by clumsy hands.

The leaders of AKEL and their fanatical Communist followers had also been freed by this time, in the hope that they would oppose our struggle. This meant that EOKA had to fight three enemies, the British, the Communists and the Turks, while measures against the population were intensified. The people were harried by fines, curfews, searches, and new laws were brought in, at the end of November, making the death penalty mandatory for a large number of new and trivial offences, and stifling criticism in the Press.

These harsher punishments were combined with a new series of operations in the mountains. Early searches in the Kykko area were a total failure, while others at Troodos ended with the arrest of three men. At the end of November 3,000 more men were poured into a manhunt in the Solea valley: this coincided with Harding's departure for London, where he had to explain his recent setbacks to the Cabinet. Again the operation failed but, since some good news was needed for London, ten innocent men were arrested and given out to be dangerous EOKA members.

There was no change in the army's tactics. The only innovation was the use of a new type of tracker dog, specially trained in Malaya and Kenya. It was announced that these animals had been sent to the mountains to rout out Dighenis, but all they did was annoy villagers, bursting into houses where a bitch was kept, or where some meat had been slaughtered. The one British measure which had some success was the formation, at the end of 1956, of what they called 'Q patrols' – small mobile units of strong-arm men from the Special Branch, both British and Turkish, which relied on Greek traitors and informers for their leads into the Organisation. They were independent groups with their own methods, transport and equipment, but we soon took their measure and we were able to neutralise their activities without difficulty.

Because of the lack of informers in Cyprus, the British imported some 150 Cypriots, mostly Turks, from the criminal underworld of London, in the hope that they could infiltrate EOKA. There was a first group of youths between eighteen and twenty-five, whose task was to mix with the villagers; a second group of older men and women who were to take work in coffee shops (always the centre of gossip); and a third which would act as liaisons, forwarding the information gained by the others to British intelligence. Other spies were dressed as peasants and sent through the villages on donkey-back pretending to be EOKA members. A full list of agents' names fell into my hands, but when I sent copies to area commanders they said they had spotted most of them already and thought them too obvious to be worth shooting. The authorities also allowed Cypriot criminals to escape on condition that they would attempt to penetrate the Organisation; a few of these were able to betray some of our members before I had them executed.

The best informers, the most callous traitors, were well paid and protected, and when they had outlived their usefulness they were flown to Britain where they lived in luxury on the thousands they had earned. London Cypriots were infuriated to see these men driving new cars, eating at expensive restaurants and generally showing that crime paid. They also set a bad example to the weak-minded. I therefore decided to organise an execution group in London to deal with them. There was no question of action against the British public; my only purpose was to eliminate the gang of idlers, drunkards, gamblers and criminals who had sold their own country. When they had worked their way through the bribes given them in Cyprus these men often turned to crime. Among many others the case of one traitor is well known: he was a man on whom British intelligence relied in many operations against us, undoubtedly the best informer they ever had. When he was finally taken to London, his pockets full of money, he lived a wild life for a few months until it ran out. It was not long before he was serving a heavy prison sentence for attempted murder and the armed robbery of a woman he met in a London street.

Although I intended to send the execution squad from Cyprus, it was to be led by a well-known London Cypriot who knew his way about in England, for very strict control would be required. The shooting of even three or four Cypriots in London would create an enormous sensation, but the results would be well worth while. Later I planned to organise groups in Australia and Africa, where other informers had taken refuge.

However, when I put the scheme to Archbishop Makarios, soon after his release from the Seychelles in March 1957, he disapproved and refused to finance it. I was deeply disappointed. If I had been able to obtain funds from any other source I should have ignored Makarios and gone ahead by myself. As it was we threw away a splendid chance to punish traitors, humiliate their patrons and show the strength of the Organisation on an international scale.

*

As 1956 drew to a close we plunged into a final, bitter duel with Harding and violence became a weapon of the 'security forces'. Violence during interrogation came before the public eye in April 1956 when two British army officers who had fallen foul of their police colleagues were found guilty of beating a Cypriot prisoner with an iron chain.

The forms which interrogation took differed widely, according to the interrogator and to the type of prisoner being questioned. A mountain guerrilla knew that, if he was captured, he would be taken to one of the isolated mountain interrogation centres; but different handling would be given to an EOKA member who was, say, a lawyer or a doctor.

There were, of course, men who broke down under interrogation and I gave much thought to the difficult task of deciding how they should be treated by the Organisation. These men fell roughly into three categories: those who confessed out of fear, or after some mild rough-handling; those who told everything after more prolonged interrogation; and those who spoke, yet were cunning enough to mix the false news with a few true but unimportant facts so as to mislead their interrogators and throw them off the scent. Men from the first two categories might be executed, depending on circumstances: they were, after all, playing with the lives of others, and many of their comrades had kept silent, although they knew much more and were treated far worse. Men in the third class did not count as traitors so long as they did not let slip anything of consequence. There were, of course, many risks, but the Cypriots are inventive and imaginative and very often they could lead the police into a wilderness of half-truths that was far more troublesome than a blunt refusal to talk. (Yannakis Droushiotis, for example, spun a long and detailed story describing how he had witnessed my departure from the island by submarine on the Paphos coast, which had the British roaming the seashore for days, looking for confirmatory evidence.)

Regrettably, it was sometimes necessary to execute men who had once served the Organisation; but I never gave the order unless there was direct proof of guilt. I knew the British often played tricks on prisoners, threatening to denounce them as informers, or displaying them to the public in police cars, in the hope that we would kill them. Often I found that there was no need for an execution: disgrace was punishment enough and the humiliation of being dismissed from EOKA was a harsher sentence than death to many people. The whole village of Akanthou turned its back on one informer: strangers were warned not to speak to him; even his wife looked away when he came near. The man went mad and was taken to the asylum.

*

As the United Nations debate on Cyprus approached, preparations began for a major British offensive. Harding's first year in the island had brought him no victories and scant success; his pride spurred him on. So, no doubt, did the British Government, who wanted to convince the UN General Assembly that our revolt was collapsing and sway the delegates towards another non-committal resolution.

The months of December 1956 and January 1957 were hard for EOKA: we took the full force of Britain's power in a steady series of blows and we were shaken, but very far from crushed. Trouble began when the Limassol smuggling network was broken and the EOKA customs team arrested, along with several important Limassol leaders, including three men who knew my whereabouts. These were Manolis Savvides and Andreas Papadopoulos, who had helped to build the hideout I was living in, and Dafnis Panayides, whose house I had stayed at from June to September of that year. If any of them broke down under torture my life was in grave danger. Yet my long study of human nature under stress told me they would not give way and I did not trouble to move. My faith was justified: although these men were ill-treated over a period of a month, they told nothing.

As for the arms-smuggling net, I at once sent a message to Deacon Anthimos Kyriakides, a priest recommended to me by Antonis Georgiades, my aide, instructing him to find a new system and staff it with new men. He contacted a leading Nicosia businessman, Socrates Eliades, and between them, after many trials and difficulties, they arranged a very successful network which was never discovered by the British.[1]

Harding's mountain operations began with probing attacks, led by the Q patrols: bands of Cypriots, Turk and Greek, under British officers, who had only one task – to get information. On the last day of 1956 one of these patrols surprised Afxentiou's group while it was resting at Zoopiyi, in the Pitsillia. Afxentiou himself had a narrow escape and Michael Georgallis, a courageous young guerrilla of twenty-one, was killed.

The group were staying at the home of Minas Constantinou of Zoopiyi when, soon after midnight, soldiers entered the village. Someone had obviously betrayed them, for a patrol went straight to Minas's house, where Afxentiou and another guerrilla were on guard. Afxentiou prepared to open fire when, to his surprise, the patrol walked past up the village street and started thumping on the door of Minas's father's house. They had made a small mistake! Minas's father, hearing his son's name shouted, opened the door and was confronted by five armed men, two Turks and three Greeks in British pay. At first he tried to pretend that he could not understand whom they wanted, but when the Greek traitors seized him and started to push him about, he shouted a warning. Afxentiou and Georgallis ran out and were about to shoot, when they saw that Minas's father was in their line of fire. In the split-second pause one of the Turks brought his automatic up and fired a burst from the hip, wounding Georgallis in the face and body. As he collapsed in the road, Afxentiou fired over his body, hitting the Turk. Then, as both groups ran through the dark, narrow streets, there was a fresh exchange of shots before the enemy agents made off in a car. Georgallis had meanwhile dragged himself painfully over the ground, leaving a thick trail of blood: he reached Minas's door and pulling

[1] We brought arms in through Limassol customs in suitcases for more than a year before the system was discovered. A total of 43 light automatics, 12 pistols and quantities of bullets, grenades, time pencils, detonators, etc., were imported up to October 1956.

himself upright, to his knees, shouted, 'Leader, I am dying. Long live Greece!'

He was buried in the village cemetery that night and the guerrillas escaped to Papoutsa, a 5,000-foot-high peak some miles away, before the army arrived in strength next day. Georgallis's shallow grave was found and the body exhumed. A major operation began to capture his comrades.

Another piece of treachery led to the arrest of three men from the Marathassa group at their mountain hideout in January 1957. Markos Drakos, whose own hideout was nearby, was given warning and decided to move out of the area. Two days later he ran into a British patrol and was killed by a lucky shot. At midnight Drakos was leading his group through the forest: he had gone slightly ahead of the others when he suddenly came face to face with soldiers who were just changing guards at an ambush position. Some of them ran for cover, yelling as they went; others opened fire at random. The gallant Drakos was shot through the heart by a stray bullet, and the man directly behind him was wounded in the leg. Had the patrol given chase he would certainly have been captured, but they chose to dig themselves in for the rest of the night and wait for our attack; the wounded man was carried to safety by his comrades. All Cyprus mourned Drakos as a brave and selfless fighter and I, who had known him well, was consumed with grief. I wrote in my diary:

19 January[1] 57: MAVILIS (Drakos) was killed shortly before midnight yesterday in an encounter with the enemy. EOKA has lost a brave and honest soldier. May his memory be eternal. His self-sacrifice and patriotism will be an example to all.

The operations in the Pitsillia mountains, which had begun with Georgallis's death, continued with increased intensity, and the British were able to mark up two new successes, both after treachery. Three days after the loss of Drakos, the group under George Matsis were arrested in a hideout at Sarandi.[1] A few hours later a traitor led troops to another hideout at Omodhos, where, in a tiny dugout hidden under the fireplace of the village rural constable, Polycarpos Yorgadjis had taken refuge with another group. All these men were trapped underground with no chance of fighting back. This was a grave blow: two guerrilla groups had been wiped out at a time when we were short of good men. But I was sure that the tide would soon turn, and Afxentiou shared my faith. He wrote to me after these arrests:

[1] George Matsis was the uncle of Kyriakos Matsis, leader of the Kyrenia district.

I understand the size of our misfortunes, but we will not retreat; on the contrary, we shall throw ourselves into the fight with greater determination than ever and fill the gaps that have been created. Our faith in victory is unshakeable.

I told him, in my reply, to take great care, regroup and return the enemy's blows so that we could show we still had plenty of fight left in us. I wrote:

In time of trial the true fighter shows how he can face trouble with courage and calmness. If our ranks have been thinned, they must remain unbroken. The gaps will soon be filled and the Organisation will continue its mission. If everyone stays at his post and does his duty the wheel will turn once more in our favour.

So far Harding had concentrated on destroying our guerrilla army, but at the start of February 1957 several leading members of my Nicosia groups were arrested, among them the town commander, Andreas Chartas, the execution group leader, Nicos Sampson, and the head of the courier network, a young theologian called Phidias Kareolemos. Harding was throwing everything into this attack on every sector of the front. My own headquarters in Limassol were endangered on 7 February, when the area was searched for several hours. Patrols passed the house repeatedly and a guard paced up and down over the roof of my hideout until late in the day, when the search was called off.

That evening I heard over the radio that two more brave young men, George Papaverkiou and Takis Sofocleus, had died. Obedient to my order that groups should attack at whatever cost to themselves, they had gone out, completely unsupported, to ambush a convoy of seven army trucks. They had blown up the first vehicle with a mine, then opened fire with their automatics, but they had been mown down by a merciless hail of bullets from the troops. Neither of these heroic boys was yet twenty years old. So our darkest days were lit by acts of incomparable bravery.

On 17 February I lost another of my few remaining guerrilla leaders when Stylianos Lenas's group clashed with an army patrol. Lenas, badly wounded, was captured and died six weeks later. His men escaped during the night, but encountered two more patrols and another two fighters were killed. A British lieutenant was also killed in the exchanges.

While thus raining blows on our frontline the British were also attacking behind our backs, with the Turkish mob as their weapon. Large-scale riots by Turkish Cypriots were engineered to begin on 23 January, to coincide with the period of maximum pressure on our ranks by the army, and they lasted until 3 February, without the arrest of a single Turk. Greek civilians were killed and wounded, their shops and houses set ablaze: the 'security forces' simply looked on complacently. All this was accompanied by a never-ending stream of propaganda. On the radio EOKA was presented as riddled with doubt and dissension. Forged letters attacking us purporting to come from anonymous priests, sorrowing mothers, bereft widows and 'true patriots' were constantly broadcast. We countered this poisonous rubbish by leaflet and word of mouth. I ended a typical proclamation with the words: 'Let us give one more slap to the unblushing cheek of the tyrant. Let us write across the length and breadth of our country, "All for the freedom of Cyprus!"'

Our troubles had not yet come to an end. Harding had rounded up the majority of our guerrilla bands in the mountains and now he could gather all his forces together in one great hunt for the target that had so long eluded him: Gregoris Afxentiou.

For many weeks the group had been harried by the army, but had always kept one step ahead, moving from village to village through snow, rain and icy winds, until finally they took refuge at Makheras Monastery, 3,000 feet up in the hills, where they had often been given hospitality. They built a hideout in the mountainside half a mile down the valley, knowing that they could always rely on the monks to bring them food and drink. A big search began around the Monastery on 29 February; and three days later, by their usual methods, the British persuaded a peasant to tell them where the hideout was.

At dawn on 3 March 1957 a patrol reached the entrance of the hide and called on Afxentiou to surrender. He did not reply to their calls at first, but looked round at his comrades and with his face lit by a radiant glow, said: 'I shall fight and I shall die.' Four times he repeated this and, with a grim smile, he told the other guerrillas to leave; when they had given themselves up, the troops warned him that they would throw grenades in if he failed to surrender. Afxentiou replied with a burst of automatic fire, killing a corporal. The British tossed a grenade into the hideout and again they called on him to come out. One of the captured guerrillas, Avgoustis Efstathiou, said: 'What's the use of shouting. He is dead.' A soldier seized him and thrust him towards the entrance, with orders to drag out the body. Avgoustis moved towards the hide, shouting to Afxentiou not to fire but, as soon as he was inside, he called out in English: 'Now we are two! Come and get us!'

The grenade had given Afxentiou some minor cuts and his leg was bleeding freely, but for the next eight hours the two fighters repelled assault parties with a hail of automatic fire and bombs. At one stage Afxentiou tried to make a break for it, sending a smoke grenade into the midst of the soldiers to cover the escape, but when he tried to fire his gun jammed and by the time he had unblocked it the smoke had cleared.

Between the exchanges of fire there were pauses while the British discussed what to do next. In the hide, the two men talked about the past and the struggle to which they had dedicated their lives. 'The flame we lit years ago has spread through the hearts of all Greeks,' Afxentiou said. 'Nothing can extinguish it now. Freedom will not be long in coming, for our death will fan the flames still higher.'

The British were desperate at the unexpected resistance, because crowds of newspaper reporters had now reached the scene and were watching their humiliation. Yet they had not the courage to take the hideout by storm, despite their abundant weapons. Instead, they poured hundreds of gallons of petrol down the hillside, so that it flowed into the hide and soaked the two fighters' clothes and ran down the walls. Then, from a safe distance, they set it ablaze with tracer bullets and the two heroes vanished in a sheet of flame. Afxentiou called out his last words to his comrade: 'Don't be afraid!' and Avgoustis, his hair and clothes blazing, ran from the hide. Afxentiou stayed where he was and died in the flames, amid a fury of exploding ammunition and grenades.

Many hours later the soldiers tried to enter the hide, but the heat and smoke drove them back. They grabbed Avgoustis again and told him to go in and drag out the corpse. He tried to shift it by pulling the feet, but the leather of the shoes burnt his hands and, choking in the thick, evil-smelling smoke, he staggered out into the daylight again. Not until next morning could the troops get inside; and then they had to tear the roof from the hideout to drag out the hideously charred remains. One leg had been completely severed by a grenade and a huge wound gaped in the head. When Afxentiou's father was taken to identify his son's body he saw only a blackened, unrecognisable shell of burnt flesh in the shape of a man.

Had the British realised how Afxentiou's fate would inspire the Cypriot people, perhaps they would not have acted in this way.

I heard the news of Afxentiou's death with pain in my heart, but also with great pride. Marios and Georgiades sat silent all evening and could not look into each other's eyes, until I said: 'Why are you so sad? People get killed in a war, and that is what we are fighting. We shall have many more as brave as he.'

The enemy tried to make propaganda from this 'victory', but the sneers of his radio commentators merely aroused the Greeks to fury. The Field-

Marshal, however, was flushed with success and felt sure that at last Dighenis was in his grasp. His intelligence chiefs tried many tricks to find my hiding place or tempt me out of it. The only one which gave me reason to think twice was attempted four days after Afxentiou's death, when at 8 pm I had an urgent note from my central courier in Nicosia, saying that my hideout had been betrayed. The note gave no other information, but it was obvious that if I was going to move, it would have to be that night. I quickly decided that none of the very few persons who knew my whereabouts would speak. As for the couriers, they knew only that they carried messages to certain shops and houses in Limassol. The British might have reason to guess I was somewhere in the town, but I was sure they had no proof. They had planted this information in some way to panic me into moving without proper preparation and precautions through streets crowded with police and soldiers and spies. I decided to stay where I was, remaining on the alert all night and taking turns on guard. Early next morning I sent Mrs Dafnis Panayides to Nicosia to discover the source of the information. When she returned to say that it had been obtained through a Turkish policeman, my suspicions that the whole thing was just another intelligence trick were confirmed. So, by keeping cool, I avoided a move that might have proved fatal.

I must here confess that whenever my life, and thus the fate of the Organisation, depended on a rapid decision under pressure of events, the steps I took were later proved to be correct; and today I myself wonder how it was possible for one man, a man fatigued in body and mind by long years of harsh struggle, to make decisions which were so consistently right. Napoleon said it was not God who inspired him at difficult moments, but prudence. I cannot believe that, in my case, it was solely my personal abilities which brought me success and supplied me always with correct decisions: this I ascribe rather to divine providence.

CHAPTER EIGHT

The Uneasy Cease-fire

THE UN debate of February 1957 was the most important international discussion of Cyprus that had yet taken place, and a turning point in the struggle. Even before it opened Mr Averoff wrote me from Athens that the outlook was unfavourable because America saw the Radcliffe Constitution as a basis on which we should negotiate with the British. At the best, he said, we might have to accept a compromise such as the Indian proposal for independence; at the worst the discussion would be postponed indefinitely. I told the Greek Foreign Minister that I had many objections to his policy. We could not allow our claim to be shelved; we expected more courage from Athens, particularly at a time when Cypriot morale was at its peak and everyone was prepared to fight to the last bullet. It was for Averoff to bang his fist on the table if he really hoped to get the results which we had shed our blood for. In return, he suggested another cease-fire. I objected to this because I knew that the British would try to exploit such a gesture as a sign of weakness and defeat; however, I agreed to scale down our activities without an announcement during the period of the debate.

The debate in the UN began on 18 February and ended five days later with a resolution calling on the principals to resume negotiations in a peaceful atmosphere. Next day the Greek Consul urged me to declare a cease-fire at once. He believed – and in this he was supported by the Bishop of Kitium – that we should be the first to set an example of goodwill in the spirit of the resolution; he also suspected that the British would use any delay to involve Turkey in negotiations which should in our view concern only Britain and Greece. Before I could reply Harding bombarded us from the air with leaflets claiming yet again that the days of EOKA were numbered; meanwhile he pressed on with his operations against us. I wrote on 28 February to the Consul that it looked as if Harding had advised London to force through the Radcliffe Constitution, and I feared that the Government would now try to do so.

Every time Britain has an opportunity to try a more reasonable line in Cyprus, Harding puts on a big show: he launches new operations, rounds up a lot of harmless people and tells London that he has us licked. All this has its effect in influencing British policy. Harding is now so infatuated with his own prestige that he cannot imagine any way out unless it is publicly conceded that the solution has been brought about by his campaign against EOKA. In these circumstances what is the use of calling a cease-fire? The enemy will probably ignore it and we should then have to accept his blows without being able to hit back.

Although, then, I had little faith in a British response, I finally decided to offer a cease-fire. I meant to see that this time nobody would claim that the move was a cry for mercy and so I made the offer conditional on the release of Archbishop Makarios, with whom negotiations should be resumed. My proclamation said on 14 March:

In accordance with the spirit of the UN resolution, which expressed a desire for the just and peaceful solution of the Cyprus problem on the basis of UN Charter principles; and in order to facilitate the resumption of negotiations between the British Government and the only representative of the Cypriot people, Archbishop Makarios, OUR ORGANISATION declares that it is willing to order the suspension of operations as soon as the Ethnarch Makarios is released.

EOKA,
The Leader,
DIGHENIS.

Harding retorted by flying immediately to London where I believe he assured the Cabinet that since Dighenis would soon be captured there was no need to treat with him; at the same time he accompanied a fresh military drive with officially-inspired rumours that I would be caught in a matter of days. Day after day Ministers delayed their decision, hoping my end would come. Lord Salisbury, leader of the reactionary group in the Cabinet, violently objected to the release of Makarios, even though it was by now generally conceded that his imprisonment was doing Britain great harm in the world. In the end it was announced that Makarios would be freed, though not to come to Cyprus, and Salisbury flounced out of the Cabinet, never to return. At the same time the British Government publicly offered me, and other EOKA members, a safe-conduct out of the island if we wished to leave. Nobody accepted this childish proposal and I ordered that during our suspension of operations everyone should be ready to start again if diplomacy proved fruitless. Picture my astonishment to hear from the Greek Government on 5 April that they considered the struggle to be over: they were expecting me to pack up and return to Greece! This bombshell was contained in a letter from the Consul dated 2 April which said:

If you agree, the Foreign Ministry would have no objection to announcing the cease-fire on the day when the Archbisop comes back to Athens. . . . About the matter of your departure, we are waiting until he can be consulted.

I replied at once:

Your letter is astonishing. In no way did I suggest that I was prepared to lay down my arms and leave Cyprus. To abandon the struggle without being given guarantees for a permanent solution would be nothing short of desertion and I am not capable of such behaviour.

While I puzzled over what might be behind this extraordinary attempt to rush me out of Cyprus, the Consul replied on 8 April:

I am not in a position to know exactly what gave rise to the message which I passed you. I can only suppose that the thinking behind it was influenced by Press reports that you are being continuously pursued by the enemy and was doubtless concerned with averting a tragedy.

Another surprise! Anxiety about my safety was now, for the first time in two years, suggested as a reason for calling off the campaign. I immediately wrote to the Consul:

My personal safety cannot be made a bargaining counter. It would be better to fall honourably than accept the British offer of a safe-conduct if I give myself up. What is more, if the enemy does not leave us alone, I shall resume action very shortly. I can easily carry on until the next UN meeting. I shall fight; if need be I shall die, but they will never have my surrender.

My protest brought an unctuous response from the Foreign Minister, writing on 12 April:

I have come to no decision and cannot say anything before seeing the Archbishop when he arrives here, except that I am desperately anxious on your behalf. This is not merely a question of sentiment, filled as I am with emotion in thinking of your achievements, it is one that concerns the whole future of Cyprus. Your loss now would be a most grievous blow to the cause. Since the Field-Marshal has so far failed to defeat you this amounts to a major victory for the Cypriot people and yourself. Your presence in the field is in itself a threat which allows us scope for negotiation; if anything happened to you we would not have this scope and all the legendary feats you have accomplished would not be of any help to us. . . . Once more I take the opportunity to say that you have shed lustre on the name of the Greek soldier.

The Archbishop arrived in Athens with his fellow-exiles from the Seychelles on 17 April, and on 22 April I opened two letters from the Consul. The first said, in part:

The Foreign Minister is in agreement with the views you put to me: as things are today you would do better to remain in Cyprus. Nevertheless, we

have always in mind that your loss would be a dreadful blow to the cause. . . .
If you were killed Britain would be victorious and we should become
suppliants. . . . I beg you in God's name to take care.

I found it hard to credit that my correspondents should be more concerned for my safety than I was myself; nor was I pleased by the contents
of the second letter, which reported that Makarios wanted a strict cease-fire
no matter what the provocation. I pointed out in reply that our entirely
one-sided restraint was giving the enemy all the advantage.

While Makarios was still on the way to Athens I wrote a letter to await
his arrival in which I complained that the Greek Government seemed to be
trying by a series of manoeuvres to trap us into laying down our arms before a settlement was arrived at. What made it so much worse, I said, was
that they were doing so for the sake of staying friendly with their allies:
allies who cared nothing for Cyprus so long as it was kept quiet. On landing
in Athens the Archbishop wrote back, under the code name 'Haris', and
his reply reached me on 24 April:

I am proud of you and most satisfied with the splendid fight which you have
put up. I need only add that you have become a symbol and a legend. . . .
The cease-fire is an excellent idea and the one remaining question is whether
it should be made permanent. I am not yet fully informed about Cyprus, but
from what I hear it seems that we must find a means of bringing all fighting to
an end, without, of course, injuring your prestige in any way. I have various
things in mind which the Consul will explain. Meanwhile, I should welcome
your opinions.

I replied, before hearing from the Consulate, that in my view Athens
had failed to make good diplomatic use of our struggle during the Archbishop's absence from the political leadership:

Greek Ministers have behaved like mendicants, asking for favours instead of
putting forward dignified demands. The Government cares only for its
alliances with people who grovel for our help when they are in danger and
spurn us the moment that the danger is past. I do not know what information
you have been given about Cyprus by the self-appointed advisers who have
rushed to Athens to gain your ears and surround you with the poison of the
towns, but I ask you to make no decisions until you have taken the opinion of
those who represent the fighting people here. As for a permanent cease-fire,
that is unthinkable before conditions for a favourable solution are ensured.
If your opinion is different I shall not oppose you because the responsibilities
of the struggle dictate that we should work in harmony.

When the memorandum from the Consulate at last arrived on 30 April,
my respect for the Archbishop's judgement was jarred by its explanation of

his views. It was nothing but a recapitulation of the arguments for peace at any price in return for an amnesty which would force my finest fighters to submit to British demands and go into exile. The memorandum wound up with the oblique suggestion that I, too, would be better out of Cyprus:

. . . although I do not expect you will agree with me, I believe that today you no longer belong to yourself, but to the nation.

This flattery left me unmoved, and more suspicious than before. Barely a week earlier the Consulate had passed on the letter in which Averoff agreed that I should stay in Cyprus, now they thought once more that I should go! I did not know what to make of these strange moves, but I did know that I must be more careful in my dealings with Athens and its agents from now on. Once more, a little later, Averoff wrote agreeing that I should wait for a reasonable solution, but asked at the same time that I should avoid action until the next UN debate at least. The subject of my departure was finally dropped when Makarios wrote, on 17 May, formally accepting my decision.

After my final return to Greece in 1959 I learned something of what was going on in Athens over this curious period. A senior army officer who had been helping from the start to send us arms told me that Makarios sent for him five days after his return from the Seychelles and asked him to stop sending guns to Cyprus. Then, after another fortnight, the Archbishop told this officer that since the Cyprus struggle would soon be over there was no need to plan further consignments. Asked whether Dighenis agreed with the stoppage of arms, Makarios replied that he was hesitating about the final cease-fire but these doubts would soon be overcome.

It had been generally supposed that the Archbishop's release was a first step towards a peaceful solution, but the British had their own ideas of the form that it must take. Not only did they try to force the Radcliffe Constitution down our throats, but they resumed their search for 'moderates' who would agree to operate it. Without in any way being a hero-worshipper of Makarios, I had to put a stop to this; on my instructions a stream of telegrams, cables and resolutions from every organisation in Cyprus declared that the Archbishop must be the sole representative of the island in any talks with Britain. Frustrated in their hunt for quislings, the British once more threatened us with partition, and were noisily applauded by the Turks – above all by the Turkish-Cypriot puppet, Dr Kuchuk, who always danced to Menderes's tune. Other voices were raised in Greece and overseas: the air became full of conflicting 'solutions': UN trusteeships, NATO condominiums, independence, self-government and so on.

It seemed that the only point on which all sides agreed was that Dighenis would be much better outside Cyprus. In repeated statements Lennox-Boyd urged my acceptance of the 'safe-conduct' to Greece. Francis Noel-Baker, the Labour M.P., quoted Harding as saying my stay was a barrier to political progress and it was even put to me that I was responsible for keeping Harding in Cyprus: if I would only leave he would consider his mission fulfilled and then he could go too. Such entreaties were proof enough that 40,000 British bayonets could not deal with me and made my duty clear – to stay where I was until I got the terms I wanted.

What would come next? Another operation, of course, directed to my discovery, and bulletins to say that it was near. I took the danger seriously enough to decide on a diversion and used the Deacon Anthimos to put out a strong rumour that I was now hiding in the Troodos mountains between Milikouri and Kykko. On 16 March Harding took the bait and began the famous 'siege of Milikouri' which went on for just under eight weeks. Thousands of troops dug up fields looking for my hide, stripped houses of their tiles in case I was nesting in the roof, pulled down walls and uprooted trees. I listened with interest on the radio to reports of the longest and most thorough search yet made – a search that I myself had 'ordered' thirty miles away. Helicopters flew over the area calling for my surrender.

Harding was a stubborn man. Drawing a blank in the mountains he announced on 24 May (appropriately, Empire Day) that 'while Grivas and his few remaining associates remain at large we cannot lower our guard', and the searches were extended to the towns. Harding never knew how narrowly he came to miss me. On 6 June about 600 troops cordoned off our Limassol suburb at about 1 am, ready to search the area at first light. I made a practice of looking carefully around the house at night to see that we left no traces of our presence before going down to sleep in the hide, and when Marios said there were soldiers near I told him to make a double check. With the trapdoor closed down over us we laid out our little arsenal: two M3 American automatics, revolvers, mills-bombs and smoke grenades. We were ready to come out shooting and had some hopes of making off in the confusion across the fields, which offered good cover. At dawn the soldiers began to search over an area of five square miles, calling at the houses and moving across the countryside in a long line as they hunted for buried weapons or hideouts. It looked to me like a routine operation and in that case all would depend on our hosts keeping their heads. After a long wait we heard soldiers' boots thudding across the concrete roof of our hide; then we heard them entering the house. After an interval they were in the kitchen over our heads; next they opened the door of the sink cupboard which masked our trapdoor and we picked up our guns for the break-out. At that moment Elli called out to the soldiers, 'Wouldn't you like a drink?' Marios brought out tumblers and a bottle of whisky kept for such occasions. The soldiers were impressed by his hospitality, and his excellent command of English; people as friendly as this couple could have nothing to do with EOKA. After some cheerful conversation the troops went on their way and at 11.30 am Marios rapped on the cover of the hide to tell us that the danger was past.

We could never fully repay the debt we owed to these people who so bravely sheltered us, and to the Panayides next door. The two wives were my guardian angels; day after day they walked calmly past the army guards carrying messages for me and when Panayides was put in a detention camp at the end of 1956 his wife was always ready to leave her work and her family if I wanted an urgent letter taken to Nicosia. Of course on this occasion of 6 June we were also saved by the cunning construction of the hide, for the soldiers actually had their hands on its cover before their attention was distracted. EOKA hides were so varied and so baffling in their design that it was rare indeed for any of them to be revealed except by treachery. One of my previous hides survived sixteen searches by men with mine-detectors after I had left it.

If the British were not idle during the cease-fire, neither were we. I spent much time in filling the gaps in our ranks and in redistributing arms and men among the various groups, including the guerrillas – and this was done while the mountains were crowded with troops. In the rugged Pitsillia area Lambros Kafkallides replaced the hero Afxentiou, while Neofytus Sofocleus, who had so nearly blown up Harding in his bed, took over the Marathassa group from Polycarpos Yorgadjis, who had been captured in January – thus becoming the first valet in history to fight as a guerrilla chieftain. I also gave careful attention to a list of unmanned targets which our saboteurs could attack without technically breaking the cease-fire. They would do so on my orders only if reasons of prestige – such as the execution of one of our men by the British – called for a gesture on our part. Since hangings were always accompanied by a military standstill on the roads, our groups were told to strike at their approved targets on the *second night* after the execution; then the cease-fire would continue as before.

Acting on orders from London, where they well understood what the consequences would be, Harding did not actually execute anyone during the cease-fire, though he delayed one reprieve for six months and another for seven. The British vehemently asserted that political considerations in no way affected such decisions of life and death; in fact, of course, they did so all the time. An interesting example of British justice at work during the Emergency was provided by the case of Nicos Tsardellis, who was sentenced to death for a killing he did not commit. The attack was actually made by Andreas Kokkinos, a member of the Larnaca execution group, in June 1956, on a British police officer. It took place in the main street by daylight. As the sergeant got into his car, Kokkinos ran up and shot him through the head at close range; then made good his escape. Among the bystanders who ran from the scene to avoid arrest was Tsardellis, a twenty-five-year-old grocer. A Turk threw a bicycle in his path and he was arrested and picked out in an identification parade. After the sentence was pronounced, Tsardellis raised his arms and cried 'Shame on British justice. This is what I would expect.' His relatives in court burst into frenzied wails of lamentation which they kept up for so long that the Chief Justice came out of his office and shouted, 'It is the duty of the police to keep people from brawling in court!' The real killer in the case, Kokkinos, asked us for permission to go to the British authorities and suffer the consequence of his action, but I did not accept his sacrifice and sent him to join the guerrilla group of Polycarpos Yorgadjis at Marathassa for his own safety. Then I waited to see what would happen to Tsardellis. His appeal in the Supreme Court was rejected and later leave to appeal to the Privy Council in London was refused. A week after this, Harding surprised everybody by reprieving Tsardellis. The Governor was at this time applying the emergency regulations at full force and riding on the crest of a series of 'security' successes in February 1957. It seems likely, therefore, that he had received information from arrested men that Tsardellis was innocent. This view of mine is supported by the fact that a few weeks later Harding hanged a youth of only nineteen, Pallikarides, on the much more venial charge of arms-carrying. No mercy was shown here. Apart from the fact that Pallikarides was caught red-handed with the guns on a donkey, the police had privately reported that he had killed a traitor, though this could not be proved. A propaganda leaflet was issued after the hanging giving a detailed description of how Pallikarides was said to have shot the man.

*

It may be asked what our friends in Athens were doing to lend us at least moral support in maintaining the cease-fire which they had asked for. Their attitude is well instanced by a letter from the Consul, Mr Frydas, complaining of leaflets in which I warned the British that my patience might be tried too far: he said that extracts were being used against the

Greek Government by British propagandists to show that we were 'threatening to resume violence'. This was my reply:

Since I cannot keep in personal touch with my men, the leaflets which I issue must be a source of courage for them. If we are to be afraid of saying anything to inspire our followers to work and sacrifice, if we are to consider before issuing leaflets what the British may think of them, then we may as well dig a grave and bury the long struggle. In my place you would think in the same way, but of course it is not easy to understand the problems of command when you are standing on the sidelines. . . . Now I understand why British and Turkish diplomacy are always more powerful than ours.

This is what I was asked to put up with. The British could ignore the cease-fire and do what they pleased, but EOKA must not even drop a leaflet that was open to misunderstanding. The Consul-General, Mr Vlachos, followed it up with a candid suggestion of retreat on the political front. In a letter which I opened on 25 July, he suggested persuading Makarios to accept independence for Cyprus on the understanding that Enosis would not finally be excluded. I replied expressing my astonishment:

For us here, of course, there can be only one kind of independence, which is to choose our own fate, but for the British the word may have all sorts of meanings. . . . There can be no question of discussing such a thing unless the period of so-called independence is agreed in advance. Personally, I have no belief at all that the British are ready to offer anything we could accept. Why do we keep retreating before their threats of force when we hold all the cards?

Regardless of my protests, the Greek Government continued to fall back, step by step, while the British, who refused to have anything to do with Makarios, were encouraging the Turkish campaign for partition, and the Americans backed the British. On 26 August, after I had kept up the cease-fire for almost six months, waiting for diplomacy to do its part, Mr Averoff wrote to me:

I regard it as my duty to see that you, whom I hold in higher respect than anyone else in Cyprus, should know about the latest developments. Most of the allies now believe that a solution must be sought on the basis of an independent Cyprus, *without a guarantee of independence for all time*. The British seem agreeable on the understanding that they keep their bases in the island and that Turkey also consents.

I called on Mr Averoff in reply to stand by our demand for self-determination, so that we could settle our own future. I added that Greek diplomacy must go over to the offensive to make Britain and America see sense, instead of always truckling to Turkey. What would happen if Harding roused the Turks against us?

You will have to come to our aid. Our wonderful Minister of Foreign Affairs should make it plain to the British and the Americans as well that any Turkish move of that kind will bring free Greece into the arena. That is the only way to restrain the Field-Marshal. But will it be done? I take leave to doubt it.

The Americans at last came into the open on the eve of our next UN meeting, when the US Government tried to prevent the inscription of our appeal. When Makarios was leaving for New York to canvass support for the cause, Washington announced that neither President Eisenhower nor Mr Foster Dulles, Secretary of State, would receive him. This gratuitous insult to the Cypriot leader, who had not asked to be received by either, was the Greek Government's reward for a policy of appeasement and showed exactly where everyone stood. I could no longer look towards Athens in the event of Turkish attack. The Turks had become even more bellicose, threatening that five Greeks would die for every one of them who was killed. Proof of their preparations was given by an explosion on 1 September in a Nicosia suburb where they were secretly making bombs: four Turks died and were given heroes' funerals by their compatriots. I felt it right to put out a leaflet – the first to be signed 'Dighenis' since the cease-fire began – raising the question of what Greece would do if Cyprus was partitioned or Turkey ran amok. This brought a pained letter from the Consul, who feared the Greek opposition might make use of it to attack the Government for inactivity. I retorted that I could not watch my people being slaughtered by Turkish mobs while the Greek Government washed its hands of the tragedy: it was not in me to keep silent at such times.

*

Operations and searches were not the only means used by the British in trying to find my hideout: interrogation and treachery were at least as important and they went on throughout the long months of the cease-fire. What saved me more than once was British reliance on routine. Generally the interrogation of an important suspect was spread over twenty-eight days – the full period for which a person could be held without trial – and this gave us time to change our code names, alter our routes and cover our tracks.

Early in September the British had their best chance of tracking me down. They swooped on the home of Niki Artemiou, an eighteen-year-old girl courier in direct contact with our mail centre in Nicosia, arrested her and seized many documents, including letters written by me. Among others arrested was Maroulla Economides, another girl who knew the area in which I lived and the few people who visited me. It was Maroulla who brought to Limassol in March 1957 the mistaken message reporting that the British knew my whereabouts: this put her in touch with the last links of the chain through which my letters came. If Niki or Maroulla was forced to betray the courier system and name its leading members the whole Organisation would be in deadly peril.

I acted like lightning in this crisis, while the British were unpardonably slow. They failed even to penetrate the simple secret of my correspondence. Each group in EOKA knew me by a different pair of code names, one for my signature and another for my address. One group would write to me as 'A' and I would sign the reply 'B'; another group might address me as 'C' and I would reply to them as 'D'. Working their way through the captured letters, the experts decided that they came from ten to fifteen different people, instead of from one. Their slowness allowed me to track down the driver of the car which took Maroulla down to Limassol in March. He was an EOKA member who knew almost as much about my courier system as Maroulla did and I quickly established that he was a traitor. I did not hesitate a moment in taking action. With the execution of the informer the chief threat was removed and the girls were rocklike in their refusal to speak in spite of everything. Niki managed to smuggle out a long report written in lemon juice, to all appearances a blank piece of paper which gave me valuable information on her interrogation and the line of Intelligence inquiries.

The months of inaction, during which we still had to be ready to strike at any moment, were very wearing to the guerrillas, yet only once was there trouble in our ranks. On 9 October Evagoras Papachristoforou, a guerrilla leader, and his courier, a youth of eighteen, were found murdered in their hide near Galata, in the Troodos mountains. Michael Ashiotis, who had shared Papachristoforou's hide, then surrendered to the British with a quantity of arms and ammunition. Much propaganda use was made of this deserter before he was shipped to England for his own safety. Meanwhile permission for Papachristoforou's father, a detained priest, to attend his funeral was refused. His fellow detainees at Pyla Camp set fire to their huts in protest; the troops fired, wounding three men, and several people were taken to hospital, including a British assistant superintendent of police. Camp K went on hunger strike and I ordered reprisals on 11 October.

CBS and RAF, Nicosia, were sabotaged by time bombs. The Government radio was put off the air and the RAF camp's electricity was cut by £9,000-worth of damage to transformers.

★

On 22 October 1957, Field-Marshal Sir John Harding, who had come to Cyprus full of promises two years before, resigned the Governorship. I have been asked so often what I thought of this adversary that I shall try here to offer a balanced view, free of the emotion which became inseparable, both in Britain and in Cyprus, from his name during the Emergency. I must say that at the start I was prepared to salute on his appointment a gallant soldier who had been honoured with his country's highest military commands. No one could rise to the post of Chief of the Imperial General Staff without a good military brain, but I have wondered whether his successes in other fields were not a handicap when he faced an army which could never be drawn up in battle array. The extent of his attempts to understand the people he came out to rule could be measured by his insistence that they should put Britain's strategic interests before their own right to freedom. Surely no one who saw the expression on Cypriot faces when the British radio bulletins were turned on in cafés could suppose that the vast propaganda service which Harding built up was doing any good. What were they to think when today his radio speakers declared that EOKA was breathing its last for lack of money and arms, while tomorrow it accused the Church of richly subsidising EOKA's arsenals?

I had expected that a Field-Marshal would come out with a flexible military plan; if he did, it was hard to discern what it consisted of. Twice from my hiding place in the mountains I watched forces of up to 1,000 troops looking for me, with helicopters flying overhead. I did not even trouble to move off as they approached, so aimless was their search. Officers, remaining on the road, shouted orders as if on an exercise. In Limassol later the strong patrols which so often passed our house went by as though on a route march. This, then, was the 'spider's web' which Harding said he was weaving for us.

In time his 'Security Forces', composed of army and police, began to work together and by June of the following year I saw signs of a well-considered, organised plan. Naturally, I changed my tactics and avoided his thrusts, which continued in the same direction. Harding disliked changing a decision, once he had made it; if the results were not all he expected he would go on just the same, thus opening the way to a series of mistakes. His soldierly bluntness, which put the whole country against him, was also a valuable index to me of his military intentions. In speeches and broadcasts, and through newspaper interviews which he gave so prodigally, I was kept in constant touch with the way in which his mind was working. No less lavish were his assurances of early victory: did he believe them himself? It seemed that he did, and thus fell into what Napoleon called the biggest mistake a General could make: to paint an imaginary picture and believe it to be true. The result was that even when he talked sense the Cypriots turned away and at Westminster his fitness for the post became a matter for debate. In my view a leader must always speak the truth; he must not gloss over his difficulties but give proof of his ability to overcome them. For my part I concealed nothing and never promised more than I could perform. Having thus won the Cypriot's confidence, my orders were obeyed by all. Even the British knew that I kept my word: when I declared a cease-fire they came out into the streets unarmed and safe.

Nevertheless, I continue to hold Harding the soldier in regard. In Cyprus he was given a task outside his powers, but he was the strongest man I faced there; there can be no comparison between him and the rest of the soldiers and politicians I had to fight. It must also be remembered that while in the military field he was lord and master, politically he was in the hands of old colonial officials. Overall policy was supposed to come from London, but Harding's prestige gilded the political advice which was given him by his close advisers and which he imparted to Whitehall and the Press; thus they had a potent influence on Ministers at home. In these circumstances if is not easy to apportion blame for British blunders. At all events the man who had come out to destroy EOKA went home in November to his cottage among the Dorset hills, where he had a special guard set over him for fear of EOKA action.

*

The Army, left in control during the interregnum before Harding's successor came out a month later, continued to harry the population with searches and curfews, and I ordered some isolated acts of sabotage to show the British that they could not do exactly what they liked. Their first shock was the explosion of a magnetic mine in the merchant ship *African Prince*, which lay at anchor off Karavostasi where she was loading copper ore from the American-owned Cyprus Mining Corporation. She was holed below the waterline and saved from sinking only by the coincidental appearance of a British warship which rushed a repair party aboard. This was followed by the most devastating single stroke of sabotage performed during the

Emergency: the destruction of five jet planes worth £4,500,000. It says little for the much-vaunted British security that the bases were regularly shaken by our bombs. The great airport at Akrotiri was the most closely guarded of all, with barbed wire, bloodhounds and sentries, but nothing could damp the ardour of our saboteurs.

The explosion of 25 November at RAF Akrotiri, is still a mystery to the British and I tell the story here as it was reported to me by Andreas Vassiliou, a seventeen-year-old electrician. With another electrician employed at the station, Yangos Kaponas, he smuggled in two bombs the size of oranges, one in a bag of grapes and the other in a pot of pork jelly, a Cypriot lunchtime delicacy. Once past the guards, Vassiliou hid both bombs in the hangar where he worked, and waited for a chance of planting them: in addition to sixty British technicians swarming over the aircraft which were under repair he was never out of sight of his Cypriot fellow-workmen, who included a Turk and an Armenian. At the lunch break, however, everyone left the hangar except one of the Cypriots, who ate the sandwiches he had brought and then settled down in a corner for his siesta. A sentry was posted near the entrance to the hangar; when his back was turned Vassiliou dodged behind a Canberra jet bomber and quickly placed the first bomb near its fuel tank. Then he waited until, nearly an hour later, the sentry came up on his rounds. They exchanged a few words, then Vassiliou said he was going to the lavatory and walked towards the exit, but instead of leaving the hangar he chose another Canberra out of sight of the guard and placed the second bomb.

Time pencils had been set for midnight. Vassiliou waited all night at his home in nearby Limassol expecting to hear the explosions. Nothing happened. When he got to work next morning the bombs had still to go off – as they might do at any moment. The hours crept by: owing to pressure of work everyone was kept in the hangar over lunchtime and told they would have to stay until 4 pm. Vassiliou was one of the first out of the door when the whistle was blown. It took the crowd of men ten minutes to reach the offices of the contractors and just as they got there they were nearly lifted off their feet by an explosion. A series of other explosions followed and flames burst out from the 60-foot-high hangar. Nothing could save it now, and no one could enter it to rescue the aircraft inside. Soon the hangar collapsed with a roar, destroying what was left of the four Canberras and the Venom jet fighter under repair and wrecking a quantity of valuable machinery. Vassiliou was among the Cypriot staff arrested, but his angry interrogators could prove nothing against him and had to let him go. Vassiliou went on working in the base for another two months; then, in a police raid on a friend's house, his name was found in a list of local EOKA members, together with a plan for blowing up another hangar. He made for the hills and joined a guerrilla group, with which he did useful service until the end of the Emergency.

The British were further alarmed by the shooting at Limassol of a senior police officer. Many thought this meant the end of the cease-fire; in fact, it was merely a necessary interruption. For some months Superintendent E. N. Peirce, of the Special Branch, had been trying to penetrate my courier service in Limassol and we had to be rid of him. His execution was no easy matter, for Peirce was alert and wary. We followed him everywhere, kept watch on his house, listed the places he visited. Our first attempt to ambush him was at a five-way junction in the middle of Limassol, but on the day when an execution group waited there for him he failed to appear. Another time they waited outside the Acropole Hotel when he was lunching there, but he left by a side street. He constantly changed his habits and sometimes we lost sight of him for days at a time. Then we found he had adopted a circuitous route to his office and waited for him at a double bend which would slow down his car – when the car came there was a Land-Rover behind it full of armed police. But next day he gave us our chance at the same spot. It was a three-man job. The first man forced Peirce to a halt by riding his bicycle in front of him; the second was ready to give covering fire if anyone tried to interfere; the third, a youth of fine spirit called Pavlos Pavlou, ran up to the car pulling out his gun. Once more a sixth sense warned Peirce: he turned suddenly towards his executioner just as Pavlou fired through the open nearside window, and received the bullet in his right eye. Our men ran to their bicycles and made off in the stampede.

Although seriously wounded, Peirce survived; but he was in hospital for many weeks and troubled us no more. His career was at an end and I slept the better for it.

CHAPTER NINE

Frauds and Fine Words

The new Governor – Labour Party tricks – A victory at the United Nations –
The Foot plan – My passive resistance campaign – Quarrels with Makarios –
Atrocities in the detention camps – Foot invites me to a secret meeting

THE advent of a new civilian Governor was widely forecast as the start
of a new era for Cyprus and politicians both in and out of the island declared that a permanent peace would soon be achieved. I was less optimistic:
indeed, I believed that we were now entering a very dangerous stage of the
struggle. Harding, a blunt and forthright man, had failed; and in his place
the British were putting a diplomat whose task would be to lead the people
astray with fine words and trick their leaders with lying promises. Their
choice for the job was Sir Hugh Foot, the Governor of Jamaica, and a
better man could not have been found.

From the outset of our conflict I lacked respect for Foot and regarded
the self-created aura of 'liberalism' surrounding him with distaste: I was
sure it was fraudulent. Very little foresight was needed to guess what was
coming when, even before arriving at his new post, he declared publicly his
hatred of 'violence, and the fear of violence'. A brave speech! I replied that
the new Governor would have our support if he sincerely intended to work
for peace; otherwise our fight for freedom – our 'violence' – would go on.

I told the Cypriot people to be very reserved in their attitude to the
newcomer. I realised that Foot, who had once been Colonial Secretary in
Cyprus, would try to make use of old friends and acquaintances and worm
his way into their confidence before revealing his true colours. To prevent
this I arranged an announcement by the island's mayors, just before his
arrival, in which they said they would not meet the Governor unless he
wanted to discuss self-determination, in which case they would refer him
to Archbishop Makarios for negotiations.

Foot flew to Cyprus on 3 December 1957. His first move was to ask
for a 'credit of time' while he studied the situation and decided what should
be done. Makarios and the Greek Government had, unlike myself, formed
a good impression of him and since, for my part, I did not want anyone to
say that EOKA stood in the way of a solution, I replied by leaflet that he
would be allowed a reasonable period to examine the problem in peace and

make recommendations to his Government. I offered the hand of friendship – if his hands were not already tied by the Colonial Office. Having given this proof of my goodwill I sat back to await developments; if, as was all too likely, Foot's promises came to nothing, we could renew the fight with the people's full approval and the understanding of the world.

I knew how to deal with the open enemies of Cyprus, but our 'friends' were more troublesome: professed liberals like Foot, professed democrats like the British Labour Party, professed allies like the Greek Ministers, changed course with monotonous regularity until it sometimes seemed that all three were combining against us. Averoff, for example, made great play at this period with a Labour resolution pledging self-determination to Cyprus within the lifetime of the next Labour Government: he said it was of 'incalculable value' and would do more for our cause than the next United Nations debate due in December 1957. I, however, had long since decided that the Socialists were in league with the Conservatives. Why else should they send MPs to Cyprus yearly, who (after being entertained at Government House) would publicly appeal for a 'cessation of violence' and advise co-operation with Sir Hugh Foot? Meanwhile the Labour leaders, contrary to the resolution passed by their own executive, urged us to take part in futile talks. Mr Tom Driberg, Chairman of their Executive and a leading spirit behind the resolution in question, even tried to form a Labour Party in Cyprus, which would have served Foot's interests.

During this critical period the Greek Government decided to criticise me publicly for 'interfering' in Athenian politics. They complained that a PEKA leaflet which spoke of the danger of war between Greece and Turkey might disturb Greco-Turkish relations: this at a time when Ankara was brandishing threats of riot, bloodshed and invasion! When I heard the news on the radio I wrote at once to the Consul:

I will not accept a slap in the face like this from anyone: I will not be gagged. . . . I have not imposed my views on anyone and the Greek Government is not bound by what I do. Statements of this kind, which show how the Government has been duped by British propaganda, merely cause confusion in our ranks.

The Consul took my protest to Athens where Averoff hastily declared that he had always extolled the Cypriot people's wonderful fight: his statement was intended only to clarify the internal political situation and had been deliberately misinterpreted by the London Press.

I closed the discussion by telling the Consul, on his return, that the Greek Government had once more given the British a chance to score.

On the eve of the United Nations discussion Averoff wrote to say that Turkey, with assured backing from the West, was in a stronger position than ever and Makarios also sent a gloomy letter: a decisive resolution on our case could not be expected, he said, because the Americans wanted a solution to be found indirectly, perhaps through NATO. When the debate opened in New York on 9 December 1957, Turkish rioters swept through Nicosia looting, burning and destroying Greek homes and property. The British did nothing to stop them and the rioting spread later to the villages. After three days of bloodshed in Cyprus and argument in the UN Political Committee, a Greek resolution was approved calling for further negotiations 'with a view to applying the right of self-determination'. This was a considerable victory for us, achieved as it was in the face of strong opposition; but it was a moral victory only and pressure continued behind the scenes. When the resolution came before the General Assembly all Greece's allies in NATO voted against her, America led the abstainers and the necessary two-thirds majority could not be achieved.

*

Meanwhile Foot was making propaganda for himself as the 'friend and servant' of Cyprus. He toured the countryside, shaking hands everywhere and listening to farmers' complaints; he lit a candle 'for peace' in an Orthodox church; he walked down Ledra Street, with plain clothes police around him, on the day after the UN riots. As a Christmas gesture he released 100 detainees and eleven girl prisoners. All this, I knew, was just a trick to keep us quiet; as I wrote in my diary at the time:

I continue to believe that the Governor is a cunning and dangerous diplomat who is trying to win the people over and estrange them from EOKA.

At the end of December it was announced that Foot's study of the situation was complete. He left for London to present his proposals and attended two Cabinet meetings. The Press was filled with speculation which led the British public to expect a quick solution, and even the Cypriots thought there might be a step forward. After two weeks of suspense, however, Foot returned to Cyprus with empty hands: the Cabinet had decided that their position was so strong they need make no concessions; the views of extremist Tories had prevailed. Foot's predecessor, now Lord Harding of Petherton, was spokesman in the House of Lords for the powerful forces opposing all dealings with Makarios, and he chose this moment to publish a series of articles in the London Press which warned that peace would never be achieved while I remained in Cyprus.

Foot's role now was to play for time and undermine the people's resistance. I saw little hope of any useful political developments and I wrote to Makarios that, since America was under the influence of Britain and Turkey, while Greece, with her dollar policy, was at Washington's mercy, the time had come to break new ground:

If my suggestions are not adopted then I must part company with the Greek Government and launch an intensive campaign to let the Greek people know what is being done in their name. I shall wait until the end of February to see what Athens does.

In the interim Macmillan sent Selwyn Lloyd, his Foreign Secretary, to Turkey and Greece, hawking a plan for self-government which was designed to encourage the Turks in their demands for partition. As Lloyd arrived in Ankara, Cyprus burst into pro-partition riots and when troops acting in self-defence killed three Turkish Cypriots the authorities offered profuse apologies and statements of regret. Lloyd later flew to Athens, where he was joined by Foot, who then had his first meeting with the Archbishop; two days later Makarios wrote to me:

The British did not put forward any concrete proposals; instead they stressed repeatedly that any plan for a solution was acceptable to them, if it also satisfied the Turks. They sounded us out on whether we would be willing to grant Turkey a base in Cyprus.

Selwyn Lloyd and Foot were now quite openly using Turkey as a lever to shift the entire situation on to a dangerous new basis, a manoeuvre which they could never have attempted if Greek diplomacy had shown more courage. The very suggestion of a Turkish base in Cyprus, although rejected at once, revealed how easily the British thought they could blackmail Greece into a settlement.

EOKA had meanwhile been kept on the alert since 11 January 1958, when it became obvious that nothing but trickery could be expected from the British. Targets, both manned and unmanned, had been selected for action within forty-eight hours and I had revised our defences in preparation for another Turkish onslaught. Foot was thus correct when, speaking at last in his true role with an abusive broadcast worthy of Harding, he declared that we had a plan for the 'resumption of violence' and that it might start at any moment. This was his first public attack on EOKA, and I replied by way of a leaflet in which I warned the Governor:

The credit of time you asked for has run out and so has my patience. The fight must go on, because there is no other way to deal with Britain's uncompromising attitude.

It was also clear, by the end of February, that we could hope for nothing from Athens, but before I could carry out my threat to part company with the Greek Government it resigned over an internal crisis on 2 March.

On 4 March 1958 I launched my campaign of 'passive resistance', which had been in preparation for some months. This was to take the form of widespread minor sabotage backed by a boycott of everything British; killing would be sanctioned only for the purpose of reprisal.

The first explosion was at RAF Nicosia, where our incendiary bombs set fire to the buildings. Night after night the destruction increased as we blew up water supply lines, food stores and any other Government property that offered itself. At the start of the attack I chose every target myself and often the time so that I could vary my tactics constantly; by 31 March, however, things were going so well that I gave group leaders a free hand.

Against this background of sabotage the boycott began on 6 March, with a leaflet banning the purchase of alcoholic drinks, confectionery and shoes from Britain. Having given the problem six months' intensive study I was certain that the campaign was not only practical but would be of great long-term value to the island's economy. The boycott proceeded stage by stage so that we could feel our way and carry the public with us, in spite of inconveniences. Week by week the list grew – cigarettes, soap, clothing, cars, cosmetics, furniture, tinned food – until it even included the football pools, which had been drawing £50,000 a month out of Cypriot pockets for the benefit of London promoters. I also stopped all other forms of gambling when we found that certain men had turned informer after losing their money at cards. The Government lottery had to be abandoned after we boycotted the sale of tickets and dynamited the lottery machines. An effective feature of the campaign was the removal, on my orders, of all British lettering and signs from shops, streets and advertisements, so that Cyprus began to look like a Greek country. British girls working as secretaries in Cypriot firms were dismissed. Greeks who still acted as village mukhtars were ordered to hand in their seals to the authorities. British airlines and travel agents lost their Cypriot custom. At last the British were made to feel the strength of Greek Cypriot resentment, and as the campaign got under way the economic foundations of the Cyprus Government were sapped. The boycott aroused patriotic sentiment, helped the sale of Cypriot products and won publicity for our struggle abroad.

Importers were given a month's notice of our intentions so that they could dispose of their stocks but, even so, there was a great outcry among the handful of powerful businessmen whose profits suffered. I did not, of course, expect to please these people, but neither was I prepared for the ruthless campaign of falsification which they initiated. When their protests were ignored they appealed to the Greek Consul and the Bishop of Kitium and finally put pressure on Makarios, with some success. Six weeks after the start of the boycott the Archbishop wrote that my policy, if extended, might damage the Cypriot economy, while it could not hope to affect Britain. He asked me to show more flexibility.

I had never imagined that the boycott would seriously damage Britain; my main purpose was to upset the Cyprus Government and this was fully achieved. I was so disgusted with Makarios's intervention on behalf of this greedy clique of wealthy Cypriots – a visitor to Athens reported that he openly supported their views – that I sent Antonis Georgiades on 28 April to see the Consul and the Bishop of Kitium in Nicosia. I wrote to the Consul, Mr Frydas:

I am amazed at the unscrupulous way in which the Archbishop has tried to convey his views. He has never sent any instructions about the boycott, yet now he tries to interfere and upset everything. . . .

And I said to Makarios:

Your informants on Cyprus have been in touch only with the dissatisfied rich, who have lost a small portion of the profits they make from the Cypriot people: these are the sharks who have been nibbling away at the brains of the Consul and the Bishop of Kitium ever since they were first asked to make some negligible sacrifices. It is shameful to waste time or thought on them.

God forbid that we should throw away the immense benefits brought by the boycott, benefits which will go on after the struggle is over, for the sake of such men. Do you want to go back to the times when we sent over £6 million to England for cigarettes, while Cypriot tobacco lay unsold? To importing all our soap and detergents from Britain at the expense of a local industry which can supply all our needs? Do you believe that we should put the interests of a few import agents before our principles, before a campaign which strikes at the ruler? If this is your viewpoint, history will be our judge.

I added that Makarios should have written to me frankly about his objections instead of leaving me to discover them through visitors to Athens and comments in the Press. The Organisation had been struck a grave blow by its own political leader. I concluded:

I am standing in the path which I have hacked out to this point and considering my next move: there is a parting of the ways ahead and I must choose which way to follow.

Makarios admitted in reply that he had been mistaken in letting his views become known in an indirect way, adding:

While I still have my reservations on this question I will not conceal from you that your letter made me very sad. You have been led to thoughts and conclusions which cast doubt on my sincerity towards you, because of what this third party has written or said after talking to me. I gave no instructions to this person to tell you about my thoughts; I simply exchanged ideas with him.

I let the matter drop for the time being, but my belief in the Archbishop's leadership was badly shaken.

The Communists provided another point of disagreement. I warned Makarios, in the letter quoted above, that they were very active politically: if we persisted in ignoring them they would reap the benefits of the harvest sown by our fighters. This warning went unheeded, and when I went on to execute a few Left-wing traitors, the Communist Mayors rushed to Athens to protest to Makarios, while crowds of Reds demonstrated under the protection of British bayonets. I learned that the Archbishop had shown sympathy towards the Mayors, but I saw no reason why traitors should be protected by a Communist trade union card.

A third source of dispute between us was the best way to deal with the Turkish mob: writing on 3 March 1958, Makarios had said that although we should not provoke the Turks, neither must we show weakness:

My opinion is that we should throw a grenade or two from some balcony and give them a sharp lesson, so that they will not dare to gather in mobs in future.

I retorted at once that I knew very well how to cope with the Turks and that if the Greek Government showed more courage there would be no Turkish problem. Makarios returned to the subject on 18 April when he wrote that, while he approved my organisation of a civil defence system:

... only EOKA can deliver the blows needed to teach the Turks a lesson. I appreciate that there are difficulties but the thing is possible. There were clashes at Limassol the other day between Greeks and Turks after a Greek was murdered. A Turk was fired on during the clash. I think it would have been possible to throw a hand-grenade or two at the Turkish mob. The same should be done in other towns. ...

All I could say was, 'God help us!' I did not want to reply directly in case my anger caused an open breach between us, so I wrote instead to Andreas Azinas suggesting that he tried to turn the Archbishop's mind to other matters:

We have passed our examinations in this kind of thing with flying colours and we have no need of advice from Athens; they must try to keep their nerve and leave us to work in peace. God help us if we here don't know what to do.

After this protest there was a lull in the dispute, but when later Makarios again tried to interfere in the same manner I broke off all contact with him for a considerable period.

*

The British were extremely worried by the success of the passive resistance campaign and our morale had never been higher. The national celebrations on 25 March, Greek independence day, and 1 April 1958, EOKA's third anniversary, were attended by huge crowds. Foot was powerless to prevent these island-wide demonstrations of enthusiasm. What most disturbed him was the prospect of a full-scale resumption of EOKA action, for he knew we were capable of striking with great force, greater even than in the days of Harding. The Governor repeatedly spoke on the radio of the dreadful consequences that would follow and at one stage he even visited Camp K in person to threaten that all releases would stop if EOKA struck again.

In their anxiety to discover our strength and intentions the British once more began to search and arrest, to maltreat the Cypriot people, and on 8 April 1958 I warned Foot in a leaflet that if this went on I would indeed give the order to attack: I said:

You bear the whole responsibility for the shameful, medieval methods used by the torturers of the intelligence services.

A week later the Famagusta execution group underlined my warning by shooting dead an interrogator called William Dear, who had been involved in the arrest and interrogation of EOKA members. In revenge the army blew up the town's biggest cinema after pretending to discover some explosives there: these had, in fact, been planted by the intelligence services themselves, following a common practice of the time.

The British did nothing to relieve this tense situation; on the contrary, they deliberately tried to provoke us to action by ill-treating the helpless prisoners in the detention camps. There were protests against the continued detention of men without trial at the Nicosia Prison, where 160 men had climbed up to the prison roof to sing and shout slogans and wave a vast Greek flag made from a bed-sheet. In Camp K 600 detainees set fire to their huts and to the gates of the camp, which they had first soaked in paraffin. The army rushed in and occupied the camp and over the next few weeks they led the prisoners a life of misery. It was four days before one of the detainees, Pavlos Stokkos, was able to smuggle out a report on what had happened.

An hour after the demonstration, when peace had been restored and the detainees had quietly returned to their normal routine, troops arrived and forced everyone out into the compounds at gun-point, insulting them and shoving them on with their riot shields. The men were roughly searched and their few small personal possessions were looted from the huts; then they were pushed back inside and locked in under guard. Two detainees were given permission to fetch water for the others and had to run a gauntlet of blows from rifle-butts as they went. No one was allowed to sleep that night: soldiers flung stones for hour after hour on the corrugated iron roofs of the huts, smashed water jars, plates and glasses, overturned tables and threw men out of their beds: in one hut a detainee had a dustbin emptied on his head; in another, a bucket of urine was poured over a man lying in bed. Police and army dogs were brought in to add to the confusion and terror.

Next morning, which was Good Friday, a monk was returning to his hut from a lavatory when a soldier let fly at him with a sten-gun: four bullets narrowly missed his head. Detained priests who asked permission to hold the usual night service for Good Friday were allowed only an hour; at the end of this time soldiers rushed into the hut used as a church and forced the detainees to leave at bayonet point. The church, including the sanctuary, was searched and priests who protested were rudely sent away. All that night the stoning continued; rocks came crashing through the windows and struck the detainees. The troops burst into the huts tipping men out of bed and shouting, 'Lovely night! Who wants to sleep? No sleep for you tonight.' Again they stole anything that took their eye, even down to a framed picture of a prisoner's child.

The camp authorities told complainants that they could do nothing since the army was in charge, while protests to the troops themselves brought only one reply: 'Get inside or I'll shoot.' For the third night in succession they were not allowed to sleep and tormented in the same way as before. Stokkos concluded his report to me with these words:

It was very moving for us to hear the church bells for Easter tolling in the nearby villages at midnight, carrying a message to our brethren outside: Christ is Risen! We stayed awake in our huts all night, molested by dogs and soldiers, wondering when the Cypriot people would be reborn.

These events were the final touch to the army's campaign of provocation and I decided that we would wait no longer. I issued a leaflet warning the Government that reprisal action would be taken unless the ill-treatment of detainees stopped immediately. Foot was highly alarmed and wanted to stop us at any cost. Two days later he made a dramatic gesture which was typical of his publicity-conscious approach to diplomacy. He called Glafkos Clerides, a lawyer working for E O K A under the code name 'Iperides', to Government House and asked him to undertake a confidential mission: he said that he feared E O K A was about to begin full-scale action and advanced various reasons why this would be disastrous to the Greek Cypriot cause; it would rouse Turkish resistance, delay the Archbishop's return and strengthen the hand of the British military leaders, who demanded stronger measures against us. In short, unless the cease-fire continued for the next few months, while a settlement was sought, the reactionaries would have their way and the island would plunge into disaster and ultimately partition.

Foot said that in this extremity he had decided he must contact the leader of E O K A personally and point out the perilous course I was contemplating before it was too late. He had therefore, acting entirely on his own initiative, written to me proposing that we meet. He had at first contemplated sending the letter through the British Embassy in Athens, who would pass it on to Makarios; but he feared the Embassy might disclose its contents to London. This would be fatal, since he had not sought official approval for his move and it was known to no one but himself and Clerides. Glafkos Clerides asked what, in that case, would happen if I made Foot's letter public on receiving it. Foot replied that he would be dismissed from his post and his career would be at an end; but he did not think Colonel Grivas was the sort of man to betray a confidence.

Clerides finally said that though he himself had no E O K A contacts it might be possible to pass the letter to someone who had, perhaps one of the E O K A men whom he had defended in the courts; he promised to see what could be done. On leaving Government House he met Deacon Anthimos Kyriakides, E O K A's chief liaison officer, who consulted with the Bishop of Kitium. They agreed that whatever subterfuge might be under way here, it would be desirable to have the letter in their hands. So, on 18 April 1958, I received the following document:

Personal.

Government House,
Cyprus
12th of April [1958]

Colonel Grivas,

I am convinced that if the present campaign of sabotage continues disaster will result for all the people of Cyprus. In their name and interest I call on you to save them from that disaster by ordering the campaign of sabotage and violence to cease.

If it would help I am prepared to go to any place at any time you nominate to meet you and urge you to act on this call. I would come alone and un-armed, and would give you my word that for that day you would be in no danger of arrest.

I make this call and this proposal to you because I believe it to be my duty to do everything I can to save the people of Cyprus from the disaster which is so near.

HUGH FOOT,
Governor

Colonel George Grivas

I sensed at once that this was no more than a confidence trick, albeit one of some daring. I was also certain that it had been concocted with the British Government's approval. British Intelligence wanted a letter from me for some reason: whatever its contents, it might help them in their hunt for my hideout. Foot's offer of immunity for one day was suspicious in itself; the time was absurdly short if they assumed that I was coming from some distance to a rendezvous and then returning the same day; nor did I believe that Foot would or could move out of sight of his bodyguards. This appeal was plainly another attempt to win time in which he would carry on with his own plans. However, since an absolute rejection might be used as propaganda against us, I issued this proclamation on 21 April 1958:

Before ordering a general attack I consider it my duty to appeal to the British Government to take the initiative in opening negotiations. . . . I am not bluffing, for deception is not part of my character; nor am I uttering threats. . . . I am simply giving a warning.

Glafkos Clerides sent me a second report on 24 April, describing his conversation with the Governor more fully and giving his personal view of the affair. I told Clerides:

I have no reply whatsoever to make to Foot's letter. The proclamation issued on the 21st makes my intention plain. I have stopped activities, but I am waiting. If I decide that the British Government is still playing tricks, I shall strike as soon as possible. Unhappily, the behaviour of the authorities towards political hostages and their continued terrorism are forcing me towards reprisals.

Our recent sabotage campaign had proved our strength; now we would wait at the ready, proving once again that we were always prepared to make every effort to prevent bloodshed. The British reaction was very different: Foot met his civil and military advisers on 22 April, the day my warning leaflet circulated in the towns – but the result, far from being a cessation of hostilities, was an increase in searches, operations, ill-treatment of detainees and the general terrorisation of the island. It seemed that Foot had lost control of the army and I wondered if he was in conflict with his Generals. I issued a final warning on 26 April that unless the cowardly treatment of detainees stopped with forty-eight hours I would hit back.

Foot then visited Camp K personally to hear the inmates' complaints and the same evening called Clerides to Government House again to assure him that the army would soon be withdrawn, visits by relatives renewed and all complaints thoroughly examined. He said he was much concerned at my ultimatum, but expressed gratitude to me for not rejecting his appeal for the continuation of the truce.

But appeasing messages had ceased to be of interest to me. I saw no sign that the ill-treatment at Camp K had stopped and so, on the expiry of the time-limit set by leaflet, I ordered reprisals, with the result that two armed Military Policemen were shot dead by an execution squad as they patrolled the streets of Famagusta on 4 May 1958.

Foot's reply was to bring back the Emergency Regulations first promulgated by Harding, which, among other things, made the death penalty mandatory for carrying arms. Even before his decision was announced the army put Famagusta through a long Sunday of terror: one thousand men and youths were arrested and a hundred of them were ill-treated severely enough to require hospital treatment. When Foot, two days later, flew to London for talks with his Government, I issued a farewell warning to him that

the black November of 1956 will seem a shade of pale grey in comparison with what will happen if the British Government tries to impose a solution to its own liking. . . .

While these talks were in progress and as they were to result in the production of a new plan to solve the Cyprus problem, I once more deprived Britain of any complaint that EOKA was barring the way to peace by ordering, on 9 May 1958, a complete suspension of activity until further notice.

There was, however, an unpleasant epilogue to the affair of the Governor's 'confidential' letter. Foot later made another trip to London at the time when the new Cyprus plan was about to be unveiled; and since he wished to appear in the public eye as a daring and determined man, willing to take any risk to bring peace to the island, he revealed the story of his letter to the British Press!

Although I had given no promise regarding this letter, I had respected Foot's confidence and kept it secret; but this did not stop him from exploiting it at the first opportunity.

CHAPTER TEN

The Turkish Massacres

ALTHOUGH I had lived for nearly two years in Limassol no one, apart from my most intimate associates, had any idea where I was. The British, believing I was still in the mountains, launched another major operation designed to kill or capture me and throughout May 1958 I followed the progress of 'Operation Kingfisher' – as it was called – in the newspapers: more than 2,000 troops were employed to comb a small area in the southern foothills of the Troodos massif; radar, mine-detectors, searchlights and bulldozers were used; fields were excavated, walls destroyed, caves dyna-mited as the ground was searched inch by inch around Mathykoloni, where my presence had been reported. Finally a whole hillside was blown up because, it was said, voices had been heard coming from the network of caves and potholes underground. The story was complete nonsense. I had good warning of the operation and told my men to leave the area long before it began.

The only inconvenience the British caused me was due to the posting of a guard on an army school nearby, where sentries saw the children on to their bus home and sat beside the driver with sten-gun at the ready. My couriers now had to come and go under the eyes of these soldiers, who became a familiar sight during the summer of 1958. They often wandered through our yard and garden within earshot of the typewriter on which we were constantly tapping out orders and announcements. Never for a day was my work hindered, although I had to be ready at any moment to vanish into my cellar and we often went through periods of agonising suspense.

My old watchdog Irma had now been replaced by a warning system almost as effective – little Myria, aged two and a half, the daughter of my host Marios. Although she was never allowed to see me, and the front room and kitchen were permanently kept out of bounds, Myria always gave me unconscious warning of everyone who approached the house by letting out a cry of 'Mama!' She had an aversion to soldiers and her high, penetrating voice inevitably rose to a shout when they came into sight. Once, when her mother, Elli, heard her calling and ran out to see what was wrong, she found a soldier climbing a fruit tree which overlooked our window. She told him that the fruit was not yet ripe and gave him some from her store. On another occasion we heard Myria's voice raised angrily and saw a truck-load of troops halted 50 yards away, preparing to start a search. We cleared up our papers and dived into the hide.

Only once did the army take us by surprise, when Myria was away living with her grandmother. It was early morning. Mrs Christodoulides was in the kitchen and Antonis Georgiades was in the bathtub when I heard footsteps and glimpsed an NCO approaching. I called a warning and told Mrs Christodoulides to try and bluff the visitor, then ran to the trapdoor over the hide, followed by Georgiades, wrapped in a towel. Ignoring the knocks on the door Mrs Christodoulides went to the bathroom and put on a dressing-gown: then she opened up with an apologetic smile, saying she had just been having a bath. The NCO made a cursory search and went off to the next house.

Elli's behaviour was typical of the courage of Greek Cypriot women throughout the struggle; on the whole, I found women more trustworthy and less talkative than men. Mrs Christodoulides and her neighbour, Mrs Maroulla Panayides, carried my correspondence for two and a half years without once losing a letter, occasionally relieved by Miss Elizabeth Nicolaou, a twenty-year-old Sunday school teacher, who took over when I wanted to change the system for a spell.

Everywhere in Cyprus I depended on women for these and other vital tasks. At Larnaca, when one male leader after another had been arrested, I came to depend on a woman, Miss Elenitsa Serafim. She was trained in the use of revolvers and the making of time bombs and in due course I appointed her leader of the whole Larnaca district. She arranged sabotage at the Dhekelia base, damaging the new £1 million military hospital and other military installations. She also formed a guerrilla group and took personal charge of the EOKA arsenal in the town – 23 shotguns, 12 revolvers, 2 stens. Betrayed in December 1956, she was detained without trial for a year. Although under constant surveillance on her release she was able to regroup the sabotage and execution squads and take command of the whole Larnaca organisation exactly as before. Several women were among her aides, including her mother, who acted as a courier when young people were under curfew.

Miss Serafim is only one example, chosen at random from the hundreds of girls who worked for EOKA, none of whom ever let me down or gave way under interrogation. I believe that women can do anything once their pride is aroused. Some girls even asked me for permission to form female guerrilla groups but this I did not allow.

*

While Sir Hugh Foot was visiting London in May 1958 the first news of a 'Macmillan Plan' was released; this was another bogus constitution with the added disadvantage of involving Britain, Greece and Turkey in the island's government. Foot's main task was to win support for the plan among his Labourite friends, so that the Opposition might be silenced.

An announcement in the House of Commons, unveiling the scheme, was expected on 22 May 1958, but the British were hoping for my arrest in 'Operation Kingfisher'. London was promised that I would be run to earth by 23 May – my sixtieth birthday – and preparations were made to celebrate the event. When the operation dragged on without result the announcement was postponed for three weeks on the excuse that the plan needed some 'finishing touches'. I issued a leaflet declaring that we would wait with patience and dignity, ready for peace or war.

The Turks did not wait: on the night of 7 June Turkish Cypriots exploded a small, harmless bomb on the steps of the Turkish Government's information office in Nicosia. This was the deliberate signal for an attack on the Greek population by hordes of Turkish thugs, led by Turkish policemen and protected by the British Army. Since the failure of the Radcliffe Constitution the British had been arming these men and inciting them to demand partition: this was the result.

During a night of terror the mob burned and looted at will. Greek shopkeepers were killed and many more injured while the 'security forces' turned a blind eye. When, after several hours, troops and police at last began making arrests their prisoners were not Turks, but Greeks. Not until next day was a curfew imposed; it included Greeks as well, to prevent them preparing their defence and while it was in force Turkish police covertly set fire to more Greek shops.

This evil joke was often repeated in the days that followed. At Larnaca there were more deaths and at Ktima and Varosha, when Greeks gathered to defend themselves, they were dispersed by the army; at Limasol, however, a mob of 2,000 Turks took to their heels when they found the Greeks waiting for them. I had no doubt that we faced a well-organised Anglo-Turkish conspiracy. It had several aims in view. First, Ankara's claim that Greek and Turk could no longer live together would be proved and the demand for partition justified; secondly, Britain would be promoted from guilty party to the position of an arbiter whose presence was essential to save life; thirdly, it would weaken Greek resistance to the point where we would accept the Macmillan Plan to gain a respite from the horrors of civil war; finally, the conspiracy would force me to fight on two fronts and thus reveal my full strength in the island.

My task was to destroy these hopes. Knowing that the Turks would stop at nothing and that the British would always back them I could apply the necessary counter-measures. EOKA fighting groups and civil defence teams in each town were united under a single command while lookouts posted along the dividing line between the Greek and Turkish quarters gave us prompt warning of attacks. Soon we could put our civilian teams into action within minutes, allowing EOKA front-line men to slip back through the unarmed crowd before troops arrived. Our speed and planning stopped the mob in its tracks and blunted the weapon in which the British had placed their trust.

We could not, of course, stop murders and isolated raids in the no-man's land between the two quarters, where night after night the marauders sought their prey, slaughtering unarmed men and women, pillaging their homes, setting fire to their churches. Nor was it easy to save our people in the countryside. The most bloodthirsty attack took place at Guenyeli, a Turkish village near Nicosia which in consequence became so notorious that it changed its name – to Menderes! A party of Greeks who had gone to the aid of fellow-villagers were arrested by the army and driven to a field outside Guenyeli – eight miles from their own village – and told to walk home. The Turks were waiting: they fell upon the Greeks with knives and axes, although some of their victims were only boys of twelve and thirteen. Nine of the party were killed and their bodies mutilated on the spot, legs, arms and heads chopped off; several others were left slashed and bleeding on the ground. The British realised that they had allowed things to go too far and after an official inquiry the Chief Justice spoke of the 'extraordinary bloodlust' shown.

Meanwhile, international tension mounted: in Turkey, mobs drunk with excitement over Cyprus called for war; Greece withdrew her staff from NATO headquarters in Ismir and threatened to appeal to the Security Council. America, seeing that her policy had only caused greater trouble, told the Turks to keep the peace. Britain, taking pleasure in her new role of 'policeman', flew in the Royal Marines and a brigade of troops.

It was in this feverish atmosphere that the British Prime Minister brought out his plan for Cyprus, grotesquely describing it as an 'Adventure in Partnership'. A Cypriot council of ministers was to sit round a table with the Governor, who would have sole say in internal security, foreign affairs and defence; representatives from Greece and Turkey would sit on either side of the Governor and help him to rule the island. I rejected this monstrosity at once in a leaflet which ended:

The Greek Cypriot people do not want counterfeit constitutions. We make one unalterable claim: self-determination. We shall fight for this to the end.

The 'adventure' was still-born, but Foot made tireless efforts to breathe some life into it. He had the advantage of backing from the United States and, of course, the Tories, who were determined to impose their will on the Cypriots whether they agreed to the plan or not, using the Turks as a weapon.

At this crucial moment Archbishop Makarios, sitting in Athens, chose to criticise my handling of affairs in both the military and civil spheres. First I was reproached for 'failing to teach the Turks a lesson'. I replied to this on 26 June 1958:

I cannot please everyone for the sake of a show. . . . I will not squander my men in spectacular but useless actions. The British have set a trap: they hope to make me expose my forces at their full strength so that they can deal them a fatal blow, but they will not succeed. Up to this moment I have preserved our ranks intact and that is why I am ready for the next Anglo-Turkish attacks.

The next day I received another letter from Makarios complaining about passive resistance and the boycott. He wrote:

Despite the success of passive resistance, the economic effects regarding the consumption of British products are probably more unpleasant for Greek Cypriots than for the British economy. The Organisation must not, of course, give the impression of admitting to a mistake on this issue, but should quietly relax the boycott both in intensity and extent.

I am very much afraid that those who are informing you and advising about passive resistance are not telling you the complete truth. They are only telling you the rosy side of the picture because they do not wish to express an opinion contary to yours.

At the same time the Mayor of Nicosia, Dr Th. Dervis, publicly declared that the Archbishop had told him, during a recent visit to Athens, that he did not approve of the way the boycott was being carried out. I was determined to stamp out this opposition, for I knew it was due entirely to the underhand plotting and complaints of the rich. I wrote to the Bishop of Kitium on 3 July:

A group of Larnaca guerrillas with Miss Elenitsa Serafim
responsible for the Larnaca sector

Teukos Loizos's group of EOKA guerrillas

Internees protesting in the Pyla detention camp

Turkish police arrest a civilian in Metaxas Square, Nicosia

I was amazed by the Archbishop's note that . . . my men report to me only things I would like to hear. There could hardly be a greater insult to me and to the EOKA fighters. It is not the first time he has made this mistake over passive resistance. . . .

I begin to doubt whether the Archbishop is capable of handling the Cyprus question and I am no longer disposed to give him *carte blanche* to express the opinion of, or to represent, the Organisation. Any and every decision on the Cyprus problem must be examined by me as well, and I will decide whether I will accept or reject it.

The disagreement between myself and Makarios arising from this interference was thus moving towards a total break, and the fact was obvious to Kitium and the Greek Consul, who both wrote placatory letters, assuring me that I had misinterpreted the Archbishop's meaning; they explained that he had complete confidence in my handling of the situation and that he was merely making tactical suggestion, not giving orders.

I told the Consul that my dispute with Makarios was, unfortunately, far more serious than he wished to believe; and it was, in fact, some time before relations between us were restored. This was not just a matter of principle: it affected my task as military leader, and this was a thing I could not allow. In another letter to Kitium I said:

I do not wish to come into direct contact with the Archbishop on this question, because I am afraid that my expressions and the whole tone of my letter are extremely severe.

I was unwilling to make any concessions over the boycott, for the people had embraced it, ignoring the cries of the few: they could see for themselves how it had swelled national pride and struck at the British. I did, however, extend the time limit set for the disposal of stocks in certain cases, to prevent hardship to the importer.

The final phase of the Anglo-Turkish offensive began in July 1958, steadily increasing its pace and intensity. The British up to this time had allowed the Turks to do as they pleased; but now they gave them active help in the attempt to terrorise the whole island. A wave of murder, arson and riot washed over everything Greek: Turks seized the markets, took over whole streets of shops and houses, drove Greeks from mixed villages and drew dividing lines across the towns at their pleasure to separate the two communities.

My defence policy was to bring our Organisation up to a standard where it could hold any attack, with particular attention to Nicosia, for events there were highly publicised and affected the morale of the rest of the island. When this was assured I would go over to the attack: I had already named the first targets and methods to be employed. We struck at the Turks through isolated killings in the meantime, but such reprisals were kept under strict control.

The army's tactics were to harass the Greek people wherever possible; and so, while the Turks went on the rampage, troops spent their time touring purely Greek villages, ordering the removal and destruction of patriotic slogans and pictures.

This strategy brought death to more than one village in July, when the populace rebelled and pitted sticks and stones against machine-guns. The first and most terrible clash of this kind occurred at Avgorou, near Famagusta, on 5 July 1958. Troops arrived in the village in armoured cars and told the first schoolboy they saw to remove an EOKA banner from a wall. When he refused, he was beaten and dragged away under arrest. Women rushed to his rescue and attacked the soldiers, who were forced back to their vehicles. Eight more armoured cars were summoned by radio and the village was quickly flooded with armed men, who began to arrest everyone they could seize. Another boy was ordered to pull down the banner and when he also refused he was mercilessly beaten. Again the women rushed forward: the soldiers fought back with batons and the village men joined in with sticks and stones. Chairs and tables from the cafés in the square, bricks, bottles and even bicycles flew through the air, forcing the terrified soldiers to seek refuge inside their armoured cars. From this safety they opened fire on the crowd, killing an elderly man outright with a bullet through the chest; another bullet from a heavy machine gun struck a young mother of seven children who fell to the ground with half her head shot away. As the crowd drew back in horror the army drove out, leaving the bodies of dead and injured lying on the blood-spattered square. Bullet holes pitted the walls around.

Some fifty villagers and thirty-five soldiers were injured in this battle, but when the Greeks tried to bring their casualties to the nearest hospital, in Famagusta, they were turned back at a road block and forced to take a roundabout route. Yet despite the tragic circumstances all Cyprus was deeply stirred by these events, not least at the courage and patriotism shown by the women of Avgorou.

I ordered immediate reprisals for this outrage, and we struck first at the army in Famagusta, shooting down two soldiers in the main street. Both were armed, but our gunmen took them by surprise as they were shopping for their regiment in a grocery. The British replied by announcing that they had found bombs in the Anorthosis Sports Club, a centre of patriotic feeling in Famagusta, and blew up the building with explosives they had planted themelves.

To pay them back in their own coin, I ordered that the Teachers' Training College, a costly new Government building in Nicosia, should also be blown up. It was a difficult operation, for a day and night curfew was in force all over Nicosia: however, a thirteen-man group defied this ban to drive in a lorry to their jumping off point, a factory whose grounds adjoined those of the College, where they had already cached their guns and about twenty bombs. Four men entered the College grounds and tied up the guards; then they signalled the others to join them. Quickly they ran through the corridors and halls of the big block, soaking the furniture and fittings with petrol, planting their home-made time bombs in strategic positions. Just as the last bomb was being placed by young Tassos Elia it exploded, shattering his hands and blasting shrapnel into his face and chest; the home-made time mechanism had been faultily constructed. The explosion brought patrols running to the scene, but our men were able to set the place ablaze; all except Elia then escaped unharmed. Later firemen arrived and carried him to hospital. The army had left him to lie where he was, answering his cries of pain with insults. One soldier, with unbelievable callousness, collected his severed fingers in a cigarette packet and handed them round as a joke.[1]

Simultaneously I turned our attentions on the Turks and for the first time they felt the full weight of our blows. I had already ordered raids on police stations, with Turkish policemen as chief targets, and waived all restrictions in killing Turks: we found that Turkish enthusiasm for bloodshed soon showed a sharp decline – they had not expected such ruthlessness on our part, knowing that we had always held our hand in the past. The slaughter reached a climax on 13 July, the most murderous day of all, when thirty-one fires blazed in Nicosia along the line between the two quarters: five Turks and three Greeks were killed and twenty others injured.

When he saw that the Turks were getting the worst of it, Foot called a meeting of the mayors and the same day broadcast an appeal for peace. I replied at once by leaflet that those responsible for the massacre could not now come forward wearing the mantle of a mediator:

. . . the fight will not stop because of emotional appeals from a frightened jack-in-office; it will stop when our right to self-determination has been ensured.

---

[1] Damage to the college was estimated later at £15,000. Tassos Elia recovered after treatment in Athens: one eye was saved and he learned to use artificial arms.

Next day I ordered the resumption of sabotage on the grand scale in military camps and installations, and reinforced the counter-attack against the Turks. This was the last straw for Foot. He announced that a month-long night curfew would be enforced, starting with a full day and night curfew over the next forty-eight hours. This measure was used not to save innocent citizens from the Turkish butchers, or churches from the incen-diaries, but to cover a mass arrest of Greeks all over the island. Nearly 2,000 men from every walk of life, doctors, teachers, lawyers, town coun-cillors, civil servants, were dragged from their homes and placed in the detention camps. All were proclaimed to be dangerous members of EOKA; but in fact there was not one important member of the Organisation among them. This vast round-up turned British Intelligence into a laughing-stock when, instead of dying down, our activity increased.

Powerless to strike at EOKA, the British turned their anger and frustration on the innocent public once more, and the Avgorou atrocity was repeated in exactly the same form at Akhyritou on 30 July, when troops opened fire on a crowd of villagers, killing two men, one of whom was blind. We replied with the execution of two British soldiers. The first of these was an army sergeant shot by one of the new Nicosia killer squads. The second, next day, was an important officer from GHQ Middle East. This execution was carried out by the team of Pavlos Pavlou, who was also responsible for putting the Special Branch Superintendent, Peirce, out of action.

Pavlou set out with two of his group at 8.30 am and they were almost arrested while looking for a target. Only Pavlou's quick thinking saved them. As they walked down the street, with guns in their pockets, an army Land-Rover approached. Pavlou started moving quickly in another direc-tion calling as he went, 'Costaki! Andreas!' as though he had just seen a friend; and when they had rounded a corner they ran along under cover of a garden wall into another street where they got a lift in a passing car. They tried again later the same day and at 6 pm they saw a Briton watering his garden with a hose. Pavlou walked up to the garden wall and shot him once at close range; then, as he screamed and fell, fired three more shots into the body and escaped with his companion. Troops and police poured into the area but the two fighters reached their house safely and hid the guns. A curfew followed and they heard on the radio next day that the man they had killed was a Colonel. I sent my congratulations on this attack.

The promptness and efficiency of our reprisals, combined with the steady decline in Turkish enthusiasm for bloodshed, made the British decide that the time had come to call a halt. At the end of July, when the death roll in the intercommunal fighting had passed 100, appeals for peace were issued by the Greek, British and Turkish Prime Ministers, and endorsed by Archbishop Makarios. I commented in a leaflet that we were not the aggressors: the British had only to call off the Turks. However, I decided that if they genuinely wanted peace – for whatever reason – I would not bar the way. On 4 August 1958 I called a new cease-fire; but I also warned, in my proclamation, that we were ready for anything:

I have given orders for all action against British and Turks alike to stop; but I declare that if provocation continues I shall consider myself free to order immediate action against both from the 10th of this month.

So, while everyone was shouting for peace, but continuing to make war, I once more led the way to pacification. Archbishop Makarios warned that it would be a tragic mistake to take this move as a sign of weakness and the news was well received abroad. On 6 August a leaflet was issued by TMT, the Turkish underground organisation, ordering a cease-fire on their side. That day the last victim of civil conflict died in Nicosia: an old Greek woman whose hands and feet were chopped off with axes after she had been shot.

*

These two months of horror were followed by an interlude of comparative calm, broken only by the Army's unceasing operations against EOKA. The British continued to talk of peace: Mr Harold Macmillan visited Cyprus on 11 August 1958, and said many pleasant things about Anglo-Greek friendship to sugar the pill he was offering. The British Premier proposed a seven-year period of self-government in which tempers would cool before the future of the island was decided; no one, he said, was asked to abandon his ambitions, merely to set them aside for the time being. This performance deceived nobody, and its failure was underlined when, on his return to London, Macmillan announced that he would go ahead with his plan regardless of our rejection. At the same time Athens submitted a new appeal to the United Nations.

Some trivial modifications were made to this plan by way of a placatory gesture, but the main Greek objections were ignored. The first step on the road to partition was taken by granting the Turks separate municipal councils. Foot visited Makarios in Athens to try and win him over: they met in the Grande Bretagne Hotel where the Governor told the Archbishop in dramatic tones that EOKA 'would destroy itself and its cause' if the cease-fire I had declared on 4 August were revoked. Makarios told me later, in a letter, that he had said the cease-fire could not be discussed in isolation;

there must be some prospect of a solution acceptable to the Cypriots. Foot had then hinted that the Archbishop might be allowed to return to the island if I could be persuaded to leave.[1] I wrote to Makarios on receiving his report of this conversation:

The Cyprus problem will not be cleared up by palavers between London, Athens and Ankara. Historic times demand historic decisions; nothing can be settled by too much niggling about possible consequences. So long as the Greek Government tries to arrange everything within the framework of its alliances with the West we cannot hope to achieve our aims.

Simultaneously I wrote to Averoff criticising the feeble policy and eagerness to compromise of his Government. I told him the time had come to assert our national dignity and refuse to accept further affronts from Turkey. He replied that his policy was dictated not by lack of courage but because he knew that if America had to choose between Greece and Turkey, she would choose Turkey, which was the more vital to defence in the Middle East. Turkish interest in Cyprus had been artificially roused but it was now a real interest, and if Menderes could not get his way by blackmail he would try to do it by bloodshed. He therefore asked me to maintain the cease-fire:

I believe that for the time being, at least until we have considered everything and while the Turks hold off and the British are reasonable, we should have patience. Do please let me have your opinions. God go with you, my dear friend. I embrace you.

I told Averoff, in my reply, that it was not Turkey's strategic advantages but her resolute policy that had won her so many favours while Greece was passed over; meanwhile our armed struggle had been wasted through lack of political exploitation. I urged that the Government and Opposition parties should form a united front to see the struggle through, as had happened at other turning points in history. This proposal, which I repeated more than once, found no favour in Athens, where ministers wanted all the power and privileges to themselves. We had many similar exchanges at this period and I did not hesitate to say what I felt. The letter of reproach I received from Averoff on 1 September 1958 was typical of his attempts to conciliate me:

My Dear Friend . . . I did not expect such a letter. Without ever having met you or known you, I felt that we were joined in mutual trust. For my part I

[1] Foot confirmed this in an address to the Commonwealth Society in London in 1960 when he said without mincing words that 'our main objective' at this time was to get rid of Grivas and bring back Makarios.

have every confidence in you. My admiration and love are such that I regarded it as my duty to find a means, without harming the Government's international standing, to do all I could for you both here in Athens and at the United Nations. I have opened my heart to you and it is a cruel disappointment to know of the doubts you express about the administration, about Greece and about myself. I want you to believe that if you are doing far more than duty demands of you, then we, at least, are doing our duty to the full.

Averoff went on to argue that he had, in fact, taken a strong line with Turkey, giving as instances the withdrawal of Greek officers from NATO headquarters at Smyrna and his refusal to loan airfields and other facilities to the Americans during the recent landings in the Lebanon after the Iraq revolution. He ended by asking me again not to end my cease-fire

as this could bring about lamentable results, hindering and halting our moves behind the scenes. . . . Hostile action at this moment will not help us and may do much harm.

I told Averoff that, while I did not wish to carp, it would not be right to hide my feelings from him. He must know that the Cyprus people were complaining at the Greek Government's inertia. I summed up the situation by saying:

I have a letter before me now from an area commander who says that what we need in Greece today is a Menderes! If I loosed the flood of complaint against Athens in Cyprus you would be deafened by the clamour.

My chief consolation at this time was that the public, however disappointed by the lack of Greek support, were more than ever united behind me after the ordeal of the Anglo-Turkish attack. The last shreds of belief in British fairness were now being stripped away by the courts, where those arrested in intercommunal fighting were being tried. The Greeks received heavy sentences, but the Turks were repeatedly acquitted of murder and arson in the face of the most damning evidence.

Now that they could no longer attack the Greeks openly, soldiers and auxiliaries in plain clothes banded together in 'vigilance squads' to arrest, insult and ill-treat innocent men and women in the streets. A British secret society calling itself 'Cromwell' handed out illegal leaflets threatening to murder Greek citizens at random.

Particularly contemptible was the British attempt to bribe our members to sell their guns, offering various sums for different weapons: the top price was £500 for a machine-gun. No Greek surrendered a single weapon; on the contrary, the only transaction of this kind was made by three soldiers who sold their guns to us!

These three men were deserters who, tired of life in Cyprus, exchanged their sten-guns for a motor-boat which one of our men working in their camp procured for them. The soldiers sailed for Turkey, forty miles away, but the engine failed within half an hour and the boat began to ship water. Rowing and bailing in turn, they were picked up two days later by a Turkish coaster and landed at Iskenderun, where they claimed to have been ship-wrecked on a fishing expedition. The truth was soon discovered and they were sent back to Cyprus for court-martial.

Incidents of this kind clearly showed how low British Army morale was and, incidentally, what poor material some of the men were: pleas entered at the court-martial showed one youth had left home at the age of eight and never returned; the second had spent years in Borstal; and the third genuinely believed that he had joined not the Army but the mercantile marine and thought the motor-boat had come to pick him up at last for his promised life at sea.

*

While Averoff pleaded with me to maintain the cease-fire, the British tried to goad me into breaking it so that they could strike at us with all their force. EOKA men were killed in two major actions provoked by the Army at the end of August.

The first was in Lyssi where, after the arrest of EOKA members who might give information under interrogation, the village arms store was being moved to a new hiding place, in accordance with my standing instructions. The weapons – a sten, a rifle, a revolver, seven shot-guns, plus bombs and ammunition – were loaded on to bicycles by a group of three which set off after nightfall. By ill-chance they walked into an army patrol almost immediately: in an exchange of fire the leading fighter was killed. The man behind him, Michael Kallis, aged twenty-four, wounded a soldier with a shot from his revolver before the patrol emptied their automatics into his body. Although dying, Kallis flung a hand grenade, killing five soldiers. As the third EOKA man tried to escape across the fields he was shot down.

Five days later I lost my Larnaca area commander, Michalakis Parides, who was living at Vavla, a hunted man. At 8 am lorry loads of soldiers arrived at the village school, which they made into their headquarters. Roads were blocked and machine-gun posts set up on the rooftops; then a house to house search began. Parides realised he had been betrayed: he could surrender, or he could fight and die. He chose to fight, although he was quite alone, one man against fifty. He stationed himself at the head of a flight of stairs in an old two-storey building where he had a good field of fire. Within an hour soldiers, guided by a Turkish policeman, burst in. Parides got in one burst before he fell, riddled with bullets. The British were very pleased at their success, for Parides was a veteran fighter: he had been arrested soon after the start of the revolution in April 1955, but escaped in December 1957, since when he had eluded capture while directing operations in his area.

Once again I was obliged to order reprisals. A British police officer was shot dead in a Nicosia street and next day an airman was killed in the same way, by our execution squads.

CHAPTER ELEVEN

The Offer of Independence

ARMY searches rolled southwards to Liopetri, centre of what the British Press called 'Terror Triangle', because of its tradition of resistance. Here, on 2 September 1958, one of the finest of all EOKA actions was fought between four guerrillas and several hundred troops and police. The four men, Xanthos Samaras, Andreas Karios, Elias Papakyriakos and Photis Pittas, had all seen plenty of action. They came to Liopetri, which stands in a broad plain of fertile red earth, on 30 August, to instruct village groups in ambush techniques and they were still there on 1 September when, at 2 am, troops drove in and loudspeakers announced the start of a curfew. All males were ordered to the school for screening, the women told to remain in their houses. The guerrillas, who were in a house on the edge of the village, decided to try and make a break for it by car through streets crowded with soldiers; but they had not gone far before they ran into the cordon and had to turn back after an exchange of shots. At 3 am they found refuge with a friendly farmer, who put them in his old, thick-walled barn.

All next day villagers were questioned until one of them broke down and betrayed the man who had given the fighters shelter. At 8 am next day the barn and farmstead adjoining it were surrounded. A platoon began the search, but when they entered the farmyard they were driven back by a burst from an automatic. The army called in reinforcements and there were some sharp exchanges of fire. When a Greek-speaking soldier called on the guerrillas to surrender they answered with another burst. The officer in charge then ordered hand-grenades to be thrown: three different types were used, but none had any effect. Next a rocket-launcher was brought up and a dozen shells were fired into the stout walls, again without breaking them. Finally soldiers rushed the building and six of them managed to enter the farmhouse; two others were killed by the guerrillas' fire and their officer was badly wounded and had to be dragged inside. As they tried to pull him in a guerrilla stepped into the doorway to shoot, but he was immediately killed by the soldiers' covering fire. The rush was fruitless, however, for the soldiers in the house were no more able to strike at the guerrillas in the barn than were their comrades who ringed the area. There was a long pause while the British debated what to do and evacuated wounded men from the farmhouse by way of a hole knocked through the rear wall. Then the battle began again.

At the end of three hours' fighting the three remaining guerrillas were running short of ammunition. But the British had run out of courage: they decided to burn their enemies alive with petrol, as they had done in the fight with Afxentiou. Policemen scrambled on to the roof of the barn by way of the farmhouse and knocked a hole through the rafters, then poured cans of petrol in, soaking the chaff. A lighted brand was tossed in and the whole barn exploded in a sheet of flame. The guerrillas ran out through the smoke, firing as they came, to be shot down before they had covered ten yards by the concentrated fire of a dozen Bren guns.

The bullet-riddled corpses lay where they had fallen in their blood for hours; then the British went into the barn and brought out the group's small store of bombs and ammunition, bread and olives. Next day the authorities, without troubling to invent an excuse, took their cheap revenge by dynamiting barn and house.

The tragedy did not end there: we knew that the traitor was Elias Samaras, who had broken down under interrogation and betrayed his own brother, Xanthos, leader of the four fighters. This man was held for a month at an interrogation centre, then flown to England. But seventeen days later he returned to Cyprus and surrendered himself to EOKA, unable to bear the pain of his guilt. His area commander sent me a report on the case and enclosed a long document written by the traitor – his confession and plea for mercy:

Dear Group Leader,

I swear in the name of God that I shall not write the smallest lie or seek to make excuses . . . [here he describes the guerrillas' failure to break through the cordon and his own arrest] . . . they had us there with our hands up against the wall for about an hour; then they called me . . . .

[PUBLISHER'S NOTE: *The exact text of this passage in Samaras's confession has been quoted by General Grivas. It is omitted in this book because objections have been raised to its publication here.*]

The barn was placed under guard until dawn. Samaras was again questioned and this time he betrayed arms hideouts and other men in the village. He was taken to Nicosia before the fight began and later heard in his cell at the interrogation centre that the four men he had betrayed, including his brother, were dead. He was taken to England and decided to return and give himself up. His report ended:

Group Leader, God forgive me if I have left out any detail of what I betrayed, but I think I have written it all. Do not torture me any more. Whatever you decide to do, do it quickly, for I cannot breathe; my breast is heavy and I have suffered enough. You are a human being too and you know about pain. . . .

If I am found guilty and the sentence is execution do not hesitate, because it would be worse to live than to die. I would like to live and work for God and my country, but if they do not allow this, their will be done.

Group Leader, I pray that God will protect you from evil: to all members I wish peace and protection from God the father; and one thing more. May they fall gloriously and honourably in battle and not into hands of the enemy. Help them to see the path of duty and God's will, so that He may not punish them as He has punished me.

I await your instructions,

Your unworthy son,
'Ekdotis'

This document was accompanied by a letter from Samaras's family asking that the traitor's life should be spared, but pledging themselves to accept my decision without complaint, whatever it might be. I was moved by the depth of Samaras's remorse and by the tragic position of his family who, torn between love and duty, had thrown themselves on my judgement. Yet I had no hesitation whatsoever in ordering the execution: first, to expiate the memory of a traitor; secondly, for the honour of the dead man's family; thirdly, as an example to other EOKA men. I sent this order to the area commander:

I see no mitigating circumstances in the treachery of Elias Samaras. He will be executed. The execution will be a lesson to everyone, showing that no one may ask for pardon on the excuse that their treachery was due to torture. The greatness of a fighter lies in not giving way to violence and physical suffering, in not being cowed by enemy bullets. As Leader, because of the family's spiritual nobility, because of the traitor's sincere repentance and because he has paid for his crime with death, I shall say no more. Everyone must judge the man for himself.

There is a comforting footnote to this tragic story. After my return to Athens in 1959 the surviving brother of the Samaras family came to see me, with his wife. I showed them Elias's last letter and they thanked me with tears in their eyes for ordering his execution. They felt that his death had expiated his crime and they looked on him as a man who, through suffering, had achieved great spiritual stature. I was profoundly moved by what they said: it was typical of their country's greatness.

*

The climacteric of the struggle was approaching with grim inevitability against a background of twittering pleas from Athens for a continuation of the cease-fire no matter what was done by the British Government, army and interrogators. The British insisted that they would impose the Macmillan Plan on the island, though how a parliament could be set up without Greek Cypriot co-operation was hard to understand. To make certain that the authorities could not use the civil service to set constitutional machinery in progress I organised an EOKA network among government employees which helped us to counter British moves before they were made. I told Foot in a leaflet on 1 September 1958:

The British plan is dead and buried. You will have to walk over 450,000 Greek corpses to impose it, but this will never happen because it is we who are determined to walk over you.

Reprisals in the form of sabotage continued through the first week of September, inflicting thousands of pounds' worth of damage on RAF, army and naval installations. Foot flew to London on 5 September for talks about the implementation of the plan and I warned him:

We declared a cease-fire on 4 August on condition that our enemies responded in kind. But from the very first day there have been arrests, curfews and torture to the point of death. . . . I warn the Conservative Government that its Praetorian guards cannot be allowed to murder and destroy unpunished.

At this stage I received an ingratiating letter from the Greek Consul telling me that Foot had said he wished to ask his Government that Makarios be allowed to return to Cyprus, but that he feared current disturbances would make it impossible for them to grant the request. I replied indignantly on 8 September:

I have ceased to listen to stories about what the Governor or the British Cabinet intend to do. They are always trying to bamboozle us. . . . I think only of how to escape from the impasse into which folly has led us. I, too, have responsibilities, greater indeed than anyone, and I mean to carry out my duty towards the Cypriot people as I think best, since my judgement and activities have never been proved mistaken.

I shall apply my plan for the armed fight because it is the only correct plan; and I shall listen to no more suggestions and recommendations. The British invented the situation which led to this prolonged cease-fire and those who support its continuance are harming our cause.

That evening I sent out an order allowing my group leaders a free hand to take reprisals wherever and whenever they wished. I felt able to relax the close control with which I supervised every detail at the start of the sabotage offensive, now that all my subordinates had proved their abilities in action.

The British maintained their policy of striking back at the innocent population, when they failed to find our men. Their savagery, indeed, seemed to increase with each new attack. A particularly ferocious revenge was taken after an ambush at Yiolou, in which eight guerrillas, armed with

M3 automatics, rifles, shotguns and grenades, shot up some trucks and killed a soldier. The guerrillas retired to Symou in the east; but tracker dogs led troops westwards to the villages of Kathykas and Theletra. People were dragged from their beds, herded through the streets under blows from fists and rifle butts, prodded on with naked bayonets when they stumbled. One villager was pulled into a yard and mercilessly beaten while his wife and seven children stood watching hopelessly. He snatched up a knife to defend his family and stabbed two soldiers, wounding them seriously; then he knocked a third soldier unconcious and tried to make his escape over the wall, only to be shot down by sten-gun fire after he had gone a few yards. Under cover of a three-day curfew further outrages were perpetrated; meanwhile the guerrillas sat safely in a village a few miles outside the cordonned area.

Such a storm of protest went up that for the first time remarks critical of the army were made in some London newspapers and eye-witness reports of the injuries and damage done in these villages were sent from Cyprus by British journalists; few, however, were printed.

*

When Foot returned from his discussions in London on 10 September 1958, it was announced that the Macmillan Plan would be implemented with the co-operation of the Turks alone; the British apparently thought the Greeks would be so consumed with jealousy at this that they would soon join in and complete the 'partnership'. The plan was to be officially launched in three weeks' time on 1 October, with the appointment of the Turkish Government's adviser to the Government. The Greek Government, of course, refused to send a representative. Archbishop Makarios appealed to the British and United States Ambassadors in Athens to prevent the arrival of the Turkish 'Commissioner', as he was to be called, while King Paul, Karamanlis and Averoff all warned that the plan would end in disaster.

The more liberal political factions in Britain saw that a serious crisis lay ahead and several Labour MPs arrived to study the situation personally; they had begun to wonder if Foot was quite the liberal diplomat he claimed to be. The first of these visitors, Mr Tom Driberg, chairman of the Labour executive, told Makarios in Athens that his party rejected partition and would give us self-determination when it came to power; then, on reaching Cyprus, he sent me through private channels a letter dated 9 September 1958. In it he suggested the possibility of an informal and private discussion on Cyprus between us. The proposition, he said, was made both as a politician and a journalist. As the former, he felt that a politician ought to have some communication with the military leaders of a cause towards which he is generally sympathetic. A journalist would of course be interested in meeting a man whom he suspected had been misrepresented by the majority of the British Press.

To reassure me, he disclaimed any idea that he might be acting as an official British go-between. He had always, he said, tried to promote the just interests of Greek Cypriots. Moreover, no one knew of his plan except for three Greek Cypriots, supporters of the Ethnarchy. He also proposed that he be kept ignorant, by means of a curtained car, of the locality of any meeting place. The letter concluded with the hope that I would at any rate reply.

The letter was sent on to me by Athanasios Papageorghiou, an Ethnarchy official who was acting as my chief postmaster in Nicosia. I did not answer it, for I could see no point in such a meeting. There was nothing to say which had not been said a hundred times before and as for propaganda, I felt quite capable of making all the publicity we needed in my own way, without taking unnecessary risks.

The second of our Labourite visitors was Mrs Barbara Castle, who brought word from Athens that Archbishop Makarios did not exclude independence, after a period of self-government, as a possible solution. After touring Cyprus, Mrs Castle saw Makarios again in Athens, where he authorised her to give this news to the world's Press.

It was a complete surprise to me, and I confess to being upset and shocked. The Archbishop had no mandate to depart from our basic claim for self-determination – the right to choose our own future and join our Greek motherland. I could not tell under what pressure he had decided to offer this vital concession, without asking my opinion, only a few days after a new appeal based on self-determination had been lodged at the United Nations. His failure to prepare the ground with the Cypriot public in advance also showed a dangerous lack of psychological understanding; I was forced to take immediate action to reassure the Organisation. This declaration could have had very grave consequences: as it was the public was both shocked and puzzled. Makarios had, unknown to me, been considering the idea for some time. He officially proposed the creation of an independent Cyprus under United Nations auspices to the Greek Government on 17 September 1958, the day the latest Cyprus appeal was submitted to the UN, although no public announcement was made. It was not until 28 September that I received the Archbishop's letter of explanation:

Sabotage at the Kykko army camp

A village home being searched by British soldiers

Limassol house blown up in October 1958 because EOKA ammunition was found in it. The owners here stand upon its ruins

The house in Kannavia where the following were killed as the result of an explosion: Alekos Konstantinou, Panayotis Georgiades, Costas Anaxagoras and Andreas Patsalides

As you will have read in the newspapers I yesterday made a statement to Mrs Barbara Castle, the MP, by which I virtually created a new situation. I declared that if the British Government abandoned the Macmillan–Foot plan, I would be willing, after a fixed period of self-government, to accept a regime of independence which could not be transformed except by decision of the UN. Although this new line could possibly be described as a retreat, it is what the situation, if coldly appraised, requires.

My latest information is extremely disheartening. . . . British public opinion has turned very considerably against us, and the British Press, including that of the Labour Party, even when not attacking us, carefully avoids any kind of publication which would damage the prestige of British troops, because of the strength of public opinion.

Barbara Castle and others among the Labour Party declared that they could not oppose the British plan unless the Archbishop offered something new which would be favourably received under the conditions at present prevailing in England. If this was done they said they would urge the Archbishop's views on the British Prime Minister and put them forward at the Party conference and through their newspapers.

I cannot now forecast the consequences, but they cannot be bad. America has completely aligned its policies with Britain and our only hope of success at the UN is to put the question on the basis of independence. . . .

We had to face up to the situation realistically and reach a decision before we were presented with a *fait accompli*, for the imposition of the British plan, no matter how bold and determined the resistance of the Greek people in Cyprus, would inevitably lead to partition, or would give the Turks rights which it would be impossible (even under different conditions) to remove later.

I sent Makarios this reply next day:

Every time I am obliged to repeat that it is impossible to achieve a favourable solution of the Cyprus question so long as the West realises that the Greek Government, with its so-called threats, is bluffing. . . .

We are fighting at this moment to prevent the imposition of a monster on the backs of the Cypriot people and we are not succeeding, thanks to Greek policy. . . . After three and a half years of unprecedented sufferings, death and disaster, and acts of heroism we are turning the people over to a slavery more oppressive than the one which they now suffer, a slavery to two masters instead of one, with every probability that they will never emerge from the tomb into which we have thrown them. Which of us among the leaders will dare to face the Cypriot people? Which of us is worthy to survive such shame?

There is absolutely no co-ordination between the diplomatic and military struggle. I feel, indeed, that the diplomats believe our struggle has created difficulties for them. If that is the case they should say so bluntly so that we know where we stand. I do not know exactly what the purpose of the Archbishop's new proposal is; if it is intended to compel a more compromising attitude on the part of the Labour Party, I am afraid we shall fall into a new trap and that these proposals will be the start of a whole series of compromises, until we arrive at some new monstrosity of a plan.

We do not suffer from any lack of plans; anyone can put forward dozens. What we lack is a man who can put his weight behind *one plan* and insist on its acceptance to the end. We can be flexible about details, but not about basic principles. We have, up to now, basically changed our views several times, with the result that we ourselves do not know exactly what we are demanding and we seem indecisive to both friends and enemies.

At all events, I declare that my opposition to the overall policy which is being followed on the Cyprus question is final. This will not show itself in any specific external form, because I do not wish it to be thought that I want to exploit the situation for political reasons – I have none. Nor do I want it said that I am trying to block the way to a political solution. However, if I conclude that the struggles of the Cypriot people will go for nothing, then I will be obliged to address myself bluntly to the Greek and Cypriot people.

The Conservatives rejected Makarios's proposal with the excuse that a period of calm must elapse before any decision was made about a final solution. The Labour Party, however, welcomed the new idea and demaded that the Macmillan Plan should be dropped. Gaitskell and Bevan attacked Government policy vigorously but with little effect. Lennox-Boyd merely repeated his worn arguments about the rights of the Turks, even going so far as to describe Cyprus as Turkey's off-shore island.

*

I now began preparations for a major offensive which would slowly increase in pace and intensity as the day for the implementation of the plan approached. First I organised a thorough propaganda campaign to warn the world that the appointment of the Turkish Government's representative on 1 October would lead to bloodshed; strikes and mass demonstrations followed, while EOKA action against the British, beginning on 8 September with controlled attacks, switched on 25 September to intense activity against manned and unmanned targets. I ordered that attacks must be pushed home even if curfews were in force, although there was to be no action against the Turks unless it was deliberately provoked.

On the morning of 26 September one of the biggest mines ever used by EOKA exploded a few seconds after the bullet-proof car carrying Maj.-General Kendrew, Foot's Director of Operations, had passed on its way to Government House. Kendrew only escaped because the lookout who signalled the approach of his car did not recognise it immediately among the stream of traffic, so that it was almost over the mined road junction before he could give the sign; as it was, the explosion caught Kendrew's escort Land-Rover, hurling it into the roadside, killing one soldier and injuring two others. This daring operation, which took weeks of planning, was carried out by day in one of the busiest areas of Nicosia.

In the days that followed we struck at the British more fiercely than ever before, although for the first week of October I limited operations to the town groups and ambush teams in the countryside, bringing in the mountain guerrillas on 7 October. There were many clashes between the army and student demonstrators, and on the day the Macmillan Plan was formally launched, 1 October 1958, there was a twenty-four-hour general strike all over the island. The attacks listed in my records for 2 October, a typical day, give an idea of the scale of operations:

LARNACA: Soldier killed by bomb; civilian agent shot dead by execution squad.

NICOSIA: Bomb thrown into police headquarters from car, casualties unknown.

FAMAGUSTA: Two army trucks ambushed, casualties unknown.

LIMASSOL: Eight Britons injured by bomb at Acropole Hotel; four soldiers injured by bomb thrown at truck.

PLATANI: Two soldiers killed, two wounded in mined truck.

PANAYIA-STAVROS: Two soldiers killed, two wounded in ambush.

PYROI: Truck ambushed, casualties unknown.

MESOYI: Two soldiers killed in ambush of truck.

PIYI: Two soldiers killed, two wounded in mined truck.

PERISTERONA: Bombs thrown at two army trucks, casualties unknown.

The Organisation was at the height of its power: our men were better armed, better trained and hardened by years of fighting. Twenty-two guerrilla groups were operating in the mountains and countryside of the west, and a large number of OKT (shotgun) groups were at work in the Nicosia, Famagusta and Karpassia plains to the east.

We made important advances in the use of explosives and our laboratories in Nicosia and Famagusta had developed new types of mine and invented new mixtures to fill them. We made our own detonators, time pencils, incendiary bombs, hand grenades and pressure mines; towards the end we even manufactured a small automatic weapon which used 9 mm ammunition.

All this was done by amateurs: men who had no professional training in handling arms and explosives – chemists, electricians, metal-workers, plumbers. The Nicosia team of scientists was under the overall leadership of the deputy headmaster of the Pancyprian Gymnasiu, Christos Papachrisostomou, and the laboratory was directed by a chemist, Nicos Servos (who used the code name 'Faust'), and his deputy Costas Economides. The chemicals used in making our explosives were freely on sale to the public and the authorities must have known, from captured mines and bombs, that we were using them; yet for some curious reason no attempt was made to prohibit their sale until the struggle was virtually over, by which time we had sufficient reserve to continue sabotage for over two years.

The most important weapon in our armoury was the pressure mine. I had urged our technicians to concentrate on its development, because it was extremely effective in flat country where ambushes were impossible and it usually caused fatal causualties, while being both safe to use and economical in men and materials.[1] I deliberately promoted rivalry between the Nicosia laboratory and the Famagusta group in producing mines, and by the Spring of 1958 we had perfected two distinct types, one made by each. The Famagusta teams under Pavlos Pavlakis and Photis Papaphotis put their mines to good use when the time came. During experiments Papaphotis was injured by an explosion but resumed work after a brief stay in hospital. He lost a hand. Members of the Nicosia group were also injured and were treated by the team's surgeon, Dr Odysseus Ioannides.

Dozens of men from the guerrilla groups were sent for training in the use of these new weapons to the Nicosia workshops, which had their headquarters at the tiny chemist's shop of Nicos Servos, in the heart of Nicosia.

Thus, thanks to our own ingenuity, we kept the fight going. I can certainly give no thanks to the Greek Government, who offered no help at all. The fact that we were eventually able to bring in a certain number of guns from Greece during this period is due entirely to the efforts of myself and

---

[1] These mines did not endanger civilian transport. They were controlled by an on–off switch of the kind used in table lamps. The operator, in a vantage point several hundred yards from the road, placed the switch in the 'on' position when a military vehicle approached, thus forming an electrical circuit which was completed by the passage of the vehicle over the pressure board buried in the road. Another useful weapon we developed was the 'cannonaki', little cannon, which was a form of mortar made from a steel pipe two or three inches in diameter, filled with shrapnel and buried in a bank at the roadside. When electrically detonated it sprayed metal fragments over a wide area.

my colleagues: Andreas Azinas in Athens, Deacon Anthimos Kyriakides and Socrates Eliades in Cyprus.[1]

Public morale was splendid, despite the everlasting operations, curfew and searches which, as the authorities intended, were destroying the island economically: villagers refused to risk maltreatment and arrest when taking their produce to market, and in the towns all shops closed at 5 pm, even when there was no curfew – no Greek could walk the streets after dark in safety. Yet the population responded to our new attack with fanatical enthusiasm. To a large extent this was due to ANE, the youth movement, and to PEKA. Wonderful work was done in the organisation of demonstrations and all forms of propaganda: ANE even published a special underground magazine called *Reveille* filled with patriotic articles and information about EOKA activities.

Perhaps the most important feature of all in this respect was the boycott, which flourished despite the unlovely alliance of capitalists and Communists against it. The AKEL leadership went to work among businessmen and import agents, spreading rumours of economic disaster, and the commercial world was glad to believe them. Some businessmen told the Bishop of Kitium that the island was drifting into bankruptcy and claimed they could not meet their obligations; but I realised that they were playing games and secretly importing British goods. I warned Kitium that I would take severe measures if this continued:

There can be no concessions on my part even if I have to walk over a few corpses, because we are serving the interests of the struggle. If these gentlemen persist in their threats, then I must say to them: it is either you or me.

Foot and his propagandists did their best to exploit the situation and discredit passive resistance, but they failed completely. I could point out that during the third quarter of 1958 Commonwealth imports were cut by

[1] A letter I wrote to the Bishop of Kitium on 10 July 1958 sums up the position well: 'It would certainly surprise everyone to learn that I never had more than sixty automatics and that, with this number I kept the fight going for three and a half years against an army of 36,000. In spite of my appeals no method was found to keep me supplied with sufficient material. I was therefore obliged to invent our own explosive mixtures, which I am still using today for mines, and to find and suggest personally methods of transporting materials – methods which were at once highly dangerous and of very limited scope. And yet, some one and a half years ago, they promised me that a way had been found which would be ready by April of 1957 – and later, they said, by September of the same year. *Up to now this method has not been found.* And yet the question of my supplies, following the appearance of the new enemy, the Turk, is one of great urgency. Generally, I conclude that there is the greatest possible indifference about the matter. . . .'

£3 million, and official figures showed an overall reduction of £10 million in trade with Britain: but the real value of the boycott was that it heightened patriotic feeling and brought the public and the Organisation closer together. Every man, woman and child could feel that he was doing something to help the fight.

CHAPTER TWELVE

The Climax of the Fight

ON the evening radio bulletin of 3 October I was startled to hear that the wife of a British sergeant had been shot dead by unknown men while shopping in the streets of Famagusta, and another soldier's wife beside her had been wounded. The news was as much a surprise to me as to anyone else; I could not imagine how it had come about and I had to wait until my leader in Famagusta, Costas Christodoulides, could get a report through the curfew which had come down on the town. It seemed that he knew nothing about the affair and to this day no one knows who the killers were. While nobody could rule out the possibility of some mis-understanding or of some hot-headed Greek seeking to revenge the fre-quent attacks on the women of our community by the army,[1] there was no evidence whatever that EOKA was involved;[2] indeed, the woman in question, Mrs Margaret Cutliffe, might have been the victim of some crime of spite or passion.

The British did not wait for an investigation. Hardly had the curfew siren sounded when troops of four regiments rushed into the town, rounded up some 3,000 people at random and let loose a night of terror. Dragged from their homes, men and boys were herded like animals through the streets of Famagusta. Many were piled into trucks face down, one on top of another, and driven off to interrogation centres and army camps. On the road and again on arrival they were savagely beaten with batons and rifle butts. Three Greek Cypriots died during those terrible hours. The first, a student of seventeen, had his skull fractured, the second, a thirty-seven-year-old shoemaker, had seven broken ribs among his injuries; the third, a twelve-year-old schoolgirl, died of shock and heart failure after witnessing the scenes of brutality. Another sixteen people were

[1] The Security Forces had killed or wounded eighteen Cypriot women and children since 1955, and the latest murder, at Avgorou, had aroused bitter feeling.

[2] EOKA harmed only those who harmed us; I never ordered an attack on a woman or child throughout the struggle and anything of the sort would have been severely punished. I ordered the release of John Cremer, the Englishman who was taken hostage in August 1956, when I learned that he was an elderly man. The British made atrocity propaganda out of the death of a Government official and his wife who were shot while driving in the Kyrenian mountains; this would not have occurred if the man had not first drawn a gun and fired.

seriously injured and altogether 400 went to hospital for treatment. The troops swarmed through the town smashing shop-windows and stealing goods. Rifle butts were thrust through the windscreens of cars, doors were broken down.

Foot and General Kendrew hurried to the town when the news of the outbreak reached them, but they were at pains to excuse the army's behaviour. For once, however, the truth could not be hidden. An Englishwoman, shocked by what she had seen in Famagusta that night, wrote to the *Manchester Guardian* denouncing the conduct of the troops; though she was afterwards victimised by the Cyprus authorities and ostracised by other Britons, her evidence left no doubt about the excesses of the army.

Here, if ever, was an opportunity for the Greek Government to expose British violence in Cyprus, but once again they went on the defensive, deploring the Englishwoman's death but finding not a single word to say about the army's barbarity and the murder of Greek women. Indeed, Averoff wrote to me as if EOKA, and not the British, stood in the dock; in a letter dated 14 October he said:

An unfortunate turn is the increased coolness of the Labour Party; with the murder of the Englishwoman and the British Press campaign about it Labour too has been expressing opposition to us, even the warmest and most extreme among them. They are criticising Makarios and regard his statement [made on 3 October, this statement called on Cypriots to resist British attempts to enforce the Macmillan plan] as having provoked the murder just at a time when the Labour Party and NATO are trying to find a political solution. If my information from London is correct they have made a confidential appeal to Makarios to denounce the murder and offer some moderate declaration; otherwise it will be difficult for Labour to continue to support us. It seems that similar attacks are being made, and by friends of ours too, on our delegation at the UN. These people go so far as to suggest that the Hitlerian orgy at Famagusta was a natural reaction by furious troops to Mrs Cutliffe's death.

Since EOKA had disowned Mrs Cutliffe's killing, I replied to Averoff that I failed to understand the tone of official statements from Athens, which simply denounced the crime without launching a counter-attack on the British for murdering dozens of our women and young children in cold blood. As for Makarios's message to the Cypriot people it had revived morale and steeled their faith in the struggle: if the British criticised it they did so precisely because they knew it had good results. 'We must meet British propaganda with determination, not fear.' I went on to remind Averoff that I had made great efforts to keep up morale but I did not know how much longer I could do so, since after three years we had nothing to show the ordinary people but diplomatic defeat and political inaction.

No one in Cyprus today can approve the handling of the national question by the Karamanlis Government. Surely, independence and dignity should take first place, even before economic advantages: it were better to be free and poor than to exchange our independence for dollars from America. A ray of light comes from de Gaulle: here, it seems, we have a leader of liberal principles who has a national policy which is completely free, instead of being harnessed to the will of the Americans and British. . . .

These thoughts are constantly going round in my head. I have no one to discuss them with in my prison and perhaps because of that they may have more value, since they are influenced by no one else. My recommendation from all this is a single-minded one: DARING and again DARING and once more DARING.

Unhappily, all my urgings fell on deaf ears; indeed, the Bishop of Kitium actually wrote to tell me that this was no time to create division, adding that EOKA should have given due warning in a leaflet to the Government if it intended to end the cease-fire as soon as the Macmillan Plan went into operation. I replied somewhat sharply that there was no need for a leaflet to renounce the cease-fire; events had done that for us. In any case, I said, we had become a laughing stock with all this talk of cease-fires while the army did whatever it liked. Another problem was presented by the constant curfews on towns and villages; their ostensible purpose was to prevent EOKA action, but in reality they were aimed at breaking the nerve of the population, interrupting education and taking away the livelihood of the people. I was amazed, I told the Bishop, at the silence of the Greek Government in the face of this provocation and the barbarity of the army; not a single protest had come from Athens.

Next day, 7 October, I issued an order for the guerrilla groups to go into action, and soon we were attacking on all fronts. The execution groups were at work in the towns; the sabotage groups were busy in the bases; the guerrillas struck out in the mountains and countryside. Another switch was due in the British command; on 11 October the burly Director of Operations, Maj.-General Kendrew, left Cyprus in a cloak of secrecy to be replaced on the same day by Maj.-General Kenneth Darling, a man of small stature who tried to make up for his lack of inches with a boastful tongue. His Press conferences were taken up with victory claims and abuse of EOKA. His language shocked even some of his fellow-officers. 'We've got those bastards on the run,' he said repeatedly. He may have convinced himself, but he convinced no one else, for everyone could see that the army under his command was taking the greatest beating it had yet suffered, worse even than the humiliation we inflicted on it during the month of 'Black November', two years before.

Darling dashed around the bases tightening up security; he doubled and redoubled guards, ordered more dogs and more patrols, insisted on hundreds of Cypriot workers being dismissed from their jobs in military zones – yet still our attacks went through. A particularly daring raid in which a Canberra jet bomber was destroyed on 20 October is worth describing in some detail. The bomber was one of ten aircraft on a disposal apron surrounded with barbed wire at Akrotiri air base. One armed airman guarded the gate, another patrolled the perimeter, a third kept a lookout over the whole area through binoculars from an observation post. Nevertheless, one of our young workers on the bases undertook to smuggle a time bomb into the airfield and this was moved with painful slowness to within 80 yards of the target. After a brief rest, the saboteur once more took up his journey, dragging himself along the ground through bushes. When he was still 25 yards away a truck drove up with a party of airmen, who began searching the area. He lay there watching but they passed him, and when the truck moved off he began to crawl forward again. Eight rows of barbed wire surrounded the apron and the saboteur had to cut his way through each of them; then, when he was inside the apron and the backs of the guards were turned, he jumped up and scurried into a lavatory hut for shelter. Luck was with him: two guards began working with a saw to warm themselves up and the saboteur ran across the open ground behind them, slipped the bomb into the undercarriage of the bomber and ran back to the lavatory. He eventually found his way back to the gap he had cut in the wire and left in the same way as he had come, crawling on his stomach. Back in the camp he quickly changed into a spare pair of overalls and left at the usual hour with the other workers, undergoing several searches on the way out. The time bomb blew up the Canberra at 3.10 am next morning. Damage was officially estimated at £800,000. While Darling's security chiefs were desperately hunting for the wreckers in their midst we broke through the elaborate network of precautions in RAF Nicosia, a week later and a bomb was planted in the baggage of an officer who was about to board a flight for England. Our objective was to destroy the plane, an RAF Comet jet transport, in the air, but it did not leave in time and the bomb exploded as the passengers were going aboard, injuring ten servicemen.

Between these two airport attacks we staged one of the biggest and most spectacular explosions of the Emergency by dynamiting army trucks as they stood at the front door of Yiallousa police station. This was an extremely difficult and dangerous assignment, but I sanctioned it in preference to easier tasks as a demonstration of EOKA power. It was effected by laying mines in a storm-drain which ran along past the front of the building for 40 yards and what made our success the more remarkable was that the army had a soldier constantly on guard at one end of the drain while a sandbagged machine-gun post had been built at the other. As usually happens, once the precautions had been put into effect the danger was forgotten and we found after a while that the sentries withdrew into the police station at about 3 am each morning and stayed there until dawn. The drain was barely wide enough for a fullgrown man to squeeze through so the job was undertaken by a nimble schoolboy of fifteen, Andreas Modestos, who after a trial run one night reported that although he could crawl through without meeting obstructions he would not be able to carry with him the two large mines we planned to detonate. This difficulty was met by putting the mines in a child's trolley, a strongly-made toy which Modestos pulled behind him by a string.

At 3 am on 23 October the boy began his crawl down the drain. He found the mines, even in their trolley, a handicap. Half-way to his destination – the section which lay under the police station verandah – the drain became so narrow that he had to pull himself along on his back; a little later he had to crush his body under an iron pipe which crossed the drain. Here the mines had to be taken through by hand. One of them hit the pipe and a small piece of metal connecting the detonator with the charge was broken off, so Modestos had to crawl back with it. The mine was repaired during the day and the boy returned with it on the following night and placed it in position beside its brother. He brought back with him a cable which, suitably camouflaged, led round the corner to a house from which, at a given signal, the explosion could be set off: in all, Modestos spent nearly seven hours in the drain.

The day passed without the appearance of a worthwhile target and so did the following morning, but at 2 pm on 25 October two trucks full of soldiers stopped before the police station and just as the men were jumping out the mines were detonated. The first truck, blown 20 feet into the air, came down on its back and the other was also badly damaged. There were nearly twenty British casualties when the smoke and dust cleared and Darling rushed over from Nicosia to fire off a barrage of threats and insults. It was an unusual aspect of this operation that almost the whole village knew what was going to happen. Several people saw young Modestos clambering out of the storm-drain at dawn and everyone was warned to keep away from the post office across the road when the trucks arrived to change the guard at the police station, yet the secret was kept by all.

Everywhere the spirit of our men was high; everywhere our people were filled with pride and the spirit of adventure. Such losses as we suffered – and they were few in comparison with the enemy – served only to raise our ardour. A few days before Panayotis Tomazos, a nineteen-year-old student, was killed on 22 October he received a letter from his father which contained these words:

Be bold, fearless, honourable and loyal. Choose good comrades for your friends and you will come out of the struggle with clean hands. Above all, never betray your sacred arms: prefer the harshest death.

With two other guerrillas Tomazos laid an ambush on the mountain road near Kakopetria to intercept troops racing to the rescue of a patrol which had been attacked half an hour earlier. Two trucks full of soldiers came into sight, but the mines buried in the road failed to explode when they passed over them. In spite of this, and facing the heaviest odds, the guerrillas opened fire on the British. The first truck was halted and several of the men in it were wounded. Not content with his success, Tomazos raised himself from the hillside to throw a grenade and was caught by a hail of bullets from the second truck. His two comrades said later that on the way to the site of the ambush Tomazos plucked a small branch from an olive tree and put it in his pocket, saying, 'If I should die they will see this and know that we are lovers of peace.'

On the British side morale was at its lowest ebb, as was proved by an encounter on 3 November between one of our little mountain groups and a patrol of some twenty soldiers. This group of four, led by Antonakis Solomontos, were sitting in their hide in the Troodos forest when they heard a warning whistle from their sentry, then the sound of shots. The guerrillas reached for their guns and when a British officer appeared at the mouth of the hide, shouting to them to surrender, Solomontos fired and hit him in the face. This was enough for the patrol, which took to its heels, leaving the officer to make his way behind them. Solomontos called on the officer to halt; instead, he tried to run off, then turned and fired. When a second call was ignored Solomontos fired a short burst. The officer was killed and our guerrillas made off with his stirling gun. They were amused to hear on the radio that night that the British had captured guns and ammunition in their abandoned hide; in fact, our men left in good order with their weapons before enemy reinforcements could come up.

To keep down casualties Darling restricted all vehicle movement to daylight hours; I replied with the increased use of pressure mines while limiting daylight ambushes to areas where the attackers had a good chance of safe withdrawal. Darling called this policy 'cowardly', which is an index of its success. It meant, for a start, the large-scale disruption of his communications: army vehicles stopping and examining the road ahead, looking for the tell-tale cable at the side; we simply buried the wires a little further out of sight: then up went another British truck. After a while Darling's men began to force Cypriots picked up in the villages to drive with them, knowing that we would not willingly blow up our own people. Of course, we could not always tell when there was a Cypriot aboard and those unhappy hostages who survived our attacks were usually beaten up by the soldiers when their comrades were killed. Like so many British misdemeanours the taking of hostages, which is a crime under international law, was ignored by the outside world which was so easily made indignant by EOKA action.

One must concede to Darling a schoolboy ingenuity which was allowed full play in Cyprus. A soldier with red paint on his face and uniform would be made to lie across a forest path, with a tempting gun beside him, while patrols hid nearby, waiting for EOKA to fall into the trap. Other soldiers on donkey-back offered themselves as bait in the mountains to our guerrillas. In the towns they crept in soft shoes through the darkened streets, climbing on roofs and sliding down drainpipes to the terror of peace-loving people. These efforts at deception were no more successful than the attempts to break down villagers by troops who descended on the country places by night in blackened faces, shrieking, banging tins and firing off their rifles: it may be said in favour of the latter practice that at least it released the men's frustration.

Above all, the enemy had no success whatever in interrupting that most delicate and important machinery which kept EOKA going: the movement of our couriers and arms-carriers. Day after day cars carrying guns passed unscathed through the road blocks, thanks to the keen wits of our agents – they knew the British, and the way their minds work, as a single incident may show. One afternoon George Economides, one of our gun-runners, left Nicosia with three pistols and ammunition in his car for Kyriakos Matsis, the Kyrenian mountain leader; he also took with him as a distraction for the troops a girl member of EOKA, Miss Lella Georghiadou. They ran into a road block outside Kyrenia and watched three soldiers, experts at the job, unscrew the boot of the car in front—just where their guns were hidden in their own car. While this was going on an officer came up, and Economides told him that he was in a hurry to take his girl for a drive in the hills. The officer was amused, his confidence was secured by the appearance of a packet of English cigarettes which were forbidden to Cypriots by the EOKA boycott, and the car passed on without a search.

By now the British were at their wits' end, and showing it. Tory MPs called for martial law, newspapers demanded that bullet-proof waistcoats should be issued to all Britons in Cyprus, secret societies were formed in the army and issued leaflets threatening the Cypriot population with bloodthirsty revenge. Soldiers often told prisoners they were guarding that they wanted to go home to England and only a small handful of the hundreds of British police who had come to Cyprus for high pay and promotion could be persuaded to renew their contracts. A final attempt to hunt me down was made by two experts sent out from Scotland Yard, Superintendent T. Butler and Assistant-Superintendent P. Vibart, but such were the quarrels in the higher ranks of the Cyprus Police that they returned to London in disgust within a few weeks of coming out.

The last pretence of decency was abandoned when Foot agreed with the army on the mass dismissal of some thousands of Cypriot workers without notice or compensation, thus dealing the collapsing economy of the island the heaviest blow in his power. Of course the Governor tried to cover his heartlessness by blaming EOKA for blocking the way to peace; he conveniently forgot that our three cease-fires had been ignored or rejected. Darling also saw to it that all Harding's emergency regulations were brought back. Property could be seized at will, 'danger areas' where troops could shoot at sight were created and back in all the panoply of power came the interrogators and the Turkish thugs. By now the number of paid informers who could supply fresh information had dwindled away, so information could only be secured by violence. I was seriously concerned not only by the brutality practised on our men when they were arrested but also the risk of fatal leaks: although many heroically underwent every interrogation, I could not expect every member of EOKA in British hands – some of them were still young schoolboys – to hold out indefinitely. I wrote on 26 October to the Bishop of Kitium, raising the question of the sufferings of our prisoners:

We must blame the Greek Government, the Archbishop and the Cypriot intelligentsia. For the last year or more I have been warning the Archbishop that if this treatment is allowed to continue all our secrets will be gradually betrayed. Yet nothing has been attempted beyond a lot of windy speeches and an exchange of notes; thus is the enemy encouraged in the direction of new excesses. One day history will name those who stood by while our men suffered and our cause was put in terrible danger. If I survive I shall be their chief accuser.

It was information procured under interrogation which led to the only successful British operation at that time, ending in the discovery and death of Kyriakos Matsis, my Kyrenian guerrilla leader. I knew Matsis well and his loss was a deep personal grief to me. I remembered so well when I had first been impressed by his strong and selfless character. It was in September 1955, on a day when he had brought messages to the house where I was living at the time in Kakopetria, the mountain resort in the Troodos. As we talked, I received word that some fifty troops had arrived in the village and were approaching our area. My little group picked up their guns and we all left together after I had said goodbye to Matsis: he was not a wanted man and there was no need for him to risk his life with us. But Matsis was not so easily shaken off. He insisted on following and covering us with a sten as we made our way up the hills. Only when we were completely clear of danger would he agree to leave.

In January of the following year Matsis was betrayed and arrested. Because the British had learned that he was a leading member of the Organisation in direct touch with me, everything was tried to break him down. Matsis always answered that he was fighting for freedom, not for money. When in the face of every inducement Matsis remained silent, escaped his captors in September and rejoined us, I was proud to appoint him leader of the whole Kyrenian range.

Now, at the start of November 1958, an army net was thrown over these mountains and Matsis sought refuge in the village of Dikhomo, where a hideout had already been prepared. Then some of the men he left behind were arrested; interrogators worked on them night and day until they had extracted the information they wanted. On 19 November soldiers surrounded Dikhomo at dawn. By 9.30 am they had reached the little bungalow where Matsis was hiding in a secret cellar with two comrades. The guerrillas heard the stamp of army boots over their heads for some minutes; then there was silence. The patrol had moved on. At noon the soldiers were back for a fresh search; again they left within half an hour but Matsis told his friends that he feared they had been betrayed. In fifteen minutes the army returned and went straight to the entrance of the hideout. This consisted of four tiles embedded in a concrete slab which formed a trapdoor indistinguishable from the rest of the tiled floor. The guerrillas heard the soldiers trying to lift the cover, then an officer cried in Greek, 'Matsis, give yourself up!' Matsis replied 'I shall come out firing.' The army again called to the men to surrender, threatening to burn them out with petrol if they refused. In the end Matsis ordered his two companions to leave and shouted to warn the interpreter that they were coming up. The troops withdrew outside the house, covering the door with machine-guns. When they had arrested Matsis's friends they went back into the house and threw grenades down through the open trapdoor of the hide. Matsis was killed outright. The soldiers found him clasping two guns, his right leg severed at the hip, his body covered with shrapnel wounds.

Matsis had often told friends that he would never be captured alive again. A month before his death, while driving from Bellapaix to Kyrenia, troops had suddenly appeared on the road ahead. Matsis told the driver to carry on, adding, 'If they try and halt us I'll open fire. I would sooner be dead than a prisoner of the British.' Even after they had succeeded in killing him the authorities were afraid of this fine young patriot. To prevent a magnificent demonstration at his funeral they refused to hand his body over to his parents. He was buried instead without Christian ceremonial of any kind in the weed-grown yard of the Central Prison, where he lay next to Afxentiou and other EOKA heroes.

In contrast to this unchivalrous treatment of a fallen foe was the emotion aroused among the British whenever one of their people was shot. Hysteria over the inability of the army and police to come to grips with our town execution groups had reached such a pitch in the London Press by November that Darling decided to issue revolvers to British civilians, who were invited in hundreds to Wolseley Barracks to help themselves from the armoury there. A very large proportion of these residents refused to take the risk of bearing arms; since the soldiers, they argued, never succeeded in shooting down an EOKA man in the streets why should they expect civilians to do their dirty work for them? It was an understandable point of view.

CHAPTER THIRTEEN

The Road to Zurich

SIR HUGH FOOT had first been brought into the Cyprus drama when the mailed fist of Harding had failed to get results; this devious civilian who offered soon after his arrival to meet me 'alone and unarmed' now tried another tactic to cover up the fresh defeats suffered by General Darling and win at least a breathing space for British diplomacy.

The United Nations was to consider a new appeal from Cyprus in December. Three weeks before this vital meeting an envoy was sent to call on Archbishop Makarios in his suite at the Grande Bretagne Hotel, Athens. He introduced himself as Mr Kenneth MacKenzie, editor of the English-language newspaper *Cyprus Mail* and correspondent for the London *Times*. Mr MacKenzie's brother happened to be the spokesman of the Foreign Office in London, but I do not know whether this fact was included among the credentials he offered; in any case the *Cyprus Mail* was notorious for its reactionary colonialist views. It was typical of British guile to use for a mission of this nature an intermediary who could always, if necessary, be disowned.

Mr MacKenzie somewhat surprised the Archbishop by assuring him that the Governor held him in high esteem and that the Premier, Mr Macmillan, also looked for his help in the sincere search which was being made in London for a solution. Foot, he went on, wanted the Archbishop to know that the British Government had now been brought round to see the Archbishop's proposal for independence in a favourable light: indeed, it was being given serious consideration. As for partition, it would be impolitic for the present to exclude this solution, but the Government thought the best way of disposing of it was to implement Macmillan's partnership plans far enough to secure the rights of the Turkish minority; after that they would tell the Turks that no further claims would be entertained. In view of these private assurances, Foot asked Makarios to persuade me to lay down my arms.

When the Archbishop inquired how the British Army would respond to such a gesture, Mr MacKenzie said that the army could not be called on for a cease-fire without precipitating a Tory backbench revolt in Parliament and infuriating Turkey. Avoiding any overt move, Foot would try to get the Security Forces to limit the scope and vigour of their operations, but the British campaign against EOKA must be seen to continue.

The Archbishop wrote to me about this curious offer, adding in his letter dated 9 November:

I replied that neither the continuation of EOKA action nor a cease-fire was a matter for me to decide. I deeply regretted the loss of life in Cyprus, but the responsibility rested entirely with the British Government. I added that I did not share his confidence in either Foot or the Government in London. . . .

The current deadlock is unpleasant for us in Cyprus, but it is no less so for the British. Once the partnership plan has collapsed for good, the British may well come to make concessions for the sake of reaching an agreement.

Makarios went on to join Averoff in asking for a suspension of EOKA attacks during the UN hearing. I objected that people would cease to take us seriously if we kept on offering one-sided truces, but I would be willing to limit my men to small-scale attacks which would suffice to keep the British on edge. Indeed, little effort was needed to do that, for enemy nerves were badly strained. On the day the Archbishop wrote the British Services dispensed with their entire force of Cypriot labour: this was their reaction to an explosion the previous night in an airmen's canteen at RAF, Nicosia. A powerful time bomb was smuggled into the airport by means of a grocer's delivery van and hidden in a settee by a waiter who had to stand behind the bar until it went off. About thirty airmen were listening to the British radio, which was remarking as usual that EOKA were at their last gasp, when the bomb went off. According to the official casualty list two men were killed and seven wounded, but our reports from inside the camp confirmed that the death roll alone was eight. Before the mass dismissals of Cypriot staff could be carried out all the Greeks at the airport were arrested and beaten by angry airmen: it was taken for granted that they were all EOKA.

On 16 November, after we had been trouncing the enemy without respite for six weeks, I issued the order to hold down attacks until further notice, accompanying it with congratulations to all ranks on their many successes. A few days later I heard from Averoff:

I am all admiration for your fight, and recent results have been outstanding. Be careful for yourself: I ask this not merely out of friendship but because I believe that your survival is essential to the struggle.

Our hopes at the UN are not brilliant. Only the Soviet Union, for its own purposes, could be expected to support an appeal for self-determination, but there is rising sympathy for the solution of independence.

It would be most helpful if you could formally suspend action for a spell of, say, ten days: you might proclaim that while the UN was considering the fate of Cyprus you would hold your hand and that if freedom is granted you would lay down your arms. . . . Naturally you will judge the situation for yourself, and if you agree with my advice it will be for you to draft the proclamation – a task you always carry out so well.

My reluctance to announce yet another cease-fire was strengthened by news of the death of Matsis, which reached me on the same day as Averoff's suggestion. In spite of my unannounced order to hold down activity, I had rejected similar appeals from the British Labour Party and I did not want to put out any statement which might be seized on as a sign of weakness. After thinking matters over, however, I decided to smooth the way for the UN appeal and on 22 November I issued a declaration that we would confine our action to retaliating against any British attacks while awaiting with calm the UN decision.

The British response to this move was consistent with the ambiguity of Mr MacKenzie's offer to Makarios: a show of toughness to please the Turks and Tories with nothing, in fact, to back it up. The Governor summoned his advisers the same night and announced that operations would go on 'for as long as is necessary to put down violence'. By thus brushing aside my goodwill gesture, Foot and Darling hoped to convince doubters that they were masters of a situation in which a handful of EOKA fighters were holding their 40,000 troops at bay. But though I understood the reason of false pride which prompted this reply and did not allow it to influence my actions I thought it proper to warn Averoff that I intended to renew the attack at once if nothing was settled at the UN. In fact, little enough came out of the debate until, at last a compromise resolution was passed on 6 December which merely called for continued efforts in the direction of a 'peaceful, just and democratic solution'. I ordered my groups on to the alert; in my view the resolution had shelved the issue for another year and, thanks to American intervention on Britain's side, we could hope for nothing practical. Averoff, however, disagreed. He wrote to me on 27 December[1]:

We were the victors at the UN: that is plain from the speeches, which all deplored partition and favoured independence. I am at present studying the minutes. . . . I don't know whether you read my impromptu reply to the Anglo-Turkish assault: it was quite an astonishing hymn of praise for EOKA. I shall send it to you.

[1] An extract from Mr Averoff's speech to the UN on 5 December 1958 is given Appendix 3.

On reading the delegates' speeches you would expect us to obtain a nine-tenths majority – yet we got nothing. (The original Greek resolution had to be withdrawn for lack of support.) I am now quite sure that what the delegates say in public is of no value; their votes are cast entirely on the basis of personal interest and the British and Turkish influence far outweighs ours.

I told Averoff in my reply that all our talk about independence was pointless so long as the British interpreted the word in a different way: the result might well be that we should end up with something which combined joint sovereignty and administrative partition. But I found to my surprise that Makarios also thought we had made progress since the delegates had spoken against partition, and he wrote to urge that, in spite of army operations, we should maintain our cease-fire:

All sides have tried to create an atmosphere of detente in the last few months, each for its own reasons. The Turks have internal problems to face. Greece wants to reduce tension and improve relations with Turkey. The British may have elections in the spring and so it is also in our interest to keep the situation steady in the hope that Labour will take office. The cease-fire must be maintained as long as possible. If, however, the British show no understanding or, worse still, try to force through the Macmillan Plan, then theirs will be the blame for forcing EOKA to hit back. A means will be found for letting the Governor know the conditions for maintaining the cease-fire. . . .

I agree with your view that Cyprus policy should be co-ordinated with EOKA activity. Any proclamation ending the cease-fire should therefore be issued in co-operation with the political leadership so that we can make the best use of the situation. Similarly, of course, the political leadership must keep you informed of all its ideas.

Under pressure of such representations from Athens, I had to keep the cease-fire going. The army took cowardly advantage of our restraint. Thousands of troops harassed the villages, looking for wanted men and arms; patrols forced people down to their knees at gunpoint to wash out patriotic slogans and a girl of eighteen was wounded in one of the clashes forced on villages by marauding soldiery. I ordered small-scale action – a few grenades and pressure bombs – to bring the army to its senses. Two of my men were in the death cells at the Central Prison at the time and Foot refused them a reprieve: the hangings were averted with only minutes to spare by a telephone message from London. In these unpropitious circumstances I received on 19 December a letter from the Consul in which he took it upon himself to reproach me for my policy of limited reprisals:

I must point out that the public find it difficult to justify the recent mine explosions. The atmosphere which has been created by political developments puts army actions – which in any case appear to be dying out – into secondary importance. Explanations should be offered so as to extend the current lull in operations into a truce.

This letter was accompanied by a message from Averoff which urged me to maintain complete calm and Mr Frydas also added some advice on the best way to justify the reprisals we had taken. These reprisals, however, were not yet at an end. Next morning two airmen were blown up by a pressure mine on the Karpass peninsula at Gallinopetra. So huge was the explosion under their truck that it disintegrated and pieces of the men's bodies were spread over 200 square yards. Even if I had wished to do so I could not have prevented this attack: it took place almost 100 miles away and no messenger could have got there in time to cancel the plan. To Mr Frydas's violent objections about this and another reprisal which took place at Agros I replied expressing surprise at the tone and contents of his protest:

The two groups which struck at the British acted within the spirit of my orders. The Gallinopetra action was taken after the army had cut off villages there for a fortnight and ill-treated the inhabitants: it was perfectly justified. In the other instance at Agros the villagers were also villainously ill-used by soldiers so the group there were also entitled to retaliate: you must also remember that Rotsides (one of my veteran guerrillas) was killed by the army in this area recently. The instructions suspending activity which I issued after receiving Mr Averoff's request had not yet reached these two groups, so in any case their actions were in order.

I went on to express my indignation that the Consul should ask us to answer for the deaths of two airmen, whereas it was the British who should have been arraigned for murdering Cypriots.

May I ask what you did to let the world know of the Greek woman who was shot lately at Letymbou or the robbery and wrecking tactics of the army during searches while we were talking about truces? These shameful military acts were never spoken of outside Cyprus, yet they alone more than justify our reprisals.

I closed this protest with a warning that if Mr Frydas and his friends in Athens disagreed with my policy towards the British then our ways must part: my honour allowed of no compromise.

The Consul apologised, saying that he should have framed his objections more carefully. I replied that I had no quarrel with him, but I had to express my disapproval of his outlook which, no doubt, was a reflection of the official mind in Athens. In any case, the matter of reprisals lay in the military sphere and I was suspicious of interference: what was the motive of this campaign?

I must protest against being confronted with proposals for dealing with the military side; I have already made it clear both to you and the Archbishop that I want no advice on how to go about my work. . . . All I see is unwillingness to back me up. What is the reason behind this? If they hope to make me give in, they hope in vain. I am ready as always to fight to the last bullet.

Since the decision on an official cease-fire could not be delayed much longer, I sent my aide Georgiades to Nicosia on 19 December to make my views clear at meetings with the Consul and the Bishop of Kitium. After careful thought I had decided that we should offer some response to the UN appeal for the creation of a peaceful atmosphere in which talks might proceed. At last, on Christmas Eve, I put out this proclamation:

LET THEM CHOOSE

The member states of the United Nations will judge between our attitude and that of the Tory Government in Britain. We have always respected UN decisions and will continue to do so. Accordingly, we shall now halt our activity for as long as the other side does so as well. Let us see how the British propose to act. We offer an opportunity for a solution in an atmosphere of peace. What will the enemy do?

My offer caught the British on the wrong foot: for political reasons it could be neither accepted nor totally rejected. On 1 January the Governor used the pretext of New Year's Day to call for the first time on the Bishop of Kitium and ask him what should be done to restore peace. The Bishop replied that EOKA had already stopped fighting and he was sorry that the British had not followed their example. He proposed that Foot should call off all army operations, free everyone detained without trial and call a halt to the partition campaign. Nothing came of the visit except a large-scale operation which Darling launched on 6 January in the Troodos mountains: this heralded a flying visit by the War Minister, Mr Christopher Soames. The result of a conference at Government House between Soames, Foot and the Service chiefs was to continue operations, while at the same time avoiding curfews and searches which would upset the population. It was only to be expected that Foot, a fortnight after his conciliatory call on the Bishop of Kitium, should now broadcast that his policy was still based on the Macmillan Plan and repeat the Harding phrase that there could be 'no bargaining with violence'.

So much for the façade in Cyprus, but behind the scenes in Athens and Ankara and above all Paris – where the Greek and Turkish Foreign Ministers were meeting under cover of NATO talks – events were moving. This movement, Averoff informed me, was in the direction of independence and such was the progress of the talks that the British feared their interests might be overlooked, especially as they could hardly reject a Cyprus solution on which both Greece and Turkey reached agreement.

For some time now I had been pressing for the formation of a widely based committee which would represent the vast mass of the people outside the actual combatant groups and would form a strong political front when the struggle was over. Its nucleus existed in a secret organisation called EAEM, the Unified National Front, which I had formed at the start of the passive resistance campaign, but all my attempts to build around it ran into resistance from the Consul and the Archbishop: they did not like the prospect of a political body which would owe allegiance to me. Now that the possibility of peace talks had arisen, I also raised the question of our representatives. To my letter pointing out that three of the five mayors who usually came forward to speak for Cyprus were Communists and suggesting that EAEM delegates should be invited instead to any such talks, the Consul replied on 8 January:

Mr Averoff agrees that we should consider how best to ensure that the voice of the fighting people of Cyprus is heard in the event of negotiations. We must also seek the opinion of the Archbishop. For my own part, I doubt whether EAEM is the best organisation to look to, but I shall say more about this later.

It may as well be said now that the Consul knew very well that EAEM members, loyal to me, would never swallow the Cyprus agreement which was even then being cooked up in secrecy. He must, like his masters in Athens, have realised that as long as I was isolated, absorbed in the struggle, restricted in my movements, dependent for information on people who could give or withhold whatever news they liked, there was a much better chance of imposing on the island a settlement of their choosing. When the time for talks came I should have accredited half a dozen carefully chosen EAEM delegates to represent the different towns and districts and they would have been armed with precise instructions, not left to their own devices to be influenced by the strongest wind which blew. As it was, I was left largely in ignorance of what the diplomats were plotting and although I sent Georgiades twice to Nicosia within the year he was told as little as possible both by the Consul and the Bishop of Kitium.

The British, especially towards the end, were far better informed than I on the sort of agreement which was being secretly prepared. Here, for instance, is an extract from a report sent me by one of our senior police contacts, Inspector George Lagoudontis, on 23 December:

I had a long talk with D'Olivera. [Chief Superintendent L. J. D'Olivera was one of the most important members of the British police in Cyprus.] He began by asking where I thought Grivas was, because a final solution was near. The Archbishop and the Greek Government would accept it, but Grivas would probably disagree and then might go on fighting. D'Olivera went on, 'We think Grivas's prestige is higher than Makarios's because he lives in constant danger in hiding while Makarios enjoys life in a luxury hotel. That's the one thing which worries us: if Makarios and Grivas fall out there will be no end to the trouble.'

A more practical concern at this time was Averoff's delays in the supply of urgently needed arms and ammunition. His excuse was that he feared they might fall into the hands of some group outside my direct control, such as the followers of the Bishop of Kyrenia, who had quarrelled with Makarios. Every underhand effort was used to delay or interrupt supplies. I protested on 19 January to the Bishop of Kitium, who was leaving for Athens, that Averoff was tricking us:

There is plenty of evidence of that. His behaviour has been very upsetting; I shall not forget it in a hurry. But anyone who thinks I shall give way for lack of arms is greatly mistaken. I can carry on for a long time yet. I wish you would take this up with the Archbishop and get some definite decision. If Athens is tired of discussing Cyprus we are not tired of fighting.

Two days earlier Averoff had gone to Paris to meet Zorlu and they had half a dozen meetings between 17 and 22 January in what was declared to be an optimistic atmosphere. Zorlu was willing to drop partition in exchange for the Turks having 30 per cent of the places in a Cypriot administration as well as military safeguards. In Cyprus itself army operations continued, but when politicians and newspapers protested that the army was endangering the peace talks, the Government said the soldiers were merely engaged in training exercises. These 'exercises' were in full swing when, on 5 February, I heard on the radio that the Prime Ministers of Greece and Turkey were flying to a meeting in Zurich where the fate of the island would be decided on lines which had now been agreed.

I decided at once to move up to Nicosia so as to follow and control events more closely. A businessman with interests in Athens, Mr Socrates Eliades, devised a compartment in one of his vehicles in which Georgiades and myself could travel secretly. The journey was described thus in my diary of 9 March 1959:

I left our refuge at 18.45 hours with Georgiades. We were accompanied by Maroulla Panayides and Elli Christodoulides to the place where we were to meet the lorry. We hid in the fields until it arrived. Niki Kyriakides was aboard and Socrates Eliades accompanied the vehicle in his car. While we were getting into the lorry another car coming towards us switched its head-lights on and we had to hide under the lorry. We left and arrived in Nicosia without trouble at 21.30 hours.

Niki Kyriakides, wife of the deacon, sat beside the driver and guided him to a new hideout which had been prepared in a Nicosia house. The Kyriakides thus became the only people who knew where I was, and took charge of my personal communications. Hardly had I arrived in the capital to learn the terms which were being considered than it was announced that the Cyprus problem was already solved. On 11 February, in the barely credible space of five days, Karamanlis and Menderes had achieved full agreement and Averoff and Zorlu flew to London to present it for the acceptance of the British. Karamanlis declared it to be the happiest day of his life. What were the terms? Through a haze of rumour, a guilty silence was maintained by the principals. Averoff announced that he had kept Makarios fully informed throughout the negotiations, but contrary to their usual practice neither of them sent any information to me. I also thought it strange that Averoff went directly from Zurich to London in-stead of returning to Athens to discuss the next step and inform those in Cyprus who were most closely concerned. What had become of the Arch-bishop's promise that he would sign no accord without obtaining the preliminary approval of at least 90 per cent of the Cypriot people? What of the pledge which Karamanlis had given to the Greek Parliament that he would seek its consent before signing anything? No more was heard of either undertaking. Instead, both parties did everything in their power to rush me into accepting their agreement before I knew what it contained. On 12 February, the day after the pact was initialled in Zurich, the Bishop of Kitium passed on to me a telephone message from Averoff in London which claimed that he had achieved all that could be hoped for in the circumstances: in his remaining task of overcoming British objections everything depended on the amount of support which could be rallied behind the Ethnarch. Averoff's message went on to say that what Makarios needed above all was an expression of EOKA's approval to show that the Cypriot people were united: this would also stop any mischief-making by the Communists.

But what *was* the agreement I was asked to approve? Here is the sum total which the Archbishop himself had supplied me with on its terms:

My information is that reports of 70 per cent representation for the Greeks are correct. It is also true that the British will keep a base in the island but untrue that the Turks will have a base of their own under NATO.

With this brief statement from Makarios the Consul sent a note of his own further urging me to offer my support. 'Serious dangers from the British side, from the Communists and from the Bishop of Kyrenia's followers could be forestalled if you repeated your declaration of the past that the Cypriot people must obey the Archbishop.' He added that the Foreign Minister would also write to me about the agreement as soon as he found time.

It was clear that my hand was being forced, and I wrote at once to the Bishop of Kitium on 13 February that I could not commit myself until I knew more about the agreement; for one thing, I could not accept the proposal to station Turkish troops in Cyprus, in whatever guise or under whichever aegis they came. I said that the leader of the armed struggle could not be expected to accept a note from the Consul which declared that the Foreign Minister had not yet found time to write and explain the agreement which had been reached. The best I could offer was to try to maintain the façade of unity while awaiting the terms. This was no easy promise, for the news from Zurich had received an icy welcome in Cyprus. To avoid further harm to the morale of the people I issued an appeal to all ranks for unity and obedience and said that I would issue my views on the agreement as soon as I was fully informed.

There can be no question of my betraying our struggle or the sacrifices of the suffering Cypriot population: all of you may be sure of that. I hearken only to the voice of Cyprus and so I ask only one duty of you: obedience to my orders. We must prove once again that we are faithful to the ideals of our motherland.

Now, on the same day, came an appeal from Makarios himself asking for my approval of the agreement, which he sketched in for the first time. Like Averoff, he argued that it was the best we could get. It would lay the foundations for a sovereign, independent state which would end the centuries of slavery. Greek soldiers as well as Turkish troops would be permanently quartered in the island; the President would be a Greek-Cypriot with a Turkish-Cypriot Vice-President who would have a right of veto in foreign affairs; Greeks would hold 70 per cent of the seats in Parliament. Makarios said that he was pleased with the agreement on the whole. His letter ended:

I think it would be as well to issue a proclamation giving your endorsement to the solution reached by the political leadership. I hope that we shall soon be in a position to meet and exchange views so that we can take joint decisions on the future. With much love, 'Haris'.

Since the information given me in this letter was so scanty, I expected further details before any more steps were taken, but on the 8 pm radio bulletin next day I was astonished to hear that the Archbishop had sent for twenty-five 'advisers' from Cyprus. As long ago as 10 November in the previous year I had written to ask the Bishop of Kitium to ensure that EOKA was properly represented at any peace talks, preferably by EAEM members, and in particular that the mayors should not be invited: because municipal elections had been repeatedly postponed these civic leaders could no longer be regarded as representing their own towns, still less the country as a whole. Yet without a word to me the Archbishop had summoned to London so-called representatives of his own choosing and the mayors were prominent among the delegates. In this way the military leader of the struggle was to be prevented from giving an opinion – his views were considered superfluous while those of nonentities were sought. From the first the facts of the agreement had been kept from me and now I was barred from nominating my representatives for the London meeting because they would never have accepted the terms, no matter what pressure was brought to bear on them.

Before I could find words to protest to Makarios he had arrived in London himself and next day, 15 February, the Consul sent me two letters, both imploring me to break my silence and approve the agreement: he offered a personal assurance from Averoff that only a small, token force of troops, in no way impairing the country's sovereignty, would be sent to Cyprus. I did not reply, and the Consul wrote again next day. He said that if the negotiations collapsed for lack of support a new breach would be opened in the West, where Russia was in favour of keeping Cyprus a trouble spot: if, however, EOKA subscribed to the agreement the Russians would draw back. There was still time to declare the support of the fighting people of the island, but the conference was due to end next day. This time the Consul enclosed a letter from Rodis Roufos, a member of the Greek Prime Minister's staff in London who had served in the consulate in Nicosia. Roufos gave me an assurance from Karamanlis that no better agreement could be obtained and conveyed his view that the presence of

Greek and Turkish troops would serve to guarantee the integrity of Cyprus. I replied without wasting words that I did not agree with the Greek Ministers that it was right to invite foreign troops to my country and I was waiting to see the text of the agreement.

On 19 February, while I was still largely in the dark about what had happened, the document was signed at a formal meeting in Lancaster House, London, by the Prime Ministers of Britain, Greece and Turkey; Makarios and the Turkish-Cypriot leader, Dr Kuchuk, added their signatures to bind Cyprus to its conditions. It was in this way, without the pretence of real consultation, in an atmosphere which I later learned was filled with promises and threats, that the fate of Cyprus was sealed. Now that it was done, Makarios wrote me what was meant to be a conciliatory letter: he had signed so as to bring an end to British sovereignty and 'create a little Greece at the end of the Mediterranean'. The Archbishop tried to explain away the concessions granted to the Turks as being 'no more than had been promised to safeguard their rights': the presence of foreign troops was dependent on the alliance which had been created between Greece, Turkey and the new Cyprus republic – if that alliance lapsed the troops would have to leave. All this led up to yet another sugar-coated appeal for me to endorse what had been done behind my back and without my leave:

Accept my warm congratulations for your splendid achievements and the heroic spirit which you injected into the people. Today's happy consummation is primarily due to your efforts. I feel sure that you will now agree that it is time for a strong statement of support for the agreement from EOKA. This will show the unity of the national front to everyone. . . .

Nothing was mentioned in this letter about the bases which had been granted to the British; this unhappy topic was left to the Bishop of Kitium, who gave me the completely inaccurate report that these military zones would be no larger than the areas occupied by British installations already and that no roads would be included. He added what he called his personal opinion that the British would soon have to abandon these bases and even suggested that under international law Cyprus might be able to denounce the very treaty which made her independent and thus get the British out! The Bishop having sweetened, as he thought, the pill, then came out with the familiar appeal:

No one has opposed the agreement except the Communists whose ostensible objections to the bases question was prompted by Moscow. . . . I hope, therefore, that you will have no more hesitation over issuing a proclamation in favour of it.

Not until 21 February did I receive Averoff's promised explanation of what he called 'the essence of the agreement', yet though he knew that no one had a more intimate understanding of the military issues than myself, his letter contained nothing of value about the bases. I replied that he had left me still in ignorance, but that if what I had heard was true I had serious objections. The answer to this – from the Consul – was a message of regret that full details were 'not available', yet it was four days since the agreement had been signed in London and twelve days since it had been initialled in Zurich. Next day the Consul sent me what he referred to as the text of the agreement, and it was not until later that I found it was not complete. These are the actual documents I received from the Consulate on 23 February:

1. A declaration accepting the agreement, signed by Harold Macmillan, C. Karamanlis and A. Menderes.
2a. The basic structure of the Republic of Cyprus.
2b. Treaty of Guarantee preserving the territorial integrity of the Republic.
2c. Treaty of Alliance between Cyprus, Greece and Turkey which allowed Greece to station 950 troops and Turkey 650 in Cyprus.

There was, however, another document which was not sent to me. It was the most important of them all: a declaration by the United Kingdom which set out two large and ill-defined areas which the British would keep for bases, together with an Annexe in which they reserved the right to make free use of roads, ports, airfields and public services of all kinds, among a variety of other privileges. Some of these points were mentioned next day in the Press and I also discovered by way of a newspaper interview with Foot that the British were demanding many other sites outside the two main base areas at Episkopi-Akrotiri and Dhekelia. I at once brought the interview to the attention of the Consul with the following comment:

If this news is true we shall have British soldiers all over Cyprus. . . . The disastrous effects of an agreement which was drawn up too hurriedly and in the absence of expert advice will soon become apparent.

The reply was a prevaricating letter in which the Consul said he did not have the minutes of the negotiations to study but he suggested that the Foot interviews might be typical of many similar British statements which were being put out to appease extremists in England who talked of a 'sell-out' in Cyprus. He argued that in practice the British would have difficulty even in maintaining camps and sites they already occupied with the 5,000 troops which, it was said, they meant to keep in the island when the garrison was reduced.

What was I to make of this answer? That the Consul was also ignorant of what had been agreed about the bases? Either he had been told nothing or he had been told not to tell me what he knew. The fact remained, as I wrote to the Consul in reply, that the British could at any time take over every key point in the island and have the use of all the roads they liked. In other words, Cyprus remained in virtual occupation of the British Army.

Such, then, was the surrender which I was expected to acclaim as the vindication of our struggle and Averoff tried later to make the Greek Parliament believe that EOKA was represented among the Archbishop's advisers who agreed to it. He used as a pretext for this assertion the fact that the Nicosia head of PEKA, our political propaganda chief, Tassos Papadopoulos, was among those called to London. As I have explained, none of these advisers was sent by me or went with my instructions, but as it happens Papadopoulos was one of a small minority who held out against the agreement to the last. After it had been forced through he wrote to me from London of the shameful flattery and promises used by the Greek Ministers to win over the Cypriot delegates, while at the same time Averoff and Karamanlis threatened Makarios with the withdrawal of all support if he rejected the Zurich terms. Under intense pressure from all sides Makarios capitulated and the delegates voted in favour of the agreement by 27 votes to 8. Papadopoulos said in his letter of 26 February:

The impression was created in London that I represented EOKA and people even avoided committing themselves in my presence. I made it clear to them that I spoke only for myself.

This statement is evidence enough that EOKA had nothing to do with the London Agreement. Once he had signed it, Makarios was as desperate as Averoff for some demonstration of EOKA approval. Papadopoulos quoted the Archbishop in his letter of 26 February:

Indirect approval even would help, such as an official greeting from the Leader on the Archbishop's return, or perhaps a PEKA leaflet hinting that EOKA was non-political but had full faith in the political leadership.

Receiving no encouragement from me, Makarios told Papadopoulos that he was worried by the chilly reception being given to the agreement in Cyprus and asked him to go there in advance of his own return so as to try and influence public opinion. It seemed that the Archbishop hoped at least to gain a few words of support from a PEKA leader since he understood at last that none would come from me.

CHAPTER FOURTEEN

The Plot that Failed

I HAVE said that every means of pressure was employed by the Greek Government and their friends to force the Zurich agreement down our throats, but I have yet to tell how their efforts in London were out-matched in Cyprus itself, where our allies and our enemies combined together against the one man who continued to bar the road to national betrayal. The story is so bizarre as to remind one of some cloak-and-dagger story, but I shall allow the facts to speak for themselves and let the reader judge.

On 19 February, the day when the agreement in London was signed, I received the following letter from the Consul, Mr Frydas:

Anastasis has notified me that from things said by the Governor and British Ministers it seems highly probable that they know the Leader's hiding place and are only refraining from arresting him on a temporary basis because of the present political developments.

Anastasis was the code-name of the Consul-General, Mr Vlachos, who had gone to London with Averoff's mission, and I soon decided that this warning was either a British trick or the result of a conspiracy between the British and Greek Ministers, incredible as that might seem. For a start, I was convinced that the British had no idea where I was living. My move from Limassol had been accomplished in total secrecy ten days before and the only persons who knew my whereabouts were Deacon Kyriakides and his wife Niki, my companion Antonis Georgiades and the owners of the house, who were completely trustworthy. To this very day no one else knows where I was staying in Nicosia and the hide which was built in the house before my arrival was completely secure. I read the warning note again and this, I decided, was the message it was intended to convey to me: 'You are in danger of arrest unless you quickly accept the agreement signed in London.' For the time being, I decided to give the Greek Government the benefit of the doubt and replied briefly that the British must be bluffing; if they really knew where I was hiding they would act at once. I could not believe they could resist the triumph of arresting me after their years of vain search and I added: 'I know how to fight. I have waited for them before and I will wait for them now.'

The British did not come. But nine days later, on 28 February, they tried another tack. Two police officers, Detective-Sergeants Wilson and Dawson, visited a Nicosia businessman, Leonidas Markides, who was connected with EOKA. They questioned him politely about Socrates Eliades: where he lived, what his work was, his political sympathies: all rather pointless since Eliades was well known in the commercial life of the capital. The real purpose of their visit emerged only when they had thanked Markides and left again.

Markides sent me a report[1] explaining that during the detectives' visit to his office one of them had opened a brief case to extract a file on Eliades. In doing so he dropped some papers on the floor, which he at once picked up. When the two policemen had gone, Markides bent down to switch off the electric fire and saw that an envelope remained, half-hidden by his desk. It was stamped in English SECRET and TOP SECRET. It was unsealed and inside were documents that appeared to be of great significance. Markides immediately passed the envelope and its contents to one of his contacts in EOKA, who saw it on his way to me.

The envelope was dropped at noon, but apart from a telephone message Markides heard no more from the detectives until 8.30 pm, when Wilson called at his home to say that he had lost an envelope containing important documents – it might be in any of eight places which he had visited during the morning. Markides volunteered to go to his office and look for the envelope. Within the hour he telephoned Wilson's hotel, as arranged, but Wilson was out. It was not until next day, 1 March, at 9 am that Wilson telephoned again. Markides simply said he had found nothing and was not troubled by the police again. On the face of it, this seemed an obvious hoax. Was I really expected to believe that experienced intelligence agents went about flinging packets of secret papers under the desks of EOKA members? And that, having done so, they did not bother to search for them, but took the EOKA man's word on the telephone instead?

The envelope was in my hands within a few hours. I found that it contained police photographs, taken from a distance, of Deacon Anthimos Kyriakides and Socrates Eliades, as well as two official documents. The first of these, dated 24 February 1959, read as follows:

SECRET

To Majr McGowan,
    Sir
Reference to the report which I sned you on 18 February I now beg to report that as you told me surveillance has been done on the priest Anthimos.

[1] Appendix 4.

A. He has been constantly seen moving about in Nicosia old city and contacting all sorts of peoples including three places which are already under suspicion about EOKA.

B. Also on 20 February he was followed by Andreas to Larnaca rd No. 22. Nearby the RAF HQ there.

C. Also on several occasions the wanted terrorist Andonis Georgiades has been watched entering into the house of the priest at Maria Singlidiki St no 1. Andreas says also he has seen the detainee person Fidias Kariolimus visiting there. This man was also in Omorphita wich you remeber.

D. I wish ti say that surveillance on the priests house is not very good to do because of the locality and the people etc but the priest Anthimos is truly careless and can be followed most easily. He has no ideas about all these things.

P S Selim Mustapha.

At the foot of this was a handwritten comment:

D/Sgt Wilson

Please see the attached report. I don't want to discourage Selim who is doing well but please try to get him to improve his standard of typing and presentation.

GMcG H.I.

The second document read:

SECRET

SPECIAL BRANCH — MEMO PAD

TO D/Sgt Wilson

DATE 25 Feb 59
REF

FROM Major McGowan

TEXT OF MESSAGE:

1. Will you please carry out discrete inquiries regarding Socrates ELIADES of 22 LARNACA Rd. As I explained to you yesterday he is believed to belong to the EOKA clique who may be inclined to oppose the 'agreement' and in addition information at our disposal leads us to believe he is in close contact with Mr. 'X'. There is also the arms issue.

2. You may remember that Anthimos, the Deacon of the Ecclesiastical Court, who is believed to be 'X's personal courier, was followed on 20 Feb to the house of S.E.

3. I would like to know soonest his political and social connections.

4. Surveillance photos are attached.

G. T. McGowan
H.I.

A study of these documents confirmed my impression that the whole affair had been staged, and not very cleverly staged at that. The clumsy attempts at verisimilitude, such as Major McGowan's comments on the standard of the Turkish constable's clerical work, did not obscure the emptiness of the supposed operation: there was no reason whatever for the British to follow my men since the agreement had already been signed and on the day the documents were dropped Foot announced a total amnesty. If this had been simply a final attempt on the part of the Intelligence service to catch me I should not have been disturbed. But there were clear indications that either Makarios or Averoff – or both men – were at the bottom of it. First, I had given my views of the agreement to no one in Cyprus except the Consul and the Bishop of Kitium, so where did the British get their idea that an 'EOKA clique' was opposing it? Secondly, there was the reference to Socrates Eliades and 'the arms issue'. Eliades had, in fact, taken delivery of a cargo of smuggled guns for EOKA in the first week of January and this was the only consignment he received: its delivery was known only to Makarios, Averoff and Andreas Azinas in Athens, and to the Bishop of Kitium, the Consul Frydas, Deacon Anthimos and the man in whose house the guns were hidden, a Nicosia dentist called Andreas Lambrou. Where did the British learn about these guns and why did they not seize them? On 19 February Eliades moved them by lorry to Lambrou's house from another place in Nicosia and Deacon Anthimos called there later: why were these movements not spotted by the police who were supposed to be watching Eliades and Anthimos?

Then there was the puzzling reference to Antonis Georgiades: after myself the most wanted man in Cyprus. Why, if he were seen visiting Anthimos's house 'on several occasions', was he not arrested? The truth is that Georgiades visited the house only once, on 17 January, for a meeting with the Bishop of Kitium and Frydas. How did it come about that the police at once recognised Georgiades, who was known to them only through a bad photograph, and yet failed to spot the Bishop and the Consul, two of the best-known men in Cyprus whom they saw every day?

I turned then to consider Sergeant Mustapha's report that Phidias Kareolemos, an EOKA member, had visited Anthimos. This again was false: Kareolemos, I found, had been released from detention on 22 February and since then had met the Deacon only once in the street, when they walked a short way together.

A final piece of evidence showed this plot up for what it was. Police-Sergeant Mustapha Selim had been passing us information for some time through Lagoudontis, so that Socrates Eliades was able to question him about the report he was supposed to have written to Detective-Sergeant Wilson. It turned out that the report was a forgery: Selim Mustapha had not written it and knew nothing about the circumstances. If, in fact, he had been ordered by his British chiefs to make such inquiries about our men or to help in faking the documents he would certainly have exploited the opportunity of telling Lagoudontis or Eliades.

That was the end of this shabby and dishonest effort to stampede me into a public acceptance of the settlement. I called Deacon and Mrs Anthimos and told them to carry on with their work as usual. They saw that my messages were dispatched safely until the day I left Cyprus without further word from the police.

Archbishop Makarios ended his exile on 1 March 1959, but my bitterness over the agreement was such that EOKA took no part in his Nicosia reception: I did not even send a representative to bid him welcome in spite of Averoff's windy phrase in Parliament the day before that 'the whole of Cyprus, with heroic Dighenis at its head, is gathering as one man to hail Makarios, creator of the independent state'. The crowds were big enough, but they were not acclaiming the agreement, merely the return of their Ethnarch.

The fighting groups were told not to be concerned over my silence, which would be broken in due course. In the meanwhile they were to ignore the amnesty offered by Foot on 28 February. I had decided that unless every one of our men was freed at once I should stay in Cyprus to share their fate.

On 3 March, having received a note from the Archbishop asking for a meeting, I sent Georgiades to see him. My aide returned next day with the following outline of what he had been told: Makarios had agreed with Karamanlis on a general framework for a settlement before the Greek Premier left for Zurich, but these limitations had been exceeded and when the Archbishop went to London pressure was used to make him accept the terms. When Georgiades asked why Dighenis had not been kept informed of the negotiations and invited to send representatives to the London talks the Archbishop replied that events had moved too fast.

The time had come for my decision: should it be peace or war? Was I to consider the struggle ended or should it be carried into another and still wider stage? To fight the British and the Turks as well was nothing new for EOKA, but since Makarios had signed the agreement he would turn against us if we renewed the struggle, taking with him part of the population, large or small. The Greek Government would also try to turn the Greek public against EOKA as well as withdrawing all diplomatic support from us. The prospect of civil war among the Greek Cypriots was a nightmare; yet if Cyprus had offered more space for manoeuvre and easier communication with the outside world for arms supplies I would have seriously considered turning Greek against Greek in the confidence that I should quickly master the situation. Unhappily I had to decide that as things were the odds against carrying on the war in Cyprus were overwhelming. There would be endlessly prolonged bloodshed, but no final victory for either side. In the end I decided with a heavy heart that I must call a final cease-fire, leaving the Archbishop and his friends to implement the agreement as best they could in the absence of my approval.

Once I had come to this decision I had to face the practical question of the amnesty. Our men who had been detained in camps without trial were released on 22 February, but Foot had tried to put conditions about the release of convicted men. His plan was to let them out of prison in two stages. Minor offenders would be discharged first, but those convicted on more serious charges, including acts of violence against the person, would have their sentences reviewed over a period of two months: there were about seventy such men, including thirty-one who had been taken to prisons in Great Britain. It was proposed that these seventy should have the alternative of serving their sentences in Cyprus or going to Greece and remaining there for the same period. Men still awaiting trial on serious charges could leave for Greece at once, but others who were on the run – having avoided arrest or escaped from custody – would no longer be pursued.

I refused outright to accept these terms and laid down my own conditions in a letter to the Consul on 28 February. 'By amnesty', I wrote, 'I mean a complete and universal amnesty without the qualification of the so-called review.' Since now, even more than ever before, the British wanted me out of the island they would have to pay the proper price:

The Leader will not leave the island before the fate of every single person has been determined. He will thus be obliged to remain in Cyprus for two months. . . .

And of my means of departure I wrote this:

The Leader desires that no British person should come near him or accompany him. The Leader will himself decide on the means of transport to be used when the time comes. Armed escort is essential: but if the Greek Government cannot supply one he will not insist, and no one need trouble further. He wishes to carry his pistol for his personal safety.[1]

[1] The full text of this letter is given in Appendix 5.

In the Consul's reply on 3 March he wrote that Averoff had told the British that I, and anyone whom I wanted to accompany me to Athens, should leave with our weapons. EOKA arms would be collected and handed over to the Republic when it came into being. While the question of the amnesty was still to be decided, Foot had listed seventeen leading EOKA men who must leave Cyprus, and Averoff suggested that I should take them with me on my return to Greece. The Consul's letter continued:

The Government proposes to send a sufficient number of Dakota aircraft or, if you prefer, a warship. Concerning the honours to be bestowed on you, the Minister says it is impossible for you to reject them because it is the general wish, a wish shared by the King and Queen, the Prime Minister, the Government and the whole people, with the possible exception of the Communists. The Minister believes that among other honours you cannot refuse your recall to active service, your promotion to the rank of lieutenant-general and the award of the Grand Cross. The Minister is trying hard to come over to Cyprus himself so as to escort you and your companions when you leave. His opinion is that if events move quickly and honourable terms are achieved for yourself and your men it would be as well for you to make up your mind as soon as possible. He fears that the prolongation of your stay in Cyprus may expose you to unfortunate incidents vis-à-vis uncontrolled Turks or British. Finally, the Minister asks me to say that he looks forward with great emotion to meeting you.

In my reply I urged Averoff to do all in his power to prevent Foot from exiling the seventeen EOKA men, adding that I would consult with Makarios about the whole question of the amnesty. I repeated that I had no wish for honours. Then I sent a firm message to the Archbishop insisting that the seventeen – of whom ten were my group leaders – should be allowed to go free in Cyprus. After hesitations and delays the Governor had to give way and on 8 March he announced new amnesty terms which were a great improvement on his first offer. Everyone was to be released at the same time, no one was to suffer years of exile and the only condition remaining was that the EOKA men serving sentences in England must stay out of Cyprus until the Republic was declared: they were, in fact, removed to Rhodes, the nearest Greek island to Cyprus, where their relatives were able to visit them, and they were made much of by the populace. At the same time arrangements for the hand-in of EOKA arms were finalised.

All that remained was to issue the order for the last cease-fire. I did this on 9 March 1959. I showed the proclamation to the Archbishop and deleted, at his request, certain phrases which he thought would undermine whatever faith the public had in the settlement achieved. I also issued a private order to the groups explaining my unhappiness at the agreements and the reasons why, nonetheless, I had found it necessary to accept them.[1]

That evening I talked for over three hours with Makarios at a rendezvous in Nicosia and listened to his personal explanation of signing the agreement under pressure. A historic struggle was ended and with sorrow in my heart I prepared to take leave of the country of my birth, the island for whose freedom I had fought. I had longed to live once more among the Cypriot people for a brief while after we had laid down our arms and I had hoped to be able to pay homage to the graves of my men who had fallen. It grieved me that the British would not allow me this gesture: even now they were unable to rise to an occasion. Instead, I had to meet some of my group leaders in secret at the home of Socrates Eliades, taking strict security precautions, for I knew that the enemy would sacrifice anything, even their honour, to capture me. Later, at the home of another leading businessman, Mr Gabrielides, I met some fifty prominent members of EOKA and shook the hand of each. Many of them had never seen me before and I was deeply moved to think that they had obeyed to the letter the orders of the shadowy, mysterious figure whom they addressed with pride as 'Leader'. They had long awaited this meeting with the man who had guided and inspired them and I was just as eager to thank them for the loyalty and self-sacrifice they had brought to the task of carrying out my orders. I entered the room where they were gathered and everyone stood up. I walked around, embracing them in turn, and in their eyes I read the pride they felt in the campaign we had fought. When I saw the glowing faces of those young men who had for years been no more to me than so many code names on a scrap of paper, when I thought of all those others who had died so gloriously in the cause of freedom, I could not restrain my tears.

When the greetings were done we had a meal together and spoke for some hours about their future, the future of the Organisation and of Cyprus. Then I took my leave in a speech of farewell and gave them my final 'order': love and concord between you all. Driving away from the house with Georgiades, I wondered if these gallant companions would find the right leader in the struggle for peace. Men of action always follow the path they have chosen to the end; but this very tenacity of purpose means that if they are set on the wrong course they cannot leave it.

Next evening I went to the Consul's house in Nicosia to prepare for my departure. My programme had already been arranged: I would leave for Athens next day in the Prime Minister's personal aircraft with an escort of the Royal Hellenic Air Force. The Minister of Foreign Affairs

[1] These documents are given in Appendices 6 and 7.

would accompany me in the first plane if his duties made it possible. I would be received on behalf of the Greek Government by Lt-Gen. Paparodos, Deputy Chief of the General Staff, his aide, diplomatic officials and a guard of honour from the Greek armed forces. At Athens airport I would be received by the representative of His Majesty King Paul of the Hellenes, the Minister of Foreign Affairs (unless he came to Cyprus to escort me), the Minister to the Presidency, the Under-Secretary for National Defence, the Archbishop of Athens with other Church dignitaries, the Commanders-in-Chief of the Army and Air Force, the Mayor of Athens with other civic personalities. The Air Force would provide the Guard of Honour and band. A popular welcome was to be arranged and I was to lay a wreath at the tomb of the Unknown Warrior, where there would be a guard of honour composed of cadet officers. After a reception by the Prime Minister I was invited next day to the Palace where King Paul would confer on me the Grand Cross of the Order of George I with Swords.

On the morning of 17 March I was driven by the Greek Consul with Georgiades to the house of a friend, where I met the Archbishop, a number of people, both men and women, who had given valuable services to the struggle, and a small group of newspapermen. I thanked them all for their help and urged the journalists to continue working for the national cause. The only foreigner there was the Editor of the English newspaper *The Times of Cyprus*, Mr Foley, and to him I said: 'In both world wars I was a firm friend of the British and fought by their side. Later Britain acquired a relentless enemy when I realised that they preferred to keep my countrymen in slavery. Now I can be your friend again, but only when you have remedied in full the injustice done to Greece and my own motherland of Cyprus.'

While I was talking to the group, news of my presence spread outside the house and a small crowd began to gather. It would only be a matter of minutes before the whole of Nicosia came to know that I was there, and so, at the Archbishop's suggestion, I left for the airport with the Consul, escorted there by the Archbishop and others in a second car. The road to the airport was quiet and few people saw me leave. An RAF officer gave us directions at the gates and we were shown into an anteroom where we waited until two aircraft of the Royal Hellenic Air Force landed at 9.45 am. Almost before their wheels stopped on the tarmac, my friends from Athens began to jump out to greet me. I was delighted to see among them Lt-Gen. Paparodos, Brig. Psaroudakis, Lt-Cols. Asymakopolos and Papadopoulos, all of whom had fought under my command during the German occupation. I embraced them affectionately and shook hands with the air crews. Then, after taking leave of the Archbishop, I boarded the first aircraft with my aide, Antonis Georgiades. Deacon Anthimos Kyriakides and the Bishop of Kitium, whom I had invited to attend my reception in Athens, also took their seats in the first plane.

As we flew over Rhodes I was put in touch by radio-telephone with the Cypriot fighters released from British prisons. At 2.30 pm we touched down at Hellenikon Airport: after nearly five years I trod the soil of free Greece again and saw loved faces before me. To all the welcoming speeches I replied with natural and obvious emotion. A million people lined the eight-mile route to Athens and packed into the squares of the capital to cheer the leader of the Cyprus struggle. Before this joyful and spontaneous demonstration I bowed my head – until we were flying over Rhodes no one but the officials concerned knew that we were on our way. When I saw the common man, the humblest worker, standing by the roadside to applaud the man who at that moment represented the glory of Greece, I knew then, as surely as I know that one day I will die, that the Greek Cypriots and the men of free Greece are one people, indivisible. How much deeper was my bitterness, then, at leaving the Cypriots before they could be given the full freedom of union with Mother Greece.

My conscience is at ease. I did my duty, as I saw it, to the end. But the Cypriot people, who fought so bravely and for so long, deserved a better fate than the shackles which were forged for them in Zurich; and those who bound the people's hands behind their backs in London carry the full responsibility for what they did.

APPENDIX I

Preparatory General Plan

Drawn up by General Grivas in Athens two years before the
start of the struggle in Cyprus.

1. THE OBJECTIVE

To arouse international public opinion, especially among the allies of Greece, by deeds of heroism and self-sacrifice which will focus attention on Cyprus until our aims are achieved. The British must be continuously harried and beset until they are obliged by international diplomacy exercised through the United Nations to examine the Cyprus problem and settle it in accordance with the desires of the Cypriot people and the whole Greek nation.

2. THE PROCEDURE

Activity will be aimed at causing so much confusion and damage in the ranks of the British forces as to make it manifest abroad that they are no longer in complete control of the situation. The campaign will be carried out on three fronts:

1. Sabotage against Government installation and military posts.
2. Attacks on British forces by a considerable number of armed fighting groups.
3. Organisation of passive resistance by the population.

Because of the difficulties in the way of a large-scale guerrilla struggle, including the unsuitable terrain, the main weight of the campaign will be placed on sabotage, and therefore the chief task of the fighting groups will be to support and cover the work of the saboteurs by upsetting and diverting the Government forces. Should events take a favourable turn and if sufficient weapons become available, armed activity might be increased in scale and intensity. Success will not be achieved by minor and intermittent attacks but only by a continuous campaign aimed at getting important results. It should not be supposed that by these means we should expect to impose a total material defeat on the British forces; our purpose is to bring about a moral defeat by keeping up the offensive until the objectives stated in the first paragraph of this plan are realised.

While this campaign proceeds care will be taken to neutralise any counter-action on the part of British agents and to punish severely any Cypriots who work for the enemy or act against our interests.

The moral support of the whole Greek nation is needed. It should be made clear to the world that the people of Greece are behind the Cypriots to a man.

This support will be shown by (1) demonstrations in all Greek cities; (2) public applause for our campaign immediately it starts; (3) denunciations of the violence and pressure used by the British against an unarmed people. Propaganda through newspapers, leaflets etc must be used to enlighten public opinion in Greece.

All preparations for working out the above plan at the proper time will be carried out by a Committee for the Cyprus Struggle to be set up in Athens for the purpose.

DETAIL OF REVOLUTIONARY ACTIVITY IN CYPRUS

A: Sabotage. Sabotage will be undertaken by special groups which will remain within the areas of their activity, living in the towns or villages where they work. Only if their identity becomes known will saboteurs be moved to places fixed in advance and from there to the mountain areas where they will become guerrillas.

Targets will be selected by the Field Commander, who will also arrange for special cover for the saboteurs by fighting groups when this is necessary. All groups will be under the immediate orders of their leaders who, in turn, will take their orders from the Field Commander.

Weapons: Saboteurs will carry pistols and grenades. They will use time-bombs, dynamite, anti-personnel and ordinary mines; also, possibly, magnetic mines.

The formation of these sabotage groups at the different centres, the securing of supplies etc will be carefully studied and decided upon by the Field Commander, who will make a personal reconnaissance of the island before the movement starts. In any case, each of the following areas will have one sabotage group to start with: Nicosia, Famagusta, Larnaca, Dhekelia base, Limassol, Episkopi, Paphos, Lapithos, Kyrenia, Pedhoulas-Lefka.

Sabotage support groups will be formed to cover the work of the saboteurs on a predetermined plan by harrying Government forces, cutting their line of communication, and attacking police stations from which help might be sent, if things go well these groups will increase their activities as time goes on, so a store of suitable material for them must be built up in Cyprus.

B: Guerrilla groups will be formed, starting with the following five: three in the Olympus area, one at Pentadactylos and one in reserve. The groups will be as follows:

Olympus groups: 1. Kykko–Stavros area: Sector of activity: the road between Lefka, Pedhoulas, Kykko Monastery and Stavros. Force: eight men. Armament: one machine-gun, two stens, eight rifles.

2. Chrysoroyiatissa Monastery area: Sector of activity: the village of Khrysokhou up to Kykko Monastery. Prodromos and Platres. Force, eight men. Armanent: one automatic, one machine-gun, two stens, six rifles.

3. Troodos village area: Sector of activity: Kakopetria, Ayios Epiphanios, Makheras Monastery, Lefkara, and west of the mountain occupied by Chrysoroyiatissa groups. Force and armament as Chrysoroyiatissa groups.

Pentadactylos Groups: Sector of activity: Kyrenian mountain range from Apostolos Andreas to Myrtou and Lapithos. Force: twenty-three men. Armament: two machine-guns, one automatic tommy gun, ten rifles. This force will be divided into three sub-groups. N.B. The formation and strength of the strike groups was based on armaments already available. They can be extended if more weapons are forthcoming in the future.

Reserve forces: One (?) heavy machine-gun, eight stens, twenty-two rifles are available to arm men who would be used either to support the strike and sabotage groups or to form new strike groups in areas which may need them as the struggle develops. The positioning of these reserves would be determined from time to time. They could also be increased as more arms came in.

Each strike group should have its own permanent centre, but this can be varied within each sector to make it more difficult for the enemy to find them. Each group must also have to decide on a place of refuge in its own area, to be used both as a jumping-off point for attack or as a shelter to hide in when the odds become too great. The tactics of groups attacked by superior forces will not be to stand and fight back unless they have orders to do so for the purposes of a special mission; instead, they will escape in dribs and drabs to confuse the Government forces to a regrouping point chosen in advance. All strike groups will be equipped with mines to blow up roads, bridges and Government property.

Note: I do not believe the number of strike groups should be increased at present, for a higher number would find it harder to find hiding places and their chance of escape under attack would be lessened: the terrain should appear empty so as to avoid attracting troops and facilitate escape. It will be possible to increase groups as the struggle goes on so long as the opportunities for concealment and escape are as good as ever.

C: Passive resistance. To attain our final objectives and at the same time to help the striking and sabotage groups we shall organise passive resistance among the population so that we can anywhere and at any time upset the balance of the enemy and raise the people's morale. The population must be organised into a single internal front to boycott the British and their Cypriot agents and take part in protest demonstrations against oppressive measures by the Government. (The Cypriot agents will also be watched and special groups will undertake the execution of anyone and everyone considered dangerous to the cause.) Another important aim is the enlightenment of public opinion through the illegal Press and an information department will send out news to the committee in Athens which will see that it is given publicity. Organisation of civilians will be arranged under a responsible leader in each district.

D: Intelligence. Special centres will amass information on the movement of British forces in Cyprus, on military targets to be neutralised; on the movements and activities of the enemy so that we can counteract their intentions. These centres will be kept informed in turn by the Field Commander of what they ought to know. At the start these centres will probably be organised by district.

E: Supplies. Each group will buy its own foodstuffs through a supply agent, who will choose a base for each group's supplies and see that it is kept stocked. This base must be moved occasionally and always kept a long way from the base used by the group itself. In addition, each group will have a reserve supply of tinned food for emergency; this must be made good as soon as any of it is used.

GENERAL: Houses and other hiding places must be found by all groups ready for the accommodation of our people, either because they are about to strike nearby or because they are in danger of arrest.

ESSENTIAL PREPARATIONS

1. The dispatch of arms to Cyprus. This is in hand.
2. A visit to Cyprus of the Field Commander who will go into the objectives of the plan in detail and draw up orders for the various groups and formations. This requires at least three months.
3. Arrangements for supplying everything required for the struggle so as to ensure that material support will never be lacking.
4. Organisation of a fund to help the families of men who fall in the struggle.

EOKA's First Revolutionary Leaflet.
Distributed on 1 April 1955.

PROCLAMATION

With the help of God, with faith in our honourable struggle, with the backing of all Hellenism and the help of the Cypriots, WE HAVE TAKEN UP THE STRUGGLE TO THROW OFF THE ENGLISH YOKE, our banners high, bearing the slogan which our ancestors have handed down to us as a holy trust – DEATH OR VICTORY.

Brother Cypriots, from the depths of past centuries all those who glorified Greek history while preserving their freedom are looking to us: the warriors of Marathon, the warriors of Salamis; the 300 of Leonidas and those who, in more recent times, fought in the epic Albanian war. The fighters of 1821 are looking to us – those fighters who showed us that liberation from the yoke of ruler is always won by bloodshed. All Hellenism is looking to us, and following us anxiously, but with national pride.

Let us reply with deeds. Let us be worthy of them. It is we showed the world that international diplomacy is UNJUST and in many ways COWARDLY, and that the Cypriot soul is brave. If our rulers refuse to give us back our freedom, we shall claim it with our own HANDS and with our own BLOOD. Let us show the world once more that the neck of the contemporary Greek refuses to accept the yoke. Our struggle will be hard. The ruler has the means and he is strong in numbers. We have the heart, and we have RIGHT on our side and that is why we WILL WIN.

Diplomats of the World

Look to your duty. It is shameful that, in the twentieth century, people should have to shed blood for freedom, that divine gift for which we too fought at your side and for which you, at least, claim that you fought against Nazism.

Greeks

Wherever you may be, hear our call: FORWARD ALL TOGETHER FOR THE FREEDOM OF OUR CYPRUS.

EOKA,
The Leader,
Dighenis.

Extract from the speech of H.E. Engelo Averoff-Tossizza, Minister of Foreign Affairs in the Royal Hellenic Government, at the United Nations on 5 December 1958.

The British and Turkish delegates here have upbraided the militants of Cyprus, calling them a band of assassins without ideals to defend. Mr Noble has gone so far as to tell us that they are gangsters. I do not know what the ideals of London gangsters may be; I suppose there are all sorts of them in the underworld. But, of course, they have nothing to do with the principles of liberty.

On the other hand, General Darling's words, unlike those usually used by a British soldier fighting a handful of young militants with his army of 37,000 armed with the most modern equipment, can be answered with the words of that great British leader whom we all followed during the war and recognised as our chief. I am speaking, of course, of Sir Winston Churchill. Here is what he wrote, among other things, in the *History of the English-speaking Peoples*, Volume I, page 21: 'It is the primary right of men to die and kill for the land they live in and to punish with exceptional severity all members of their own race who have warmed their hands at the invader's fire.'

I can only tell General Darling that this small people whom he is fighting today at the head of a mighty army were, instead of following his advice, following the advice of the greatest living Englishman. Churchill's ringing words are in harmony with a theory and practice which stand as one. As for the theory, I shall speak a few words only and they are not mine; they are 2,000 years old and come from Cicero: 'Vi vin repellere omnes leges omnisque jura permittunt', which means that to repel violence by violence is permitted by all laws and by all right.

Cicero was wrong in generalising as he did, for he did not imagine that in India men would succeed in vanquishing violence through peace and faith. He was wrong, perhaps, in not leaving the door open for exceptions. But how many of my colleagues in this Assembly represent nations which freed themselves by repelling violence with violence? How many peoples of Africa and Asia, of Europe and the two Americas, have not had to use violence, whatever violence was possible and within their reach, in order to obtain their liberty? Were they also assassins? Were they terrorists without conscience or honour? Or were they merely carrying out a duty? On the other side of this room I see my friends of the American delegation, and I cannot resist the temptation to read two small paragraphs of the Declaration of Independence which their ancestors proclaimed in 1776:

'But when a long train of abuses and usurpations, pursuing invariably the same object, evidence a design to reduce them under absolute Despotism, it is their right, it is their duty, to throw off such a Government. . . . And for the support of this Declaration, with a firm reliance on the protection of Divine Providence, we mutually pledge to each other our Lives, our Fortunes and our sacred Honour.'

Why is it that today this small people, civilised for so many centuries, which finds itself under a 'long train of abuses and usurpations', is to be denied what for others was both a right and a duty? Why should that small people now be slandered?

It will be said perhaps that this is due to the fact that Cyprus is some sort of special case. I am not acquainted with any colonies which, before their liberation, were not a special case – a special case, of course, which always militated against their freedom. It will also be said, perhaps, that the Cypriots are acting as terrorists, since they are waging a *maquis* war which General Darling despises. I should like to know how many wars of liberation were fought by means of pitched battles between insurgents and troops of a colonial Power. There have been a few rare exceptions, but in general they have always been wars similar to the one being waged at present in Cyprus. They were wars fought by *maquis* fighters who were everywhere regarded as heroes. William Tell, the national hero of peaceful and civilised Switzerland, obtained his title, did he not, by reason of having ambushed and killed the foreign governor of his country.

But perhaps it will be said that they are killing women and civilians. I agree with you in disapproving any such acts, but who killed these women? Who, several months ago, shot the American consul? Who stands to profit by the commission of such acts? Is it those against whom a loud chorus of indignation at once arises throughout the world? Who has done these killings? I dare accuse no one, because the question is indeed delicate; but meanwhile we have repeatedly requested that a commission of neutralism be set up to investigate thoroughly and fully these acts and other such matters, including the accusations that Greece is in contact with EOKA, a contact which I have always denied and which I deny officially and categorically.

My distinguished colleague from Turkey went so far as to tell us that Colonel Grivas, a member of the Greek Army, had been sent for this purpose to Cyprus. Colonel Grivas, who was born and raised in Cyprus, has not been a member of the Greek Army since the end of the war. He is a retired officer, who as a native of Cyprus where he grew up, has gone there to fight a war of liberation – if, indeed, it is true that he is at the head of the movement.

But I go back to my previous point. Why are we not given that commission of inquiry which we have been clamouring for? We have been asking for that commission, and this is sufficient evidence of our good faith. I can well imagine that there have been exaggerations on both sides, and we expect to have them judged by neutrals. What is important is the fundamental cause of these actions and the mainspring is the persistence of colonialist oppression in Cyprus. So long as this oppression and this regime continue disturbances are inevitable, and it is to this that we should pay attention. It is the cause of it all which we must deal with, and it is this that we have to extirpate in order to put an end to all violence, violence from above as well as violence from below.

Report by Leonidas Markides to General Grivas, describing how British Intelligence agents tried to involve him in a plot to arrest 'Dighenis' and deport him from Cyprus, after the signing of the London Agreement.

On 28 February at 11 am I received a telephone call from an English sergeant called Wilson, who said he was a member of the Special Branch and asked to see me about 'a matter in which I could help him', as he put it. He came to my office at 11.30 am with another Englishman called Dawson. They saw me alone. They told me that they had been in Cyprus for two years. They brought out a file with the name Socrates Eliades on the outside. They asked if I knew Eliades and what were our relations. They asked me about his partners and what sort of work he did. I said he was an agent for the distribution of asbestos etc. I asked them what it was all about and they said it was a secret affair and they were only trying to find out certain details. They continually asked me about what work he did. I told them he had lorries and was engaged in transport business. They later asked me about his political convictions and if he was a member of the Left. I told them I knew nothing about that. They asked me about his close friends and his enemies. My answer was that I knew nothing. They said they were sorry to have troubled me, but they stressed that it was essential to them to discover his political convictions, and if he was a member of the Left. They asked where his house was and departed. I must point out that as soon as they came into my office one of them put down his brief-case, from which he extracted the file on Eliades. I saw two or three documents fall from the case to the floor when the case slipped. He then picked up the documents. When they left I stayed in my office, and I saw that an envelope remained on the floor underneath the desk. The desk we had been sitting at has a projecting flap and it is probable that the envelope escaped his attention. It is certainly a fact that from where he was sitting it was impossible to see the position of the envelope. I saw it when I went to pull out the plug of the electric fire. I saw two or three British stamps including the words SECRET and TOP SECRET. I examined the envelope, which was not sealed, and looked inside. I saw a photo of some church deacon, I think his name is Anthimos, two photos of the entrance to Socrates Eliades house and two letters. . . . I put the envelope back on the floor in case they returned. I thought it very likely that they had left it deliberately, since one of them could have seen it from where he sat. Probably it was all a plot, because the questions about Eliades had been so purposeless and stupid. If their idea was to leak information to EOKA via the envelope, so that the organisation might make hurried moves on learning the contents of the envelope, then their plan would be easy to understand.

I went to find Kyriakos Markides and told him that they had dropped an envelope, but said nothing about the contents. Kyriakos suggested that I leave the matter in his hands. Immediately after this Miss Loulla Kokkinou came and took the envelope and, she told me, went off to copy it. We agreed that I should leave the office and come back when she had finished and replace the envelope where I had found it. Nobody got in touch with me, but when I returned to my house at 5.30 pm they told me that some Englishman had telephoned and asked for me two or three times without leaving his name. Suspecting that this was about the envelope I went to Miss Kokkinou and asked her what had happened. She told me it was impossible to return the envelope as it contained most important documents.

At about 8.30 pm the Englishman called again and told me that he had lost an envelope containing important documents, but he was not sure where he had lost it, since, he said, he had visited about eight different places. I said that I would go to my office and have a look. I then got into touch with Miss Kokkinou who repeated that it was impossible to return the envelope. I returned to my house and telephoned the number he had given me, 2026 (that is the Acropole Hotel),[1] to tell him I had not found the envelope, but the Englishman was not at the hotel. Next day, 1 March, at 9 am the Englishman phoned me again and asked what had happened. I told him I had looked in my office but had not found it. I heard nothing more about the envelope.

I should note here that I had staying in my house a wanted man with the pseudonym 'Chris', who, I understand, is the assistant of the man responsible for PEKA in Nicosia. I thought it would be right to tell him that I had found an envelope and given it to Miss Kokkinou, since I suspected there would probably be a search at my house. But I told him nothing of the envelope's contents and he told no one what I told him. I forgot to mention that during the interrogation about Eliades they asked me repeatedly to what extent he was of the Left and I denied it.

L. Markides.

[1] Where British police were stationed.

Letter from General Grivas to the Greek Consul in Cyprus, Mr Frydas, rejecting the British terms for an amnesty, 28 February 1959.

I received your letter of the 27th.

1. Concerning your statement about the amnesty and following the Governor's announcement of terms, I have the following general observations to make:

(a) There is discrimination between condemned and wanted persons. The case of persons condemned to death is subject to review, which is to be undertaken within two months; whereas those *wanted* for crimes, including those which would incur the death penalty, may ask to be allowed to leave at once for Greece.

(b) The nature of the procedure (amnesty in two stages) and the time set for its completion make me suspect that the Government had hidden motives. Each individual case is very well known and it is quite unnecessary for so much time to be taken in reviewing these cases; indeed, this review should already have started – immediately after Foot's return from London. If it had been, the whole procedure would have been almost finished by now.

(c) Who will judge each case, exactly? This is a relevant question in the light of all we know about the behaviour of English judges during trials and the false testimony on which so many charges have been based. I refer to one out of many such cases, as an example: Tsardellis, who was condemned to death and whose sentence was later commuted to life imprisonment, is entirely innocent. Another person was responsible. The charge against him was based on false testimony given by an auxiliary who undoubtedly agreed to give evidence on the suggestion of the British, who had to find a scapegoat. Concerning wanted persons, especially those the Government wants to get rid of as undesirable, any kind of charge can be cooked up.

(d) Those exiled will not be able to return to Cyprus before the date on which their sentences would have ended. When, therefore, will a man sentenced to life imprisonment, or to fifteen years, be allowed to come back? I hope I will not be told once more about expediency etc., to justify these ridiculous terms, because we also have reasons of expediency on our side.

(e) The Leader will not leave the island before the fate of every single person has been decided. He will thus be obliged to remain in Cyprus for two months, because if the English tradition is for leaders to abandon their men, the Greek tradition is for a leader to stay and suffer and fall with them. In any case, why is there so great a hurry to eject the Leader from Cyprus before the review of cases is complete? The amnesty terms are quite unacceptable to me and, in application, will be absolutely degrading. By 'amnesty' I mean a complete and universal amnesty without the qualification of a so-called review.

2. The question of the Leader. If the amnesty were to be made universal, nobody would accompany the Leader to Greece. In that case the Leader desires that no British person should come near him or accompany him. The Leader himself will decide on the means of transport to be used when the time comes. Armed escort, however, is essential; but, if the Greek Government cannot supply one, he will not insist and no one need trouble further. He wishes to carry his pistol for his personal safety.

3. Weapons. These will be handed over in small batches in many different places, so as to avoid difficulties.

Dighenis.

Copy to the Bishop of Kitium.

EOKA leaflet ordering a cease-fire, 9 March 1959.

*(Passages in italics were deleted from the original text at the request of
Archbishop Makarios.)*

TO THE GREEK CYPRIOT PEOPLE

When, on 1 April, 1955, I raised the flag of the revolutionary liberation
movement I declared that our purpose was the liberation of Cyprus, and
I asked for the support of the Greek Cypriot people and the help of the
whole nation. This was given completely throughout four years of hard
struggle.

Now, after the agreements between the Governments of Greece and
Turkey at Zurich, which have been ratified in London by the Ethnarch
Makarios *and by those appointed by him as representatives of the people*, I am
obliged TO ORDER THE CEASE-FIRE.

*

Refusal to accept the agreement and the continuation of the struggle
would divide not only the Cypriot people, but probably the whole nation.
The results of national division would be incomparably more disastrous than
those which some people believe will flow from the solution *of 'compromise'
which, undoubtedly, does not satisfy our desires.*

I therefore believe that this solution is preferable, even if it is not the one
we expected or the one which satisfies our wishes, to national division, because in such a division we would lose all.

So, instead of a battle cry, I call today for concord, unity and love, in order
that you may build the new structure of the young Republic on the ruins and
ashes of the Cypriot epic, which has glowed with such glory and national
majesty. Those who led this epic now have the task of leading the Republic
along the road to prosperity and progress. So far as I am concerned, determined as I am not to be involved in public life either in Cyprus or in Greece,
I shall anxiously follow, from a distance, the steps of my much-suffering
fatherland and share with you its joy and its pain *the fatherland which, in
spite of all my efforts, politics has failed to give the complete and untrammelled
freedom I wanted. Cyprus is very small in extent, and it would be difficult for
me to achieve any more alone, faced with an all-powerful Empire.*

My conscience is quiet, for I know that I have done my duty. It was the
politicians' task to exploit the epic struggles of the Cypriot people and ils
l'ont exploité selon leur capacité ou comme ils ont cru mieux.

NOW IT IS THE DUTY OF US ALL TO OBEY.

Gather round, all of you, united in support of the Ethnarch, who is today the symbol of unity and strength, and support him in his difficult task. This is my wish, and I call on everyone to comply.

EOKA,
The Leader,
Dighenis.

Letter sent by General Grivas to all EOKA fighters on the declaration of a
cease-fire on 9 March 1959.

TO THE EOKA FIGHTERS

The moment has come when, instead of war-cries and battle orders, I must
tell you my thoughts on the agreement reached for a solution of the Cyprus
problem. It is recognised throughout the Greek world that EOKA has performed a great task and has given Greek diplomacy a number of trump cards,
so that the settlement which has been reached is, in large measure, due to
the heroic resistance of the Organisation. The task which you have performed in these four years is great and your glory shrines throughout the
world. The whole Greek world has recognised your sacrifices and your
struggle: this must be your greatest satisfaction and your greatest badge of
honour.

An agreement has been signed which determines the future of Cyprus.
It does not fully satisfy our desires, but it is a step forward, breaking the
bonds of slavery. It is the agreement that diplomacy, as it claims, was able
to achieve in current international conditions. Arms alone, especially in a
small island which faces an all-powerful empire, cannot, as you will understand for yourselves, obtain a final solution; and our politicians say that they
have done everything they can, and that it is impossible to achieve more.

I confess that from the day the Zurich Agreement was announced I have
passed through moments of anxiety and I have carefully considered my
responsibilities to you, to Cyprus and to all Greece. I have asked myself
whether we should accept an agreement which does not completely fulfil
our desires, and whether I should reject it and continue the struggle.

On the criterion of national interest alone, unmoved by prejudice or
obligation or pressure, I have reached the conclusion that the continuation
of the fight would have the following disastrous results:

1. It would not have the unanimous support of the whole nation or the whole
Cypriot people, since the agreement has been approved by the Greek
Government and the Ethnarch.
2. It would divide Cyprus and perhaps the whole Greek people, with disastrous results.

I shudder to think of the results of national division such as the conflict
between King Constantine X and Eleftherios Venizelos, a division through
which I lived and which not only destroyed the dreams of a greater Greece,
but was a burden on the whole nation for decades after 1915, with tragic
consequences which culminated in the Asia Minor disaster. Greece today

has still not entirely recovered from this. It is preferable to accept a solution, even one that is not entirely good, than have civil discord which must inevitably raze everything to the ground. Because of the probability of such dreadful consequences, and because the continuation of the struggle without the people's unanimous support would have such doubtful results, I have been obliged to accept the agreements which have been made.

My single-minded patriotism, my love for Cyprus, my duty not to destroy what we have fought for, my responsibility to prevent the tragic consequences of civil strife had led me to take this decision. I did not think I should first ask your opinion for the following reasons:

1. You did not have the necessary information which would enable you to judge the agreement as a whole – an agreement which has to be judged in the light of international realities.
2. My desire as the military leader is to bear the entire responsibility alone and not move it on to the shoulders of my subordinates.
3. The Organisation, as a military body, must obey the orders of the leader. I therefore call on you all to obey your leader's order to cease fire. This order is contained in the leaflet already sent, which you are to circulate. My wish is that this order be faithfully obeyed and that there should be no last-minute breach in our ranks. We must maintain the unity and iron discipline which aroused the admiration of even our enemies. We must not, at the last, lose what we have won by discipline, in four hard years of struggle. . . .

In an independent Cyprus the future of EOKA fighters is wide open. It is they who tomorrow will be the supports of the Republic. I shall watch and help you. I thank everybody for their valuable co-operation which will always be the greatest memory of my life and will make a strong spiritual bond between us. Each of you will always be able to look to me as his leader, always ready with concern and affection; and wherever I may be I shall always welcome an EOKA fighter with joy. For I shall never forget those who helped me in time of danger and anxiety and those who helped to win our VICTORY. Now my thoughts turn to those who are no longer here: who fell bearing the sacred banner of the Cyprus freedom rising. I await that blessed hour when I shall hang golden offerings and unfading wreaths on their immortal tombs.

EOKA,
The Leader,
Dighenis.

Index

Index

224